Philip Harland

TRUST ME,
I'M THE PATIENT

Clean Language, Metaphor, and
the New Psychology of Change

Wayfinder Press
London, England

Copyright © 2012 Philip Harland

ISBN 978-09561607-1-3

All enquiries to info@wayfinderpress.co.uk

No journey of the mind is impossible;
it is only a matter of navigation.

Reviews of Trust Me, I'm The Patient

"Trust me, this is a superb book, a substantial contribution to the field. It explains in great style why and how a 'clean' approach supports individuals to liberate themselves from their constraints without *any* interpretation, intrusion, or suggestion. Read this book and your ideas about how people can change themselves will never be the same again." **James Lawley and Penny Tompkins**
psychotherapists, authors of Metaphors in Mind:
Transformation through Symbolic Modelling, www.cleanlanguage.co.uk

"Entertaining and informative, an impressive, accessible guide with a depth of insight around Clean Language that few people in the world possess. Philip uses a light touch to get his messages across, but this is a substantial piece of work, well referenced, with practical real-life examples. It will be a firm favourite for me to refer to for years to come." **Angela Dunbar**
author of Essential Life Coaching Skills, www.cleancoaching.com

"Philip Harland has written an important book for the healing arts. He has captured the essence of the work of the late David Grove, in my view one of the greatest theorists and therapists the world has known for decades. Not only has Philip delivered the primary tenets and methods of David's work, he has enhanced the information through his own voice and elegant writing. Readers will learn how to use language in a way that does not contaminate the personal, pristine elements required for true healing and in ways that conventional therapy would never resolve. Allow yourself to be guided into this new world of change, tremendously well presented here." **Rob McGavock**
professional counselor, longtime student of the work of David Grove

"A beautifully and brilliantly written book, a treasure for anyone in the fields of coaching, therapy, and counseling. If you know nothing yet of Clean approaches, you will soon have a deep understanding, and if you already know and love Clean you will be further inspired and better able to use this simple and powerful methodology in so many ways. Trust Me, I'm The Patient is a counter to the negative aspects of older methodologies in which the practitioner had the power. Practitioners are urged instead to start trusting their clients and patients and to support them in exploring their own inner worlds. Feast on Philips's knowledge and experience!" **Judy Barber**
Clean facilitator, author of Good Question:
the Art of Asking Questions to Bring About Positive Change, www.judy-barber.com

"The title says it all. This is a book about the astonishing ability people inherently possess to chart their own paths towards healing. Enthralling, clear and readable, and utterly convincing to any sceptics who are not familiar with Clean Language. It ranges across a broad spectrum of therapy, science, and philosophy, but in spite of its profound topics, this is an easy and enjoyable read, of incalculable importance to therapists, coaches, parents, and anyone who finds themself involved in another person's journey." **Carol Wilson**
author of Best Practice in Performance Coaching:
A Handbook for Leaders, Coaches, HR Professionals and Organizations
www.performancecoachtraining.com

"Written for facilitators of all sorts from psychotherapists to parents, this is a very rich book, packed with a range of examples. It proceeds from one convincing point to the next, starting by pinpointing the pitfalls that all well-intentioned facilitators fall into. The book offers a range of models for adopting David Grove's approach, which honours the client's inner experience, puts power with the client, and uses the client's symbols and metaphors with a set of questions to liberate the client to be the best they can be. Harland suggests that this is the future for change work and therapy and he argues the case compellingly." **Wendy Sullivan**
psychotherapist, coach, trainer, co-author Clean Language:
Revealing Metaphors and Opening Minds, www.cleanchange.co.uk

"Philip Harland's latest book is a more than welcome reminder that those with problems, illnesses, or unfulfilled objectives have not abandoned their human right to be respected by the professionals who treat them. This is a wholly excellent demonstration of how Clean techniques are truly empowering for both the facilitator and the user. The book is a political challenge to the abuse of rank in the caring professions. Read it and talk about it!" **Maurice Brasher**
teacher, researcher, translator of Ken Wilber
The Integral Vision, and Robert Dilts, From Coach to Awakener

"One of my abiding memories of Philip is a brilliant session he conducted for me using Clean Language. It remains to this day a turning point. Clean Language is a life-changing technology and Philip has written a book that should be read by everyone in the helping professions. With typical style and elegance, he makes therapists feel both pride and humility. Trust Me, I'm The Patient is a major contribution to the discipline." **Jack Stewart**
healer, psychotherapist, author and broadcaster, www.healingthespirit.eu

"Presents an innovative counseling approach that explores clients' metaphors in a way which allows the facilitator to minimize the addition of interpretations and assumptions to the client's words. The book begins by contrasting Clean Language with other counseling approaches, then moves to exploring various functions of metaphors and symbols, and follows with the propositions and structure of a Clean Language session. Illustrated with rich case studies and useful observations and strategies for conducting counseling sessions, this book will appeal to professional coaches too. Clean Language is a strong and effective approach that taps into clients' internal resources and allows them to be unfolded at their own pace." **Keiko Izumi**
professional coach at the World Bank, www.cleancoachingUSA.com

Contents

This book is dedicated to my wife Carol Thompson and to my friend and mentor, the late David Grove, creator of Clean Language. Many years ago, Carol suggested that she and I should go into psychotherapy, which led to my becoming a psychotherapist, which led to my meeting David, which led to this book.

Acknowledgments

My grateful thanks to James Lawley, Clean Language psychotherapist and co-creator of Symbolic Modelling, Maurice Brasher, systems and linguistics researcher, and Caitlin Walker, educationalist and innovator, for their unstinting support and constructive comments. They helped me decide what I wanted to say and ensured that my explanations more nearly conformed to my intentions.

Thank you also to Angela Dunbar, John Martin, and members of the Clean and Emergent Research Group for their contributions.

Foreword by Jennifer de Gandt

Thank you, Philip, for proclaiming the patient's right to be trusted; their right to access, process, and use their own personal experience without expert interference. Thank you too for showing in a practical way how 'Clean' processes can be used to facilitate people so that their rights are respected.

It is up to us as therapists, coaches, managers, and teachers to realize how important this challenge is at the present moment in evolution. We have daily reminders that populations are demonstrating for their rights to be trusted in the way their countries are governed. It is for us in the helping professions to ensure that every client who comes to us is facilitated in their own learning instead of being force-fed our learning.

It is for us to take this next step in the 'client-centered' movement and to move to what Philip calls, "a fourth kind of power relation — not sovereign, not disciplinary, not auto-repressive, but shared, mutual, and independently exercised." This book is an important contribution to the future of counseling, therapy, and education, and has a wider relevance to society at large.

Jennifer@innovativepathways.net
Paris, January 2012

Notes for the Reader

Almost all the Clean Language dialogue in the book is taken verbatim from real cases. An asterisk * at the start indicates that it is either imagined or adapted for the purpose of illustration. In most examples, the full Clean Language syntax has been abbreviated so that the dialogue is easier to read. The syntax is set out in full in Chapters 13, 14, and 15.

Identifying characteristics of clients have been changed to protect confidentiality. The word 'client' or 'patient' is used to refer to anyone working with a 'facilitator', who might be a colleague, counselor, health professional, coach, parent, psychologist, therapist, teacher, manager, or trainer.

Rather than use 's/he' or 'his/hers' etc. to refer to gender-unspecified persons, I use the traditional singular forms "they" and "their", as in "ask a friend if they can help" or "each to their own." And rather than 'himself or herself', the old gender-neutral "themself" that is making a comeback, as in "helping someone help themself" or "asking the client themself."

Spelling follows the generally simpler U.S. model.

Reference notes in the text are expanded at the end of each chapter.

A complete set of Clean questions will be found in Appendix C at the end of the book.

The material here, and more particularly in the second half of the book, is based closely on David Grove's original work. Some I have embellished or developed a little and some comes from his work with others. I give credit here and there, but David was adept at accepting contributions from his collaborators and this makes it impossible – and, I think, unnecessary, given his open-source philosophy – to identify and reference them all. As his co-practitioner in the world of coaching, Carol Wilson, said to me:

> David used to say that his work was a tree, with various branches running from it. He valued each branch equally and as all were open source, they could not be owned by anyone, including himself.

The work represented here is one branch.

Introduction

The age of speculative analysis is long gone
Oliver James

> Master Lao Tzu asked Gatekeeper Yin, "How can I walk
> underwater and not drown, move through fire without burning,
> and pass amongst the multitude of forms of life without fear?"
>
> Gatekeeper Yin replied, "You must learn to move within limits
> which have no limit and to journey to where both the start and
> the end of all life is."
>
> "How can I do this?" asked Lao Tzu.
> Gatekeeper Yin replied, "You must nourish your original breath."

I have two objectives in these chapters: to present the case for achieving healing, change, and self-knowledge with minimal outside intervention; and to outline a number of new ways of doing that which are simple, practical, powerful, and proven. What you will learn here, I trust, is to nourish your original breath and to move within limits which have no limit.

This book is for everyone who finds themself working with others in the medium of verbal and nonverbal language. It will have value for health and personal development professionals, but also for anyone who has wondered what to say to a friend, a colleague, or a child with a problem. The interventions readily translate into lessons for business and education too.

I shall argue the case for a 'clean' purpose to your intervention that does not contaminate the other's experience. Quantum physics tells us that how we measure things influences what we find. Equally, how we question people determines what they learn. I shall illustrate the perils of 'unclean' questioning practice (assumption, suggestion, direction, and the rest) and consider how seductive and unproductive they can be. And I shall take you step by step through a facilitative process that lends itself to the most profound therapeutic transformation and yet can be used informally at home, at work, or in the queue for the bus.

Clean Language is a medium for the delivery of self-knowledge and healing. It is what its creator, the innovative therapist David Grove, called "a sacred language set apart from the profane language of everyday speech." A basic knowledge of the art and science of Clean questioning will enable you to enter another person's world almost unnoticed and once there to tread very, very lightly. And what will happen as a result is that the person you facilitate will get to know − and change, and heal, if that is their aim − themself.

Health and well-being are not only about fixing things when they go wrong. They are also about taking pre-emptive measures to maintain vitality, boost the immune system, and pursue a mission or passion that gives our lives purpose. The point is to help ourselves be the intelligent, insightful, and delightful people we know at heart that we are. Sooner rather than later, the urge to know more about ourselves in order to be more use to others will become a prime strategy for survival. One of our leading cosmologists, Britain's astronomer royal Martin Rees, suggests this could be humanity's last century unless we sort ourselves out.

Clean Language and Therapeutic Metaphor are practical, respectful, non-directive, non-suggestive, non-intrusive, non-interpretive ways of facilitating people to lead fuller, freer lives and be the best they can be. They invite conscious and unconscious self-knowing to come together in such a way that the system learns to recognize its own organization so that change is self-generated.

These are *non-directive* procedures, in that the facilitator issues no instructions at the level of content. Questions are directed instead at the level of process, which is concerned less with the meaning of what we say and more with its underlying construction: how we came to create our problems and how we may resolve them.

They are *non-suggestive*, in that the facilitator makes no recommendations and offers no advice.

They are *non-intrusive,* in that the facilitator does not dispute or challenge anything the other person might say.

They are *non-interpretive,* in that the facilitator offers no personal version of what the other might 'mean' by what they say.

And what happens as a result is that people relax into their own process. They are not being asked to explain themselves. They are not obliged to learn another language or to adapt to another way of thinking. People report, again and again, how liberating this is: unsettling at times, reassuring at others, demanding on occasion, but ultimately liberating. Clean Language guards against the contamination of the questionee's experience by the questioner's conscious and unconscious assumptions and preconceptions.

At a professional level, Clean Language is a counter to the continued westernization of mental illness, the bias by which health professionals diagnose conditions, attach labels, and prescribe treatment in accordance with predominantly western-originated standards. Clean processes allow that the cultural expectations and beliefs of the sufferer shape their suffering as much as their personal circumstances. We all suffer differently and should be treated distinctively.[1]

At a socio-political level, Clean Language is a counter to our continuing dependency on restrictive structures of authority and to the distressing lack of attention we give to educating the young in self- and other-awareness. 'Clean' is a psychology of liberation. It takes its inspiration from the human quest to be free of ignorance, fear, and oppression in all its forms.

Ignorance, fear, and oppression were the chains that bound the families in which I was raised. They linked generations of absent or silent fathers, anxious or thoughtless mothers, and deprived, disturbed, or traumatized children. I saw the psychological shock waves appear, often many years later, in a succession of aches, pains, diseases, behavioral problems, and mental disorders. And I despaired at the reluctance of the victims to break the chains and acknowledge the reality of their lives and relationships.

Deceit derived from denial of this kind begets shame and in the process reinforces itself.

denial » shame about the denial » denial of the shame »

A familiar example of a self-reinforcing 'loop'.[2] Circularity of this sort causes huge discombobulation in individuals, families, and communities. How readily its effects are passed on and how narrow is the range of our knowledge of ourselves and others!

When I first trained as a psychotherapist, I was frustrated to find that the models of therapy I was studying were intent on interpreting people in ways not very different from the ways I had always interpreted them – ways that derived more from the myopia of my own worldview than from the limitless prospects of theirs. Psychoanalysis relied too much on generic explanation and explicit suggestion for my liking. 'Humanistic' methodologies were not as equable as they sounded, and could be confrontational and manipulative. Cognitive-behavioral techniques were short-term, perfunctory, and rarely, if ever, got to the root of the problem. Neuro-linguistic approaches taught me how to deconstruct my clients' subjective experience, but still obliged me to hallucinate what they required in order to lead them in the direction I chose. Each of these methods has its own legitimacy and many patients have benefited from them, but none were complete or congruent enough for me.

David Grove and Clean Language were something of an oasis in this psychological desert. Every day I saw Clean processes helping people resolve their problems and transform their lives in natural non-authoritarian ways that the old therapies would never have thought possible. And every day now as I work cleanly with clients I remember why I came into therapy.

The experience has qualified me many times over to question the knowledge I have of myself and the assumptions I make about others, and to facilitate people to answer these questions for themselves. Grove's family were Salvation Army evangelists and mine were Wesleyan Methodists, so I guess we couldn't help wanting to spread the word; not about anything ordained from above, but about our conviction that healing and change proceed best from within, and with the least possible outside interference.

If the age of speculative analysis is long gone, as psychologist Oliver James maintains, and if the era of directive and suggestive changework is coming to an end, as I suspect that it is, then Clean Language may be our best bet for the future. My hope is that you will find something of value here for your own journey.

Part I of the book (*Trust Me, I'm The Patient*) is concerned with the basis and genesis of the Clean psychology of change.

Part II (*Inside Information*) deals with the pivotal role of self-generated symbol and metaphor in Clean Language changework.

Part III (*Symptoms and Solutions*) sets out the principles by which Clean healing and change are activated.

Part IV (*Coaxing into Consciousness*) outlines a number of practical ways in which Clean healing and change are achieved.

Appendix A is a universally applicable exercise utilizing Therapeutic Metaphor.

Appendix B consists of edited transcripts of Clean case histories.

Appendix C has a complete list of Clean questions applicable to almost any situation.

Notes to the Introduction

1 Westernized classification and treatment of mental states: depression, grief, post-traumatic stress, and personality differences are heavily influenced by local beliefs and customs, and their meaning and management will vary significantly from place to place. 'Clean' treatments, unlike more prescriptive methods, are culturally neutral and wholly adaptive.

2 The self-reinforcing 'denial–shame' loop: denial in turn may be said to derive from fear, as does pretty much every unwanted emotion, so the circularity would go from fear to denial, to shame of the denial, to fear of the shame, and so on.

Part I

TRUST ME, I'M THE PATIENT
The New Psychology of Change

*If you do not change direction, you may end up
where you are heading.*   Lao Tzu

Introduction to Part I

What is happening to your brain right now? Everything you are doing, thinking, and feeling is changing it physically. Delicate patterns of electrical signaling and chemical processing are affecting and being affected by your actions, perceptions, and emotions – patterns that are easily disrupted by anxiety, neglect, abuse, poverty, stress, hunger, fear, guilt, shame, anger, smoking, unemployment, environmental pollution, and a host of other factors that can deactivate protective genes and make you more susceptible to mental illness and disease.

Drug therapy can temporarily reduce or ameliorate some of the symptoms, but talking therapies have been proven time and time again to do the same job, and to go further, into realms of personal transformation, without adverse side effects and in ways that last. Your mind can change for the better without doing much more than responding to questions.

> What kind of questions?
> *Those that make no assumptions, offer no interpretations,*
> *contain no hidden agendas, and honor your individuality.*

Chapter 1
Internal Affairs

I don't know about you, but my mind has a mind of its own.
Michael Frayn

A personal mind – Difference and divergence – Identical twins Laleh and Ladan –
Importance of first person reporting

"A personal mind", the 19th century American psychologist William James called it. You live in an extraordinary labyrinth of neural networks made up of some hundred billion brain cells with perhaps five hundred trillion synaptic connections between them; a web of measureless threads that give you an enormous capacity for difference from the five hundred trillion or so in my brain.[1] Given that countless numbers of your cells and connections are varying their intimate couplings from one micro-second to the next, it is evident that every new combination will conspire to make your mind wholly, unknowingly, and qualitatively different to any other. You are, no doubt about it, exquisitely and exceptionally yourself.

Difference and divergence
Where do individual differences come from? Charles Darwin declared that "divergence of character" derived from the process of natural selection, and with good reason.

> During the incessant struggle of all species to increase in numbers, the more diversified these descendants become, the better will be their chances of succeeding in the battle of life.[2]

The survival of the species depends on our divergent natures. Evolutionary psychologist Steven Pinker notes the way that sexual reproduction results in a unique scrambling of the genes of unrelated people; how random variations in our neurology produce brains that differ structurally; how our inimitable biographical histories and unreplicable collections of memories and desires make each of us qualitatively unalike.[3] Preliminary results from the One Thousand Genomes research consortium reveal millions of previously unknown variations in DNA between individuals. Detailed examination of the genomes of two nuclear families found that each child had around sixty mutations in its genome that did not exist in either parent.[4]

Laleh and Ladan

Identical twins are a case in point. They share the same DNA, but it only takes a few different genes to be activated for them to have quite different personalities. The brains of identical Iranian twins Laleh and Ladan Bijani fused together over the twenty-nine years they spent conjoined at the head, but they felt like two completely separate individuals. "We have different worldviews," said Ladan in 1983. "We have different lifestyles. We think very differently about issues." They even pursued different careers. Ladan was studying law and Laleh journalism when they died after an operation to separate them. They were buried in separate graves.

First person reporting

Personal minds work subjectively. You might suppose this to be self-evident, but it has not always been thought to be so. Scientists have only recently begun to recognize the subjectivity of all data, including that gathered for scientific research. In a 1996 paper, *Neurophenomenology,* the Chilean biologist Francisco Varela made a plea for the validity of subjectively sourced information. He called it "first person reporting" and suggested that the detailed phenomenological examination of human experience – that is, via the senses rather than by intuition or reasoning – required a revolution in scientific thinking and a complete change in the way that science was taught. "We need to introduce new first person methodologies way beyond those we have at the moment," Varela observed. "We are extremely naïve. It's like people before Galileo looking at the sky and thinking that they were doing astronomy."[5]

David Grove's Clean Language is indivisibly linked to first person reporting. Subjective information is elicited from the client directly, using a model of questioning that effectively neutralizes the unconscious beliefs and intentions of the questioner and sidesteps the distortions and re-interpretations we habitually place in the way of our communications.

*What would you like to have happen?
To use all my senses.

And when you use all your senses, then what happens?
I'm creative. I'm myself.

And when you're yourself, then what happens?
I trust my own process.

Clean questions such as "What would you like to have happen?" and "Then what happens?" make an assumption that something is going on in the questionee's bodymind — and that is all.[6] They do not attempt to suggest what that could be or what it should be. They bring ideas and somatically sourced feelings to experiential life by supporting the client to access an inner dimension to their experience in ways they may not have done before. And what appears is 'clean' information, different in kind and quality to any other.

Clean questioning elicits and facilitates the first-person reporting of internal truth uncontaminated by the fanciful assumptions, presumptions, and suggestions of others. This is not the universal truth that Plato attempted (and failed) to define and it is not the empirical truth about patients to which Freud and his followers aspired. It is personal intelligence that none but the person concerned may retrieve.

There is exemplary richness, depth, difference, and divergence in the classified information each of us holds behind the closed doors of the unconscious. Clean questioning is the key to this extraordinary underground store. It offers a means of accessing its contents that is simple, scientific, chivalrous, and subversive.

Simple in that anyone can begin to engage effectively with Clean Language after no more than a day or two's practice.[7] *Scientific* in that it is rigorous, methodical, and evidence-based. *Chivalrous* in that it is, I believe, one of the most respectful and companionable of language-based modalities. And *subversive* in that it constitutes a radical challenge to our traditional, frequently manipulative, habit-of-mind methods.

In chapters to come, we shall look at each of these modest claims. First, what is it like to be 'unclean' and unaware of it?

Notes to Chapter 1

1   Brain power: *Science* magazine calculated that in 2007 all the world's computers could together perform 6.4×10^{18} instructions per second, which roughly equals the number of nerve impulses produced by ONE human brain each second (*The World's Technological Capacity to Store, Communicate, and Compute Information*, April 2011).

2   Divergence of character: Charles Darwin, *On the Origin of Species*, 1859.

3   Inimitable histories and unreplicable memories: Steven Pinker in *How The Mind Works*, 1999. Pinker calculates that in addition to whatever incalculable *inexpressible* thoughts we might have, each of us can entertain something like a hundred million trillion different *expressible* thoughts, or about a hundred times the number of seconds since the birth of the universe.

4   Millions of genetic variations never observed before: pilot phase of the international One Thousand Genomes Project reported in *Nature* 27 October 2010.

5   Validity of first person methodologies: Chilean biologist, philosopher, and neuroscientist Francisco Varela in an interview with Susan Blackmore, *Conversations on Consciousness*, 2005. He was not the first to make the case. In *World Hypotheses* (1942), American philosopher Stephen C. Pepper argued that there was no such thing as data free from interpretation and that objectivity was a myth. Yet we can never perfectly communicate our experience of subjectivity. Author Oliver Burkeman (*Help! How to Become Slightly Happier*, 2011) points out that. "Even the best scientific studies can't fully penetrate the experience of being you." This is because science, like all external enquiry, is nominally 'third person'.

6   A full set of Clean questions will be found in Appendix C.

7   The basics of Clean Language can be learned in a day or two. A more complete training takes several weeks.

Chapter 2
Unseen Snares

Assumptions are things you don't know you're making.
Douglas Adams

Assumptions – Incomplete information – The rush to judgment – Supposition – Implication and inference – Presumption – Interpretation and insight

Assumptions are unseen snares that life sets before us daily, hourly, every waking moment. They are tricky neuro-linguistic states compounded of a little reasoning, a measure of ignorance, and two kinds of belief: one cognitive (about what we think we know), the other affective (about what we feel is right). They lead us into making inaccurate guesses from incomplete information and calling them, among other things, 'gut instinct', 'intuition', and even 'common sense'.

Einstein said that common sense was nothing more than a set of prejudices laid down in the mind before the age of eighteen. Malcolm Gladwell, in *Blink: The Power of Thinking Without Thinking,* suggests that making common sense or intuitive assessments by "thin-slicing" our experience is an effective strategy for getting where we want to be more efficiently. Yet the book is full of counter-examples in which people did just that and got it wrong. Unconscious gender and racist stereotyping was at the root of most thinly sliced assessments. Decision making based on 'expert evaluation' was responsible for the rest.

Our minds have not yet evolved to give consistently accurate first impressions. Neuroscientist Joseph LeDoux emphasizes that the information we receive in every micro-moment of the day is processed by brain systems that give rise to *conscious and unconscious content simultaneously.*[1] Yet as curious, intelligent people, we like to know what is going on around us and that leads us, and through us, others, to conclusions based on hidden and implicit, rather than verifiable and unequivocal, evidence.

Incomplete information

The infamous trial of Derek Bentley and Christopher Craig in Britain in 1952 hinged on the jury's interpretation of five words used by Bentley to Craig, who had been challenged by a policeman to drop the revolver he was carrying. Bentley called out, "Let him have it, Chris." Craig fired and the policeman was killed. At the trial, Bentley claimed that he meant, "Give the man the gun," but the jury inclined to the prosecution view and found both men guilty of murder.

In law, of course, the truth is whatever a judge or a jury decides. Things are so or they are not so. Yet anyone who has served on a jury knows that the 'facts' of a case are determined on the basis of the lowest common denominator of the jurors' opinions of what may have, or is likely to have, or at best probably, happened. We can all be persuaded to adopt one version of events over another if the arguments in its favor are consistent with a pre-existing worldview we happen to hold.

The problem lies not so much in our wanting to believe in a single truth as in acting as if there were such a thing. Appeal courts continue to overturn verdicts based on uncorroborated or irreconcilable evidence, yet trial judges and jurors alike continue to deny that their feelings – constructed involuntarily, operating unconsciously – color their analysis of the evidence at least as much as their reason. "On the basis of mere feelings, then," the author Michael Frayn said of one case he attended, "a man is going to spend ten years in jail or else go home and have supper with his wife."

Several times in my spell as a prosecuting officer on military service I would draw the attention of a court martial to *prima facie* ('first impression' or 'on the face of it') evidence I had assembled and suggest to the court that in the absence of incontrovertible proof it was nevertheless sufficient to convict. On several occasions, the tactic succeeded. Senior officers sitting in judgment would as readily be swayed by an appeal to their imagination as to their discretion. The fact that these were relatively minor cases of insubordination and absence without leave did not make the assumption of guilt I was advocating any more defensible.

Decisions taken on the basis of incomplete information have had shocking results. In July 2005, less than twenty-four hours after the London suicide bombings, anti-terrorist police shot and killed an innocent young Colombian, Jean Charles de Menezes, because he fitted their prejudgment of how a potential suicide bomber would look and act. In an ambiguous situation, they made a series of intuitive decisions that escalated into a tragic mistake.

Another name for this innate ability of ours to imagine a complete scene from the scantiest of descriptions is 'associative patterning'.

Figure 1 Lines on a page

Notice how readily the brain fills in the gaps to imagine a familiar figure. Or two. Or five. Or even eight. The figures we 'see' when we look at Figure 1 are hallucinations.

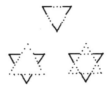

Figure 2 Associative patterning: the invisible triangles

We fill in the missing bits from unconsciously held, pre-existing memory patterns that are *similar*.

The rush to judgment
We evolved this knack of rushing to judgment because there were advantages in being able to predict a precarious future. Those ancestors of ours who reacted instantly to that rustle in the grass as if it were a predator were more likely to live long enough to pass on their genes than those who stopped long enough to consider their options. Pattern detecting was so vital for survival that we learned to err towards 'false positives' rather than miss a genuine one.

We continue to make these 'worst-case scenario' judgments when we are feeling sensitive to criticism or jumping to premature conclusions. We see and hear what we have been conditioned to see and hear, and make assumptions and suppositions accordingly.

The fact that normally we cannot *not* make assumptions and usually have no idea we are making them has huge implications for changework. Every well-meant comment we make as health professionals to our patients and clients originates in the heart of darkness. Every word we think we have conscious control of was actually constructed in the unconscious.

Supposition

The only difference between an assumption (a mixture of reasoning, ignorance, and belief) and a supposition (a mixture of belief, ignorance, and reasoning) is that suppositions contain a smaller proportion of reasoning. When I suppose something, I am even more convinced that I am right. It can be a dangerous game for that trio of fraudsters, ignorance, belief, and reason, to play.

In a speech to the British Parliament in 2003, Prime Minister Blair insisted that Saddam Hussein had weapons of mass destruction that he would not hesitate to use offensively without prior threat. A former Deputy Chief of Defence Intelligence remarked at the time that Blair was piling supposition upon supposition – even if Saddam had such weapons, it did not make him the threat that Blair implied and many listeners inferred.

Implication and inference

A speaker implies; a listener infers. "There's nothing like eating hay when you're faint," says the King in Lewis Carroll's *Through the Looking Glass*. The inference his courtiers make is that if they feel faint, they should eat hay. "I didn't say there was nothing *better*," the King goes on. "I said there was nothing *like* it." In other words there is no connection at all.

Therapists and coaches who practise the technique of creating and delivering 'implication' – verbal interventions that *imply* the outcome they want their clients to *infer* – are difficult to challenge, because clients tend to process the implications unconsciously and make the inferences themselves. Take the hypnotherapist who tells a new client, "Your conscious mind may be very confused about what I am saying." The implication is generated by the client inferring that their *un*conscious mind will understand perfectly.[2]

Therapist implication may be well intended, but as part of a pattern of influencing the client in the light of the therapist's beliefs, it can affect the therapeutic process fundamentally. No part of a therapist's input, whether assumption, supposition, or implication, exists unsupported. The unsubtle supposition in the statement, "Your conscious mind may be very confused," is that your conscious mind *is* very confused. This is the part that captures our attention, while the larger pattern of the therapist intervening to further an agenda of their own goes undetected.

The Clean facilitator may entertain any number of fantasies about what the client has said, but will copy them into a mental drafts file until the client, and only the client, updates the formation. The 'unclean' agent of change will have no such qualms and will give voice to whatever happens to be feeding their imagination at the time.

Presumption

It is a short step from assuming something to be so without proof to speculation that might be deemed vain or improper. In his book *Troublesome Words,* Bill Bryson declares that "to assume means to put forward a reasonable hypothesis" (I would qualify "reasonable" with 'apparently'), whereas "to presume has more an air of sticking one's neck out, of making an assertion that may be contentious." I agree, though I would put it more strongly. There is a lot of contention about.

My colleague James Lawley quotes an example from an experience at 30,000 feet:

> The stewardess hands me a lemon tart. I cut it in half and pass half to Penny. I cut a small slice off the remainder and eat it. I don't like it, so I leave the rest. The stewardess comes back to collect my plate a few moments later and says, "Ah, that went down a treat." I was speechless. There was nothing to reply to such a presumption of my experience!

If one presumes, one takes liberties. The eminent psychoanalyst Irvin Yalom admits to presumption in his interpretation of patients' dreams. "Sometimes it is useful to react spontaneously, to express some of your loose associations to the dream," he writes in *The Gift of Therapy.* The inference I take from this is that reacting spontaneously with loose associations sometimes isn't very useful. If that is so, how does a therapist determine in advance when it is useful and when it is not, when by definition spontaneous reactions cannot be predetermined or controlled? Clearly, we can only have an inkling about the usefulness or otherwise of a spontaneous "loose association" *after the event,* when we make a subjective assessment of the patient's reaction.

Dr. Yalom goes on to subvert his own case: "Of course, that may bias the work, since it is the patient's associations, not yours, that lead to a truer vision." Tut tut. Has he been selling his patients short? In my dictionary, 'bias' translates as 'unfair influence'.

I wish this were a trivial issue. The assumptions and presumptions we make about what others have said and the inferences we draw as a result are a frequent cause of anxiety and confusion. Language theorist Alfred Korzybski pointed out in *Science and Sanity* (1933) that

> The reader should not take lightly these structural and semantic
> issues [...] they are unusually important for sanity.[4]

Some years ago, my mother collapsed with an infection and was
admitted to hospital, where she was wired up to heart, respiration,
and blood pressure monitors, and connected to catheter, saline drip,
diamorphine, and oxygen. Two doctors told my sister and I that she
was dying. We consulted a third. They were all in no doubt. After a
few anxious hours, mother woke, showed signs of distress, and
whispered, "I've had enough." The doctor on duty at the time
presumed this to mean that she was ready to die and suggested
that she could be 'helped' if the drip were withdrawn and the dose
of diamorphine increased. My sister and I were appalled and agreed
to nothing. Several hours later mother woke again and I asked her
what she had meant by "had enough". She indicated the wires and
tubes she was hooked up to, complained about the discomfort they
were causing, and said she had had enough of them. The less
essential ones were removed, she rested easier, and a week later
she was in rehabilitation, well enough to grumble about the level of
care she was receiving.[5]

Not all the guesswork of experts has such dire implications, but
the incident is a reminder to me not to jump to conclusions about,
or to take in any way for granted, the meaning of anything my
clients might say. My mother's doctor presumed to ignore the limits
of his competence when he said, in effect, that "I've had enough"
was the same as "I want to die." He imagined an equivalence
between what she said and what he believed her to mean. The first,
he was saying, *is* the second.

Philosopher-poet George Santayana warned us of the perils of
equivalence:

> The little word 'is' has its tragedies: it names and identifies
> different things with the greatest innocence; and yet no two are
> ever identical, and if therein lies the charm of wedding them and
> calling them one, therein too lies the danger.[6]

The conventional language I use in this book is, I trust, adequate
for its purpose, but if you were to dissect it for some other purpose,
you would find it riddled with equivalence – generally benign, given
the conventions, but occasionally less so. When you find me using
'is' and its derivatives, make allowances and read with the
appropriate skepticism. The point I want to make in the context of
facilitative language is this: every intervention has intention and
effect, and deserves critical analysis. This is particularly so when it

comes to the need many agents of change have to 'understand' their patients and clients: to have insight into their pathology, motivation, and behavior. To 'understand' or to have 'insight', we must first interpret.

Interpretation and insight
Yalom acknowledges in *The Gift of Therapy* that

> *therapists place a far higher value than patients on interpretation and insight* [his italics] ... and *we grossly overvalue* [mine] the content of the intellectual treasure hunt; it has been this way from the very beginning, when Freud got us off to a bad start.[7]

The author reminisces about "the search for insight" as "the perfect therapy mating task," which keeps patient and therapist intimately connected "while the real agent of change – the therapeutic relationship – is germinating." This may be all very well for patients who are content to keep mating until the relationship germinates, but doesn't say much for those who have difficulty affording the time and money that psychoanalysis typically takes.

Therapists with access to the deepest needs and fears of others pursue insight too easily. We need to remind ourselves constantly of the hidden arrogance of power. No agent of change in the exercise of their profession is making normal conversation. To bring the presumptions, delusions, inconsequentialities, and circumlocutions of everyday language into a facilitative exchange is to put the delicate balance of the client's psyche at risk.

Many agents of change acknowledge the risk and employ discreet linguistic tricks to temper their interventions.

> I wonder if ...
> Let me put it this way ...
> You might want to consider ...

Indirect interjections soften the edge of presumption. I wager you cannot name me one counselor, lawyer, probation officer, filing clerk, or long-distance lorry driver who has never made meaning on behalf of someone else in this way. Yet meaning is a subjective experience before ever being a shared one. It is not *conveyed* by speaker or author, but *evoked* in the mind of listener or reader.

This raises what seems to me to be an insurmountable barrier for direct interveners: the impossibility of understanding their clients on the basis of the clients' cognitive reporting of their mental and emotional states. Language comes some way after the complex concatenation of parallel processing, involuntary association, serial selection, and symbolic representation from which our conscious states are constructed (see Chapter 8, *The Making of Metaphor*). It means that conscious states are colored indelibly by unconscious designs well before language appears, which makes any client's retrospective access to the cause or construction of their cognitions and emotions at best pretty feeble and at worst implausible. Self-reporting in response to conventional questioning can only be relied upon for what it is – hearsay, conjecture, evidence that is unlikely to stand up in court.

The rules of the Clean exchange ensure the emergence of genuine self-information. And they are unambiguously protective of the client. Most change modalities aim to maximize their influence and to establish a relationship with the client in which the balance of power is tipped, often heavily, in favor of the agent of change. The aim of Clean questioning is different: it is to facilitate the client's relationship with what only they can know.

There is, after all, no single, certifiable reality out there. The world is a personal movie projected onto our private screens. Facilitators who form a view of the client based on their assessment of the partial information available to them are likely to be misjudging their own worth and prejudicing the client's.

When assumption, presumption, and interpretation shade into suggestion, a threshold is crossed and something irrevocable happens.

Notes to Chapter 2

1 First impressions based on conscious and unconscious content arising simultaneously: Joseph LeDoux, *The Emotional Brain*, 1998.

2 The delivery of 'implication': acknowledgments to Steve Andreas, *Verbal Implication*, March 2004 edition of *Suppose*, the journal of the Canadian Association for NLP.

3 'Assume' and 'presume': Bill Bryson, *Troublesome Words*, 2001.

4 Semantic issues important for sanity: Alfred Korzybski, *Science and Sanity: An Introduction to Non-Aristotelian Systems and General Semantics,* 1933.

5 Patient Concern, a patients' rights group in Britain, points out that the medical profession opposes the principle of patient or family consent to 'Do Not Resuscitate' orders "because it transfers power from the medic to the patient."

6 "The little word 'is' has its tragedies": George Santayana, *Skepticism and Animal Faith*, 1923.

7 Over-valuation of interpretation and insight: Irvin Yalom, *The Gift of Therapy*, 2002.

Chapter 3
Double Agents

They'll take suggestion as a cat laps milk.
Shakespeare, *The Tempest*

The power of suggestion – The boy, the wife, and four men in a boat – The helping dilemma – Directions in disguise – Compliant clients – Attachment patterns

The power of suggestion carries heavy responsibilities and these apply to many more people than copywriters, head waiters, and hypnotists. Suggestions are double agents who serve two masters: the conscious state and the unconscious state, neighboring nations who are frequently at odds. In attempting to play one off against the other, we make decisions based on subconscious reasoning and then find ourselves inventing fictions to justify and rationalize our choices.[1] In these circumstances, the assessment of the most experienced counselor become open to question.

"Let me offer you a few ideas," one might say (i.e. "Here are some suggestions based on the assumptions I have made related to my outcome for you"), or "I understand what you say, let me put it in my words" ("I don't understand you, and it would be easier if you were to see things my way"). Whatever its avowed purpose, the deeply held intention of all suggestion is the desire to maintain a precarious hold on fugitive reality: that is, to be in control. And the basic tool for the manipulation of reality is everyday language.

The boy, the wife, and four men in a boat
In the feature documentary *Être et Avoir*, the junior school teacher comforts a young pupil who has been bullied by another pupil.

We just have to take no notice of these things, eh?

The seven-year old nods in agreement as he weeps.

We can rise above this, can't we?

The boy nods again.

Come on. Can you show me what a strong little boy you are?

The boy says nothing, but breaks into tears again.

∾

My wife is telling me about the evening she has just spent with a girlfriend.

> *She was late again. She didn't say sorry. She just smiled and said 'Hi', and I had to smile back and say how great it is to see you.*

I am indignant on my wife's behalf.

> She obviously doesn't respect you. You should confront her over this.

My wife responds in a flash.

> *I don't need you to tell me what to do. I just wanted sympathy!*

∾

A young man is talking to an older man in a room overlooking the Regents Canal in north London:

> *There were four of us: a lawyer, a laborer, a young boy, and someone else. We were all in a boat.*
> Whose boat was it?

> *I think it was mine.*
> That's fascinating. And who are you?

> *I suppose I'm the fourth man.*
> What an interesting dream. Do you usually catch on so quickly?

He doesn't wait for an answer.

> Let me guess. The laborer wanted a brain, perhaps. The lawyer, a heart. And the child needed courage.

The young man considers this. He's not so sure.

> Remember Scarecrow, Tin Man, and Lion in the Wizard of Oz?
> Who do you think the characters in your dream are?
> *I don't know.*

Could they be parts of yourself?

It seems obvious now that he's said it.

> *Ah, yes. Of course.*
> Negotiating how best to work together during this voyage on
> which you have embarked?

> *Yes. I see.*

And so it came about that in only my second session of
psychotherapy, I was embarking on the therapist's journey rather
more than my own. I was pleased to have fascinated this older man
and to have caught on so quickly. He was a Jungian analyst,
gratified, I'm sure, to have such a willing assistant. The voyage on
which he was the benevolent skipper and I was first mate was to
last three years.

The helping dilemma
The schoolteacher seemed genuinely touched by his pupil's distress
and may have thought that as long as he sounded sympathetic, it
hardly mattered what he said. In fact, he ended up asking
counterfeit questions ("We just have to take no notice of these
things, eh?"), of the sort that are worthless in a genuine
transaction, because the value of the answers has been decided in
advance.

I claimed to be consoling my wife, but in fact I was trying to dictate
her response ("You should confront her over this"). I wasn't helping
her find a personal solution to the problem.

A suggestion is nothing less than an attempt to impress an idea on
the mind of another. "Let me guess," said my analyst. "The laborer
wanted a brain, perhaps. The lawyer, a heart. And the child needed
courage." It is entirely possible that the characters in my dream
wanted these things. It is equally possible that they wanted to go
ballroom dancing or stay at home with a cup of cocoa. The analyst's
"perhaps" was too little, too late. My mind was already impressed.

At the heart of all helping is a genuine dilemma: how to assist
others to be the best of themselves in ways we believe to be best for
them? It is a conflict few agents of change have ever satisfactorily
resolved. Should I be nudging my client from behind, urging them
from alongside, or hauling them up from somewhere ahead? Or is it
really enough – is it possible – just to be there?

The problem is that our minds were designed by natural selection to surmount the obstacles our foraging ancestors faced, which more often than not meant outwitting things – animals, natural hazards, other people – in an attempt to stay ahead of the game. I came out of psychoanalysis relatively quickly, but the experience kept me puzzled for years. Some people spend fifty minutes twice a week for half a lifetime under the influence of another person's view of how their past impacts on their present. At that rate, they may never catch up with themselves.

A therapist colleague quotes a maxim that should be tattooed on the forehead of every facilitator:

> All human unease can be reduced to four causes: incomplete communications; unfulfilled expectations; thwarted intentions; and people who try to help.

Many of our words in everyday use have outdated associations and 'help' is no exception. Five hundred years ago, Old English *helpan* or *holpen* meant 'cause to be otherwise.' Its general sense now is to aid or assist, but it still carries traces of its original, more intentional role. Today if you consider yourself as helping someone, you are heir to an obligation to cause them to be otherwise.

'Facilitate' has a fine but distinct difference. It comes from the Latin *facilis*, 'easy of access'. In English four hundred years ago it meant to lessen the labor of, disburden, free from difficulty, and it means much the same today. We ease the birth of a baby, we ease the revolutions of an engine, we ease the helm of a boat a few spokes in a head sea. 'Facilitating' has fewer implications of direct causality than 'helping'. It enables strain to be less severe so that the system works more efficiently. Once the helm has been eased in a gale, the rest is up to the boat.

Directions in disguise

In Shakespeare's *The Tempest*, Antonio conspires with Sebastian to usurp Alonso, King of Naples. Antonio says he will present the plan to his cohorts in a way that will engage them emotionally. "They'll take suggestion as a cat laps milk," he says. We learn from neurobiologists that emotional engagement increases oxytocin levels, which facilitate the release of dopamine and serotonin, neurotransmitters associated with reward and well being.[2]

It pains me to say this, but the word 'suggestion' derives from dishonest purpose. It is a conflation of the Latin, *sub,* 'below', and *gestus,* 'brought': thus 'brought from below' or 'by underhand means'. Three hundred years ago, a suggestion was 'an incitement to evil, an insinuation into another's mind of the false idea that ...' A false idea can stimulate a feeling of reward and well being as well as any other kind.

Even therapists who work content-free, without direct reference to a client's own narrative, do not all claim to practise suggestion-free facilitation. Some cover their tracks by giving embedded commands that work at a subconscious level in the client. "I wouldn't want you to *feel obliged* to consider ..." Or they make a suggestion one stage removed by composing an anecdote corresponding in form to their perception of the problem in the hope that the client on appreciating the analogy will see the same light. "Once upon a time there was a young prince ...," "I know a woman your age who ..." But what if the client gets the point of the story 'wrong'? There can be unexpected effects with any prescription. In any case, why go to the trouble of making up metaphors when clients come up with their own all the time?

I feel churned up inside.
Whereabouts inside?

It's like I'm behind a glass wall.
What kind of glass?

I need to break out of this cage.
And then what happens?

Suggestion-free questions minimize the misunderstandings that arise naturally in everyday language. At best, they eliminate them entirely. If I wish to suggest something to you, I first have to construct an internal model of how I think you ought to be, rather than being mindful of how distinct and original you actually are.

"Let me guess," said my analyst. "The laborer wanted a brain, the lawyer a heart, and the child needed courage." Three suggestions lightly dressed as speculation, with the analyst's personal mix of reasoning, ignorance, and belief attached to them. He is drawing my attention to something he reasons is relevant that I might not have considered. But the world of my imagination has rules of its own that do not conform to his reason. These shadows, these chimeras I have created have some kind of role to play in my mental well being, but I cannot be sure what that is yet *because I haven't been asked.*

It is impossible to tell how much of the information in the frame after a therapist-dominated exchange like this is genuinely self-generated and how much is the result of a contaminated mix of the therapist's suggestions and the client's suggestibility. An assumption that leads to a conclusion that happens to fit the original fantasy is really a delusion. Korzybski claimed that assumptions like these were qualitatively no different from the delusions of the insane.

It only takes one unclean question ("Do you usually catch on so quickly?") or one not-so-innocuous aside ("Let me guess ...") to create a radical diversion in the course the client's unconscious had been intending to take.

Compliant clients
The unconscious is easily diverted. In general, we are an obedient lot who like to be led. You will have heard of the notorious experiments at Yale University in the nineteen-sixties when volunteers were required to administer what they believed to be electric shocks to other volunteers when an authority figure in a white lab coat required them to do so.[3] The psychologists conducting the experiments were exploring the relationship between authority and obedience, and concluded that for the majority of people obedience is deeply ingrained behavior. I think they might have reached the same conclusion by other means.

My analyst's "Whose boat was it?" may not be in quite the same league as "Now increase the voltage to 'severe shock'," but is similarly geared to my tendency to do as I am told. His question implies there is some significance to the ownership of the boat. If I go on to make the inevitable inference, that someone of significance *to the analyst* owns the boat, then my attention has shifted from my inner world to his. As the compliant client, I assume that the analyst knows something I don't. If the significance of the ownership of the boat is not immediately apparent to me, perhaps I should seek it.

"Fascinating", he says in reference to my response. A harmless enough interjection, you might think, but it comes from someone in a position of privilege with the unconscious impulse (at best) or conscious desire (at worst) to control the exchange. "Fascinating" is a judgment with complex connotations. For in my susceptible state, I am now hooked into what the therapist finds fascinating. If I wish to continue fascinating him, I should attune myself to his further response. And so I find myself wondering what he might *not* find fascinating. I should learn to avoid those things.

Attachment patterns

Client-therapist attachment patterns are many and varied, and provide both parties with the potential for what some theorists call 'a corrective relational experience.' For therapies based on this relational experience, the risk of engaging the emotional vulnerabilities of both parties – client *and* therapist – is clearly higher than for a process where the emphasis is not on the client's relationship with the therapist, but on the client's relationship with their own information.

An elderly prioress welcomes a young supplicant at the start of a forty-day retreat in a Franciscan convent.[4] She offers a few words of advice.

> Prioress   The word I want to introduce here is purity of heart.
> Young woman   (Jokingly) *Ooh. That sounds scary.*
>
> Prioress   That may be because you do not have a pure heart.
> Young woman   (Shocked) *Oh.*

The prioress would doubtless claim that her intention was to expand the young woman's awareness, but when suggestions like this are concocted from an undifferentiated mix of assumption, presumption, and interpretation, supplicants will need a highly evolved talent for picking out the best bits.

Most of us find it difficult to do this and should not be expected to try. The bodymind is a highly sensitive instrument whose job is to keep us alive and at critical times it becomes vulnerable to the attentions of experts and charlatans alike. Sometimes, as we shall see, it can be difficult to tell the difference.

Notes to Chapter 3

1 Inventing fictions to justify and rationalize our choices: Jessica Marshall reporting on neuroscientific research into internal narrative, *New Scientist* 12 February 2011. When conscious and subconscious thoughts are at odds, the fictions we tell ourselves help us create a sense of a unified self (another convenient fiction).

2 Neurobiological reward: clients who find self-reflection distressing may readily 'lose themselves' in the therapist's stories and become susceptible to emotional manipulation.

3 Obedience to authority: Yale psychologist Stanley Milgram wrote up his 'electric shock' findings in the *Journal of Abnormal and Social Psychology* in 1963 under the title *Behavioral Studies of Obedience.*

4 The prioress/supplicant scene was filmed in 2006 for a BBC documentary series *The Convent.*

Chapter 4
Faith in Authority

Faith in authority is the worst enemy of truth.
Albert Einstein

Woody Allen has gone off Freud.   Zoe Williams

Authority and the unconscious – Power relations – The language of control – Diane and the analyst – The problem with experts – Paraphrase and conflation – Self-management and the transfer of power – The true authority

"What would authority look like if it acknowledged itself to be driven by the unconscious?" asks Jacqueline Rose in *Psychoanalysis and the Modern World.* We need look no further than Lord Hutton, the judge who conducted the 2003 inquiry into the death of British weapons expert David Kelly. Hutton found himself unable to rule out the possibility that Prime Minister Blair's desire for a convincing dossier on Iraq weapons had "subconsciously influenced" the government intelligence chiefs' wording of the dossier. This was the same judge whose faith in the benign motives of politicians was likely to have subconsciously influenced the writing of his own report, which exonerated the government completely. The commentator Max Hastings observed at the time that Lord Hutton

> might have done well to consider that precise legal minds such as his own have inflicted some colossal miscarriages of justice in modern times, not least because of judges' willingness to swallow official evidence.[1]

As a consequence, I suggest, of an unconscious desire to enhance their own official status. Once authority acknowledges itself to be as driven by the unconscious as the rest of us, it might look and sound (indeed, it might even be) a lot less presumptuous.

Power relations

The 20th century French philosopher Michel Foucault charted the historical shifts between three eras of power relations: from the sovereign power of the absolute ruler – visible, autocratic, repressive ("there is no law, only power, *this is how you will be*"); to the disciplinary power of the state – unseen, overseeing, judgmental ("the law is above the state, *this is how you should be*"); to the auto-repressive power of institutions establishing 'norms' against which we police each other until, behold, we are so imbued with establishment norms that we police ourselves ("I believe in the law, *this is how I should be*").

Foucault was concerned less with the conventional power that is concentrated in the hands of individuals and corporations than with the more pervasive and insidious mechanisms by which power

> reaches into the very grain of individuals, touches their bodies and inserts itself into their actions and attitudes, their discourse, learning processes and everyday lives.[2]

Health professionals are both the subjects and the instruments of this kind of power. We act with short-term intentions and ignore the long-term effects. We measure norms of physical and mental health, for example, against a 'deficit model' that focuses on a community's weaknesses rather than on its members' individual strengths. The bodymind teacher Moshe Feldenkrais was critical of all such assumptions:

> In behavior, what matters in individual cases is not what most people do, not the statistical average, but the individual's personal experience.[3]

I like to think of the Clean community as working towards a fourth kind of power relation – not sovereign, not disciplinary, not auto-repressive, but shared, mutual, and independently exercised. There is no one truth in this radical new realm; no norm; no deficit model. Our expertise is not of the kind to be exercised dogmatically or definitively. At best, it eases clients' entry into the matrix of their own expertise.[4]

It may be the first time they have entered this thrilling and occasionally disconcerting domain. The ground rules are unusual. Seekers learn that the key discoveries are theirs alone. Their guides participate neither to convey information nor to control their progress.

Clean facilitation is much like education at its best. As novelist Muriel Spark has Miss Jean Brodie say:

> To me, education is a leading out of what is already there, in the pupil's soul. To Miss Mackay it is a putting in of something that is not there, and that is not what I call education, I call it intrusion.[5]

The best teachers offer opportunities for learning while ceding control of what is learned to students themselves. The analogy extends to any kind of supervising, parenting, or counseling. If I wish to control your learning, I offer you a stark choice: to acquiesce and subvert your imagination and vision to mine; or to resist and in the process – because resisting consumes precious energy – learn very little. (There is more on teacher control in Chapter 10 under *Limitations of Metaphor*.)

The language of control

The footballer Danny Blanchflower used to tell a story of his time in the nineteen-fifties as captain of Barnsley. One day he plucked up the courage to ask the manager if the players could be allowed to practise with the ball during training, only to be told that denying them the ball during the week "made them hungrier for it on Saturday." This is just the kind of hollow logic ("it's for their own good," "tell them only what they need to know") employed by those who wield arbitrary power. The tactics might work for a game or two, but by the end of the season are likely to have confined the players to the lower leagues of achievement.

The language of control comes readily to those who believe the truth to be knowable and the world to be a place of shared meaning. If you went to someone in the helping professions who held this view, they might claim to be able to help you adjust to reality because they knew the world better than you. Metaphors of authority quickly become self-fulfilling descriptions of reality. The client acquiesces. The expert view prevails.

In the standard talking therapies – cognitive-behavioral, psychodynamic, humanistic – the expert aspires to take an objective view of the client's information. Yet even 'client-centered' Rogerian counselors, wary of interpretation, attempting to reflect the client back to themselves, are predisposed in common with these other therapies to paraphrase clients and to install non-client material unwittingly.

*Client   *She was angry, I don't think she liked me.*
Counselor It sounds as though at heart you hated your mother.

Client   *I hadn't thought of it that way.*

Inch by inch, the client is enticed into the therapist's embrace. Escape from its intimacies is never easy.

Diane and the analyst

A male psychoanalyst is counseling a female patient suffering from 'body dysmorphia', an unrealistic sense of how she looks. The transcript below is taken from a television program that centered on the work of a respected organization of analysts, so we can take it that the therapist chosen to be featured was not unrepresentative. The patient, Diane, has been seeing the analyst for several months.

Analyst Good to see you again, Diane. How many hours a day would you say is spent thinking about your appearance now?

Diane *Probably about six.*

Analyst Six hours a day. So it's still ...

Diane *Yeh.*

Analyst Very significant.

Diane *Yeh. It's a lot less. It used to be seventeen, maybe more. But within those six hours, a lot of that will be positive. I'll still be preoccupied, but I'll be thinking good things, just sort of how I'd like to have my hair next and that sort of thing. And also thinking about how I'm happy with my hair or how I'm happy with something I've got on.*

Analyst OK. I haven't seen that so often, where you're saying, you're saying it's not negative things, it's things where you're comfortable with. As if you're trying to reassure yourself.

Diane (Pauses for several seconds) *Yeh. Maybe. Yeh. Mm. Now you say that I don't know if that's such a good thing, but I was under the impression that it was all good.* (Uncertain laugh) *Even though I was still preoccupied, it was ...*

Analyst Well, it does suggest you're still quite vulnerable.

Diane *Yeh.* (Nods) *Yeh. I suppose you're right.*

I confess to a feeling of mild nausea when I first heard this exchange. As part of my treatment, I have attempted to deconstruct it from a Clean perspective.

Analyst Good to see you again, Diane. How many hours a day
would you say is spent thinking about your appearance
now?

The analyst sets the agenda and immediately installs three notions
of his own: that Diane is still "thinking about appearance," that
she is doing it "many hours a day," and that she is doing it "now".

Diane   *Probably about six.*

The patient answers politely in the analyst's terms. She has not
been invited to say what she wants from the session or to review
what she has learned since the last.

Analyst Six hours a day. So it's still ...

With that one word "still", he re-associates the patient into the
problem pattern she was in when she first came to him.

Diane   *Yeh.*
Analyst Very significant.

A further installation of non-patient material.

Diane   *Yeh. It's a lot less. It used to be seventeen, maybe more.*
But within those six hours, a lot of that will be positive.
I'll still be preoccupied, but I'll be thinking good things,
just sort of how I'd like to have my hair next and that
sort of thing.

Diane is attempting to re-set the agenda.

And also thinking about how I'm happy with my hair
or how I'm happy with something I've got on.

Analyst OK. I haven't seen that so often, where you're saying,
you're saying it's not negative things, it's things where
you're comfortable with.

She *is* saying it now. This is a key moment. Diane is trying on a
new sense of herself, but this is neither acknowledged nor
developed by the analyst. Instead, he regains the initiative by re-
installing the notion of "negative things", and then risks adding
insult to injury with another blatant suggestion:

As if you're trying to reassure yourself.

Diane   Pauses for several seconds) *Yeh. Maybe. Yeh. Mm. Now you say that I don't know if that's such a good thing, but I was under the impression that it was all good.*
(Uncertain laugh) *Even though I was still preoccupied, it was ...*
Analyst Well, it does suggest you're still quite vulnerable.

He, not "it", is making this suggestion. He is attempting to conceal a personal judgment under a thin cloak of objectivity: a small, but dishonest, trick.

Diane   *Yeh.* (Nods) *Yeh. I suppose you're right.*

In the space of two minutes, the analyst has made three statements of opinion – "It's very significant," "You're trying to reassure yourself," "You're still quite vulnerable" – in the guise of incontrovertible fact. George Orwell warned us of the effects of this kind of rhetoric. "Who controls the past controls the future," he wrote in *Nineteen Eighty-Four*; "who controls the present controls the past." Diane is trapped in the analyst's thesis. If at some time in the future he is proved to have been correct in his assessment, it may well be the power of suggestion in the present that was responsible. It is the kind of language that could maintain Diane in an unresourceful state for years.

Clearly, we don't know the full history of their work together, but the analyst's attempt to fit a here-and-now encounter into a general, theoretical template allows at least as high a possibility of being helpful to Diane as the guesswork of the average clairvoyant. Not all models of therapy operate in this way. In cognitive-behavioral work, the suggestions will be more transparent. In humanistic interventions, they may be more provocative.

These undeclared assumptions concealed in the therapist's baggage, the tacit presumptions that the therapist knows best, the penciled suggestions that leave an indelible mark on the client's interpretation of their own information, all point to an unresolved need for control. There is a consistent failure to deliver what I believe to be the most important outcome of any client-facilitator exchange, which is uncontaminated, potentially self-determining information *for the client*. Diane has been exposed to the virus of speculation instead.

Analyst Well, it does suggest you're still quite vulnerable.
Diane   *Yeh.* (Nods) *Yeh, I suppose you're right.*

She offers no resistance. Her immune system is already compromised.

The problem with experts
The exercise of power needs constant vigilance. I am writing this at a time when a British appeal court has called into question the concept of expert evidence in a case involving cot death syndrome, where the confident assertion of an eminent professor ("One cot death in the family is a tragedy, two is suspicious, three is always murder") has been judged to be fundamentally wrong. A Criminal Cases Review Commission found the professor guilty of abusing his professional position by presenting theory as scientific fact. The Commission noted that his conclusion had been based on "an unacceptable level of speculation."

Many highly educated professionals have an aversion to doubt which may lead them to 'false positives'.[6] Diane's analyst would have felt there was honor in his authority and that he intended no disrespect, but in making no distinction between theory and certainty in a highly sensitive situation, he took control of the truth. And vulnerable, dysmorphic Diane, with her unrealistic sense of the appearance of things, compounded the offence by allowing it. She gave up trying to say what she wanted to say in the face of the therapist's relentless domination of the exchange. The effect was to deny her ownership of her own process.

Experts often share an unspoken belief that the vulnerable and disempowered are by definition inadequate and cannot be trusted to know what is good for them. This justifies a strategy of holding on to information that others 'will not understand' or which might 'upset' them. And what happens, inevitably, is that the others do not understand and sooner or later are upset.

Psychoanalysis depends more than most therapies on the theoretical expertise of the therapist. Here is Irvin (*The Gift of Therapy*) Yalom again, with an offer the average patient might find difficult to refuse.

> If I can make observations about you that might throw light on what happens between you and others, I'd like to point them out. Is that okay?

Patients who can say "no thanks" to this kindly offer are likely to be tagged as difficult or resistant (or perhaps having no need to be in therapy), while those who agree to it give the therapist *carte blanche* to make illuminating observations all night long.

Yalom is like the salesman who puts a foot on the step as you open the door – he is half-way to crossing the threshold before you can say, "not today, thank you."

A typical observation might be an attempt to throw light on what you have said with a helpful

So what you are saying is ...

before going on to paraphrase what you have said: that is, to use other words.

Paraphrase and conflation

The pioneer of so-called 'non-directive' counseling, Carl Rogers, would regularly rephrase his clients' words to achieve what he felt to be greater rapport. There are any number of examples of what he called "the mirroring of emotional communication" in his influential work, *On Becoming A Person*.[7] Here is just one:

> Client   *I wonder if I've been going around doing that, getting smatterings of things, and not getting hold, not really getting down to things.*

> Rogers Maybe you've been getting just spoonfuls here and there rather than really digging in somewhere rather deeply.

The client's "smatterings" have metamorphosed into the counselor's "spoonfuls". The client's "not really getting down to" is translated as "rather than really digging in". The differences could be deep. Later in the same encounter:

> Client   *I'm feeling it internally now – a sort of surging up, or force, or outlet. As if that's something big and strong. And yet, uh, well at first it was almost a physical feeling of just being out alone, and sort of cut off from a – a support I had been carrying around.*

> Rogers You feel that it's something deep and strong, and surging forth, and at the same time, you just feel as though you'd cut yourself loose from any support.

The counselor has modified every one of his client's metaphors in an attempt to empathize. "Something big" is reshaped as "something deep", "surging up" becomes "surging forth", and "cut off" is "cut loose". These are tiny linguistic differences, but any one of them could have a major effect on the client's self-understanding, or misunderstanding, of what is going on for them. The client's response to all this, not surprisingly, is:

Client   M-hm. Maybe that's – I don't know ...

Paraphrase as often as not is a means of establishing the speaker's own agenda and in that sense it can be intrinsically manipulative.

*So what you are saying is it upset you to have a mother who cared more for your sister?

An example of both paraphrase and conflation, combining two or more bits of information that the client has supplied at different times – she has a mother, she has a sister who was given a lot of attention – into one gratuitous 'affect suggestion'.[8] "What you are saying is it upset you" invokes an emotion that the client may or may not have felt at the time, though probably will now, while the proposition "a mother who cared more for your sister" supposes an emotionally fraught state of affairs that may or may not have been the case when the client was a child, but could easily become part of the family folklore now.

Para-phrase derives from the Greek for 'faulty or improper speech'; con-flation from the Latin *flatus*, 'an excess of air'; while sug-gestion, as we have seen, once meant 'brought from below'. The counselor who paraphrases or conflates a client's words could be introducing faulty or improper ideas into their process and generating surplus gas, quite possibly from below.

Self-management and the transfer of power
"If you want to understand the deepest malfunctions of a system," said the American environmentalist Donella H. Meadows, "pay attention to the rules, and to who has power over them." Health self-management changes the rules. Research shows that patients who use professionals as consultants and make their own decisions about treatment get better more quickly.[9]

The revolutionary Athenian teacher, Protagoras, argued that knowledge and virtue could neither be dispensed nor imposed from outside, but could only emerge from within. He was followed by that eminent soldier-stonemason Socrates, son of a midwife, who I like to think of as an early progenitor of Clean Language – partly for the way he challenged the suppositions of the day without ever presupposing the answers, and partly for his lack of vanity. He believed that the formulaic and scientific procedures of the craftsman applied as much to enquiry into matters of belief, morality, and behavior as to the manufacture of shoes or corsets. He proposed that education, like scientific enquiry, was a "drawing out" of knowledge that was already there, not a shifting in of something that was missing. Centuries later, Miss Jean Brodie would agree. Above all else, Socrates anticipated one of the key tenets of 21st century facilitation when he maintained that the tutor was the servant, not the master, of the pupil.

The true authority

Initial desires are formed from within existing limitations. They are likely to mature as clients get to know their authentic needs. The client is the true authority in these matters. Anyone who finds themself unable or reluctant to answer a facilitator's question is not thereby 'resisting', but merely, as Grove would say, teaching the facilitator to ask a better question.

The great philosopher-scientist Thales of Miletus was once asked for advice. He answered:

What is difficult? To know oneself. What is easy? To give advice.[10]

I like to think he left it at that, though he was only human. How then do we humans get to know ourselves?

Notes to Chapter 4

1 Judges' willingness to swallow official evidence: political commentator Max Hastings writing in *The Guardian*, 31 January 2004.

2 Power relations. Michel Foucault (1926-84) examined the way that systems of knowledge such as psychiatry had changed humans into subjects: *Surveiller et Punir*, 1975, published in English as *Discipline and Punish*, 1977. See also michel-foucault.com

3 What matters is the individual's personal experience. Moshe Feldenkrais, *Body and Mature Behavior: A Study of Anxiety, Sex, Gravitation and Learning*, 1949.

4 Clean questioning eases our entry into the matrix of our own expertise. At worst, like all innovations for the common good, it can be abused. I know of a couple of websites offering a corrupted technique supposedly based on Clean that professes "to control people's emotions and to get them to do things your way." This is not a Clean intention.

5 "Education is a leading out of what is already there." Muriel Spark, *The Prime of Miss Jean Brodie*, 1961.

6 Expert suppression of doubt. When questions are raised, the desire to have an answer can be overwhelming. Even a wrong conclusion can be seen as preferable to remaining in a state of confusion or ambiguity.

7 The examples of paraphrase in which the therapist replaces the client's metaphors with his own are taken at random from Carl Rogers, *The Process of Becoming a Person*, pages 120-121 of the 1961 Houghton Mifflin edition. On page 102, another client says, "I'm prepared for some breakdowns along the way" (a metaphor for some kind of mechanical conveyance), which Rogers paraphrases as "You don't expect it will be smooth sailing" (unilaterally identifying the conveyance as a boat). On page 101, the therapist summarizes a long speech by a client without using one of the client's words and the client responds (not entirely convincingly) with "Yes, something like that." There are many more examples.

8 'Affect suggestion' inserted into ostensibly reflective counseling. Acknowledgments for this example to the first truly 'Grovian' psychotherapist, David's former partner and collaborator Cei Davies Linn.

9 Patients involved in their own treatment. Research for the independent Health Foundation and the health research charity The Picker Institute shows that engaged patients "stick to their chosen treatments better, take up appropriate screening, and on the whole choose less interventionist and therefore less costly treatment paths." *The Guardian*, 21 September 2007.

10 "What is difficult? To know oneself. What is easy? To give advice." Thales of Miletus quoted by Diogenes Laertius in *Lives and Opinions of Eminent Philosophers*, 2nd century ACE. Thales is also quoted as saying, "Of all things that are, the greatest is Space, because it holds all things. The swiftest is Mind, because it speeds everywhere. The strongest is Necessity, because it masters all. The wisest is Time, because it brings everything to light."

Chapter 5
New Science, New Psychology

You know more than you think you know.
Dr Benjamin Spock

Knowing thyself – Linguistic revision – Quantum potential and psychological individuation – Vicky and the vibrating peach – The self-system learns from itself – Anna's tree, John's knee

Gnothi seauton, 'Know thyself', was inscribed over the entrance to the temple of Apollo at Delphi and became the most enduring of the maxims of the Seven Sages of ancient Greece. For Thales of Miletus and his fellow philosopher-scientists, the desire to synthesize human knowledge and psychology was the ultimate human quest – what the Romans would call *maxima propositio*, a proposition from which all human duties, obligations, and decisions derived.

A century after Thales, reformist Chinese philosopher K'ung Fu-tzu (Confucius) was reminding the rulers of the Zhou Dynasty that the harmony of the state depended on the value it placed on the psychology of the individual.

> From the emperor down to the mass of the people, all must consider the cultivation of the person the root of every thing besides.

Two and a half thousand years later, Sigmund Freud re-imagined human nature fundamentally by the light of his own projections and led us into an age of speculative analysis from which we are only just emerging. "Most of Freud," said philosopher Colin McGinn in 2003, "is ingenious fantasy, unsupported by factual evidence dubious in itself, and often lacking in theoretical coherence."[1] Yet the debt we owe Freud is that he legitimized the concept of the unconscious, that obscure domain of the mind in which memories and beliefs are stored and conflicts assembled without the least knowledge of the owner.

The question then became, 'How do we gain access to this remarkable reserve?' The orthodoxy of the greater part of the twentieth century dictated that we could only do so via the vision and conviction of professionals who maintained that their training equipped them to know better than their patients; that confronting a patient's erroneous belief system was the best way to change it; and that the loss of a little dignity and autonomy on the part of the patient was a small price to pay. To these ends, everyday language patterns were employed, deliberately or by default, to intervene at a fundamental level with the patient's experience. Yet everyday language is a severely limited system. It is often impossible to say what we mean or mean what we say, so we circle endlessly, like flies around a shuttered room.

Linguistic revision
In the early nineteen-thirties, the visionary philosopher-scientist Alfred Korzybski was declaring that almost all progress in human affairs depended on radical linguistic revision. It was obvious to Korzybski that Planck's formulation of quantum theory (1900) and Einstein's theory of general relativity (1905) could not have emerged without revolutionary departures from the scientific and semantic conventions of the day. New models had to be created. They required a fundamental revision of old attitudes and practices and their replacement by something with a more naturalistic foundation.

Language affects our natural perceptions materially. Korzybski called for a new world order in which everyone would be taught to question the limits of language and to re-evaluate its assumptions for themselves. He condemned the old language for what he called its "misevaluations", which he considered to be the prime source of our emotional tensions, mental illnesses, and flights into mysticism. The old language is the one we still use. Korzybski died a couple of years before David Grove was born, but I believe he would have endorsed Clean Language without reservation.

Quantum potential and psychological individuation
Korzybski found a metaphor for his notion of psychological individuation in quantum theory. If the particles of which our bodyminds are composed have no fixed form or position, if they are able to spin in opposite directions at the same time, if they can continue in communion while being physically apart, if indeed nothing is certain or determinate, or fully specifiable, or has exact

and discernible limits, then psychologically each of us has immensely – immensely – more potential than we know.[2]

It can be scary letting go the familiar order, but for mind-set and language to transform together, there has to be a fundamental shift. As scientists attempt to reconcile the structure of cosmic spacetime with sub-atomic scale events and to find life beyond the solar system, it cannot help but affect our sense of our place in the universe and ideas about self and identity. The next scientific revolution will be a linguistic and psychological one too.

The old vocabulary of Freudian theory was based on a model of the world that became so deeply embedded in our cultural unconscious that its figurative basis – those metaphors of "defense mechanism", "Oedipal complex", "transference", "repression" and so on – became the received wisdom. The ideas in Freud's *The Interpretation of Dreams* (1899) became as influential and familiar as Darwin's and Einstein's, and for the better part of a century we took them for granted. We failed to seek out new metaphors or to question what the old ones were obscuring or denying.

It has been said more than once that Freud's heart was less in attending to what his patients said than in refining his ideas. He took the knowledge he had gleaned from certain mentally ill patients and applied it to humanity in general. Yet later in life, he came to revise and discard many of his theories. He accepted that the new sciences of biology and neurology – to which we might now add cosmology and quantum physics – would one day blow away his earlier work.

Today, physicists readily admit exceptions to the formal laws of physics, which are perceived to be more averages, approximations, and probabilities than absolutes: generally, but not totally, applicable. Having the same degree of predictability as, say, the arrival of swallows in Spring. One of the founders of modern quantum science, Max Born, proposed that the relativism of the new physics freed us all from the shackles of belief in a single, indivisible, authority-driven truth.

Here is an IQ test that was once given to schoolchildren in the presumption of a single truth.

Figure 3 Which pair is the odd one out?

The conventional answer is the third from the left, because it is the only one without 'mirror symmetry'. In fact, you could legitimately have chosen the first on the basis of its comparative size, or the second for having no curved edges, or, at another level of abstraction, the fourth, on the basis that it is the only one you would have no logical reason to choose! No one reality fits all.[3]

Einstein maintained that quantum entanglement, in which the same information can be held instantaneously by two particles no matter how far apart they are, was impossible. Science since has shown him to be wrong. The physical 'laws' have exceptions. You will recall the first law of cartoon physics, which states that any character who walks off a cliff will continue walking until they notice that there is nothing to support them.

Figure 4 The first law of cartoon physics

And the second law, which states that no matter what misfortune befalls the body of a cat, it will always return to its original shape.

Figure 5 The second law

These are just the kind of things that can happen for real in metaphor landscapes (Part II). Clients can extend the boundaries of therapeutic possibility in any direction they choose.

The constraints on our changing are nothing like as strong as we used to believe. Our mental states are capable of subtle and flexible internal negotiations. Quantum potential (the ability to have properties that exist together, but cannot be observed or measured together) translates directly into psychological potential. Therapeutically, we thrive on ambiguity and multiple meaning, and on reconciling the irreconcilable.

Vicky and the vibrating peach

Vicky is a 29-year old television presenter with a spirited public persona and a colder private persona, which are often in conflict. High energy, high achieving moods swing into low energy, depressive moods and when either spirals out of control, she feels a little crazy.

> *When I was a kid my parents always said there was a right way of doing things, but I always thought I should do things my way.*
> And that right way is like what?
>
> *The right way is like a dense vibrating nut.*
> And your way is like what?
>
> (Pauses) *My way is like a warm soft peach.*
> And when right way is like a dense vibrating nut and your way is like a warm soft peach, what happens next?
>
> *The problem is that the nut sucks energy from the peach, leaving it cold and angry, and the vibrating energy of the nut gets over-excited and goes haywire.*
> And what would over-excited nut and cold and angry peach like to have happen?
>
> (Pauses) *To come together.*
> And can they come together?
>
> *Yes, I think so.*
> And when they come together that is like what?
>
> *A vibrating peach.* (She laughs)

Vicky is the architect of her own reality. She has constructed a metaphor in which her manic state and her depressive state can be reconciled. All I have to do as her facilitator is be midwife to their offspring and assist the child to thrive. And over the next few sessions, "vibrating peach" learns to mediate between Vicky's extremes. Her over-excitement is calmed and her coldness and anger positively energized through the interaction of two idiosyncratic symbols having limitless promise.

The self-system learns from itself

As Vicky's metaphor modifies, her state of mind transforms. She alone is determining the nature of what needs to happen in order to heal.

The 17th century Dutch philosopher Spinoza proposed that

> organisms naturally endeavor, of necessity, to persevere in their own being, and that necessary endeavor constitutes their actual essence.[4]

He went on to anticipate what we accept with little question today, that most of these activities and propensities are engaged unconsciously. In the pursuit of self-determination, we need access to the deepest parts of ourselves. Once upon a time, those who sought entry to this treasury of the self would find a shaman or high priest on guard at the gate. The gatekeeper would challenge the supplicant to engage in a dialogue to prove themself worthy of entry. And at this point an awkward third party would intrude and things would get complicated. Grove put it this way:

> The problem is if I ask you to tell me directly about your experience, I start a 'trialogue' between you, me, and your interpretation of the symptom that is held within you.

Figure 6   The long way round: the traditional trialogue

Everything the supplicant/client says must pass through this third party before it can reach and be 'understood' by the gatekeeper/therapist. The client expresses themself in a cognitive interpretation of their original feelings and their words are reinterpreted by the therapist in order to be understood in the therapist's terms. The therapist needs this 'understanding' in order to have something sensible to say. Thus, every client perception is filtered through three stages or more of interpretation before it can return to source, at which point the process starts over and the cycle continues.

A Grovian exchange, in contrast, is direct. It is not 'client-centered', but 'client information-centered'.

Figure 7 The direct route: the Grovian dialogue

The therapist's question goes direct to source. The symptom gives up the information it holds and the self-system determines its value. Neither client nor therapist is required to reinterpret what is happening in order to 'explain' or 'understand' it.

Anna's tree

Freud's one-time collaborator Carl Gustav Jung took a path of his own by reinterpreting his patients' inner worlds in a way that required him, he said, to invent a new language for each patient. He meant a language of his own, of course. In fact the new language existed already: it was the patient's own.

Anna is a client whose imagination comes up with an obvious candidate for reinterpretation:

> *I see a tree. The tree has information for me. It has roots. It is solid because it has roots. And it has a direction of growth and multiple branches.*

We will find a great deal about trees in Jung's work on symbols and it can be used to spin a theory around Anna that might relate – perhaps quite closely – to her condition. And perhaps not, because as Jung himself said:

> A tree can have an incredible variety of meanings. It might symbolize evolution, physical growth, or psychological maturation; it might symbolize sacrifice or death; it might be a phallic symbol; it might be a great deal more.[5]

In other words, Anna's tree is uniquely hers. Questioned cleanly, it will be found to have a size, shape, location, and characteristics that stem from the fact that it is the only one of its kind. Every aspect of Anna's tree will hold idiosyncratic information that only she, sometimes explicitly, at other times tacitly, knows.

John's knee

John expresses himself in more obviously symptomatic terms.

> *I have twinges of pain in my right knee.*

How can he be facilitated to access the wealth of information this simple statement holds? First, by easing his entry into the subjective organization of his experience:

> And twinges of pain in right knee. And when twinges of pain in right knee ...

And thence into an altered state of his own creation:

> ... those twinges of pain in right knee are like what?

These are not any old twinges, after all. They are peculiar to John.

> *Like a splat-shaped amoeba with six or seven rays or threads coming out of it.*

Expert information that no-one but the client could have known.

In the nineteen-eighties when David Grove began working with victims of trauma, the idea of self-expertise as a condition for healing was a radical concept and Grove's means of achieving it were novel and original, even, some thought, bizarre. He would not replace what the client had said with words of his own in an attempt to achieve 'emotional rapport'. He would not interpret or analyze the client's condition by the light of a pet theory. He would not suggest a more productive way of thinking or feeling. He would not attach labels. He would not murmur incantations. He would only repeat the client's own words, scrupulously and precisely. As I do here with John:

> And like a splat-shaped amoeba with six or seven rays or threads coming out of it ...

I tread lightly. I do not muse aloud about the meaning of amoebas. The less I trespass on John's terrain, the more he will get to know it for himself.

And when a splat-shaped amoeba with six or seven rays or threads coming out of it, is there anything else about that splat?
It's got movement – a kind of flowing out from the center.

Grove's original modelers, Tompkins and Lawley, describe what is happening here as "change emerging organically as the self-system learns from itself." James Lawley says that the more he teaches and researches Clean Language, the more he realizes it is so much more than a counseling, coaching, or problem-solving process.

It enables people to 'get inside' the organization of their own minds like no other methodology I know, which allows the mindbody system to reflect on itself in a remarkably concentrated and direct way.[6]

It is a way that encourages, even obliges, the client to own their own process, while freeing the facilitator from having to make a single suggestion. What then does a Clean facilitator do?

Notes to Chapter 5

1 Freud's fantasies: Colin McGinn, *The Making of a Philosopher*, 2003.

2 Korzybski's metaphor of "quantum potential". According to physicist Victor Stenger in *Quantum Gods: Creation, Chaos, and the Search for Cosmic Consciousness*, 2009, the scale of distances involved in the brain are more than a thousand times too large for actual quantum effects to come into play in normal brain processing.

3 The 'odd one out' IQ test comes from Eric Whitehead in a letter to *New Scientist*.

4 "Organisms naturally endeavor [...] to persevere in their own being." Benedict de Spinoza, *Ethics*, 1677, Penguin Classics 1996, translator Edwin Curley.

5 Trees and their many meanings: Carl G. Jung, *Man and his Symbols*, 1964.

6 Enabling people to get inside the organization of their own minds: psychotherapist James Lawley, personal communication.

Chapter 6
The Good Midwife

*They are indeed wise who do not bid you to enter the house
of their wisdom but rather lead you to the threshold of
your own mind.*   Kahlil Gibran

Leading cleanly – Unclean leading: Ian's need for recognition – Leader-followers –
Uncommon sense – Influence and intent – Seven core competencies – De-centered
leading, self-led, information-led – Peter and the red balloon – The facilitator role

Traditionally we have always deferred to our soothsayers, imams,
and analysts when it came to getting an insight into our complex
and deeply conflicted natures. We have expected to be shown the
way to well being. Even today among agents of change for whom
Clean Language is the methodology of choice, there are still those
who feel the need to lead the exchange: to decide on a desirable
outcome and a strategy for achieving it; to initiate the tactics and to
determine the means.

What is 'Clean' leadership? Is it desirable? Is it possible? A key
criterion for the Clean facilitator is to assist the natural evolution of
the client's system without directing or distorting it. It is the skill of
the midwife. 'Midwife' is an ungendered noun: *mid* originally meant
'with' and *wife* 'woman', thus 'person with woman'. A good midwife
works with the mother, taking their cue from the baby's need to be
born and the mother's need to give birth to the baby.

The delivery of resources does not require its facilitators to be
overburdened with theoretical knowledge or conventional ideas
about 'strong leadership'. It does require them to be unusually
receptive: sensitized to small, sometimes subliminal, indications.

People need less overt intervention than many of us realize.
Generally they know for themselves – at least tacitly, at least when

asked the right questions – what is good for them. Even the most primitive of animals, the marine worm *thysanozoon*, knows which way is up. Put *thysanozoon* on its back – if you can tell its back from its front – and it will respond with alacrity and right itself.

Unclean leading

There are various kinds of 'unclean' leader. One will have an agenda that says the client should get what the leader believes they need; rather like the salesperson who identifies at the outset that the customer needs double-glazing rather than information in order to make a decision about whether they need double-glazing or not.

Another kind will extend the client's outcome to themselves. If the client says, "I want to be happy", the unclean leader's outcome would be "I want my client to be happy" or even "I want to make my client happy." Either of these is pretty much guaranteed to prejudice the exchange, because as the client discovers more about their desire to be happy, they might well get the idea that a more attainable goal, such as to improve their relationships or to do worthwhile work, would fit the bill better. Meanwhile, the unclean leader would still be pursuing their original "I want my client to get their 'I want to be happy' outcome." Every client outcome should in that sense be treated as provisional: sufficient only for its interim purpose.

Ian's need for recognition

Ian is an experienced counselor who has recently started working in Clean Language. He is having difficulty with one of his clients, a teacher frustrated with one of her students and with the student's mother. Ian reports it this way:

> *My client sees the problem as belonging to the mother and her son. The client is not stating that the client herself has a problem. She speaks at length and passionately about her student's mother's neglect and the student's passivity.*

How might the good midwife respond to this quite complex presentation? First of all, by politely sidestepping Ian's second-hand material – his report of what his client has said – and then his third-hand material – his report of what his client has said about the mother and son. We can now be more curious about Ian himself.

> And when all that, what would you like to have happen?
> *How can I lead my client to a consideration of self?*

Three self-referential words ("I", "my", "self") in a single sentence are not there for a quiet life. They are there to be noticed.

> And what kind of 'I' is that 'I' that can lead my client to a consideration of self?
>
> *The me that wants to lead is the frustrated me that wants to give my client advice. I want to lead my clients to experiences they will recognize as positive and powerful.*

Five more references to self ("me", "me", "my", "I", "my") and two more to "lead".

> And what kind of 'I' wants to 'lead' your clients to experiences they will recognize as positive and powerful?

Ian pauses for a moment.

> *I guess it's me who wants the recognition!*

This not-so-hidden agenda highlights another key criterion for leading cleanly: the capacity to work without applause. The first philosopher of humility, Lao Tzu, put it this way: "When the work's done right, with no fuss or boasting, ordinary people say, Oh, we did it ourselves."[1] Ian acknowledges his dilemma:

> *I want to help my client and I want brownie points for doing it.*

A brownie was a benevolent elf who lived invisibly in houses and did the housework at night. She did not ask for points! The information that Ian wants recognition for his housework now leads the exchange. I only have to continue to follow.

> And when you want brownie points, then what happens?
>
> *I have to find how not to short-change the client. If I want points I have to give them myself.*

Leader-followers
Researchers Posner and Kouzes[2] identify five key elements of good leadership. They apply to Clean leaders as much as to the conventional kind.

> Modeling the way
> Inspiring a shared vision
> Challenging the process
> Enabling others to act
> Encouraging the heart

Some of the behaviors associated with 'inspiring', 'challenging', and 'encouraging' could take us perilously close to imposing our own metaphors and beliefs on clients, however, so we need to tread carefully. Clean leadership is a more sophisticated business altogether. Clean leaders are themselves followers, a paradox that works perfectly well in practice. And it works whoever speaks first. This might be the facilitator:

> And what would you like to have happen?

A basic 'entry point' question that could be said to lead the exchange, but is not in itself a leading question – one so phrased as to presuppose the response. Or the client might speak first:

> *I'm feeling sad and I'd like it to stop.*

In which case, the question follows:

> And what kind of sad could that sad be?

The question can be said to be leading the client's attention – in this case to their "sad" rather than to their "like it to stop" – but in a way that can only generate an independent response:

> It's a feeling of heaviness here in my stomach.

In contrast, an 'unclean' leading question such as:

> *How sad are you?

is so pregnant with supposition that it can only give birth to itself:

> *Very sad.*

We can agree that the non-suppositional question ("And what kind of sad could that sad be?") drives the appearance of the client's information as much as the suppositional kind ("How sad are you?"), but in doing so it gives no hint of what the content or sense of the response should be. Clean questioning, whether it 'leads' the exchange or not, can only follow, or take its cue from, or at most accompany, the client's own process.

Posner and Kouzes' leadership principles can be applied to Clean leader-follower-accompanists as follows (the points are elaborated in later chapters):

Modeling the way. New clients often have severe doubts about the legitimacy of their own process. From the first exchange, the facilitator models total acceptance with the question, "What would you like to have happen?", indicating that only the client will know what that might be. The facilitator is also assisting the client to 'model' – that is, to represent and get to know – their process.

Inspiring a shared vision. The facilitator's entry point question invites the client to establish a shared vision for the session. Other kinds of 'inspiring' – articulating a vision for the client to share, for example – are unlikely to be Clean.

Challenging the process. Not in a testing or competitive sense, but in a readiness to draw the client's attention to anything they might say – even "I don't know" – and a willingness to draw attention to a seemingly trivial item – a look, a sniff, a throwaway remark – on the grounds that it too could signal the presence of important information. A specific challenge to the client to prove or justify something they have said would not be Clean.

Enabling others to act. A fundamental position designed to validate and amplify the client's natural authority.

Encouraging the heart. Metaphor (Part II) is the first language of feeling. Feelings have a location in the body – the heart, gut, throat, etc. – and are 'like' something – rocks, bubbles, rainbows – which may contain the problem, or the means to its solution, or the solution itself, and sometimes all three. Overly cognitive clients learn to recognize the primacy of emotion ('heart') in the construction of their thinking ('head'). Emotionally unstable clients learn to distinguish between disabling and enabling feelings.

Uncommon sense

A good midwife follows or accompanies whatever the patient presents and not only those elements that are obvious. They may also draw attention to elements that, as novelist-philosopher Arthur Koestler put it:

> are indifferent to the rules of verbal logic, are unperturbed by apparent contradiction, and untouched by the dogmas and taboos of so-called common sense.[3]

Koestler was describing the act of imagination some twenty years before Grove began working with its therapeutic potential. Koestler anticipated what happens when a client shifts into what he called "obscure or imagistic mode":

> At the decisive stage of discovery, the codes of disciplined reasoning are suspended – as they are in a dream, the reverie, the manic flight of thought, when the steam of ideation is free to drift, by its own emotional gravity.

This is just the kind of thing that happens when clients move into metaphor to describe their perceptions. The principles of metaphorical transformation are more akin to those of dreams or visions than of physical reality. In *Harry Potter and the Prisoner of Azkaban*, a purple bus races through the streets of London shape-shifting at will, while once a month a mild-mannered Professor Lupin metamorphoses into a werewolf. We are in the world of imaginative reality, which accepts without question that the so-called rational mind is only part of the story and knows only a very small part of the truth.

Encouraging intuitive freedom in clients requires facilitator-followers who are at ease working with ambiguity, poetry, and symbolism without getting carried away on the wings of delusion. The result can be to restore a client's faith in their own creativity. And when that becomes weary or compromised, a Clean facilitator might have to work with client dogmatism and obstinacy without being drawn into sterile debate.

These are midwives who have dispensed with the conventional trappings of authority; who are receptive and accessible; who can acknowledge deep feeling in all its forms; and who can respond to illogic, contradiction, and fantasy as much as to reason and common sense.

Influence and intent

Every Clean Language facilitator can expect to be challenged at one time or other about how Clean they can really be. Therapists and coaches with a preference for selecting the track on which their clients will travel have been known to raise a worn little flag: "How can you not influence your clients?" Given that it is impossible for two people to be together without affecting each other in some way, my answer to the question is in two parts.

Firstly, I readily accept I have influence. Clean questioning is highly influential: it has a profound effect on the questionee's brain chemistry and neural transmission. 'Influence' only describes an effect, however. What is more in question is the means of influencing, an activity that includes a colorful collection of intentions and behaviors including coaxing, coercing, manipulating, and persuading. If my intention is to 'coax' or 'persuade' you, I will not be influencing cleanly. If my intention is to solve your problem or guide you to an outcome that is not of your own making, my influencing will be at the interfering end of the interventionist spectrum. If my intention is to facilitate your system to know and determine itself, my influence is more likely to be Clean.

Secondly, I make a clear distinction between influencing the content of your process, which I am unable to do if I follow Clean rules, and influencing your process itself, which I acknowledge. 'Influence' originally meant a flowing in, as of water to land. I have some control over the inflow of my questions, but none whatsoever over the response of the land, which will adapt itself as one living thing to another, unpredictably. I exercise a certain amount of judgment in gauging the changing nature of the land and I take responsibility for my judgment, as any facilitator must. If I get it 'wrong', it will be either because I have not identified a hidden agenda (cf. Ian's need for recognition) or made insufficient allowance for it.[4]

Here is the response of one Clean counselor to the question, "How can you not influence your clients?"

> Clean language is a wonderful tool to use when it seems 'obvious' to me what the other person's issues are. Were I using a traditional approach, I would definitely be influencing the direction of the work more. By using Clean Language, I am obliged to put aside those assumptions and simply watch in fascination as the client's metaphor landscape unfolds.

A facilitator may characterize themself as watching in fascination or as being proactive; either way they have to surrender something of their ego to the process. In psychoanalytic theory, the 'ego' is a division of the mind that serves as conscious mediator between the individual and reality. This raises the question of how a leader views reality. Autocratic leaders will typically perceive the world as objectively knowable and themselves as knowing more than their followers. Even leaders for whom the ego is no more than a metaphor for an excess of self-esteem may require the client to adapt more to their reality than they to their client's. Clean leadership has an altogether different worldview: one that seeks to adapt to the client's reality.

Seven core competencies

Adaptive leader-followers need certain core competencies. In some people they come naturally. Most people can acquire them if they are sufficiently motivated. Some never quite come to terms with them, philosophically, psychologically, or practically. I can identify seven in particular.

1 The capacity for being with and reflecting the client's reality, however revealed

This requires an ability to suppress one's own ego/mediator of reality while giving priority to the client's. Not everyone can do this and many agents of change prefer not to.

2 The ability to translate sounds into words while at the same time processing rhythm and intonation

Reflecting what a client says means having language and melody skills operating in tandem, so that clients can be matched vocally while at the same time exquisite attention is paid to their actual words. There is more on listening skills in Chapters 12 and 13 and on vocal skills in Chapter 19.

3 Experience of the Clean process as a client

Those who have experienced epiphany or enhanced self-knowledge through their intuitive responses to Clean questioning will know what it is like to trust their own process and are more likely to be at ease facilitating others to do the same.

4 Readiness to contain internal contradictions and inconsistencies

The key to this is to get to know them well and to work with them. Again, it is a considerable help to have been a client oneself.

5 High self-esteem

Unaffected self-assurance is vital to maintaining the low-self state essential for attending completely to others. The best leader-followers I have observed at work were neither intent on dominating the exchange nor content to be the clients' shadow.

6 The ability to focus

Grove had a remarkable ability to switch attention from his own concerns to those of his clients in an instant, and to maintain a high level of concentration as long as was required.

7 Acceptance of uncertainty

Clean leading honors not just who clients are, but how they are. It means having no notion of how they should be. A Clean leader will never know exactly where a line of questioning will lead.

A young woman comes to a counselor in a state of high anxiety. She has several problems, one of which is her relationship with her boyfriend, and in particular their lack of interests in common.

All Nick watches is sport, I like keeping up with current affairs.
And what kind of affairs are current affairs?

The sort I'm having with Bob, he's an electrician.

One can never be sure of the next response. A facilitator must be on constant alert for the item of information that will update or augment the last one.

Some counselors characterize the position of uncertainty as 'de-centered' leading. Some refer to it as 'self-led'. And others, the Grovian kind, as 'information-led'.

De-centered leading
has been described in one metaphor as placing the client's knowledge and skills at the center of the process and the facilitator's knowledge and skills outside the center. Australian Michael White and New Zealander David Epston's 'narrative therapy' is an example.[5] White and Epston maintain that power resides in the client and in the client's various networks, and not in the therapist's wisdom. The client gets to tell and retell the story of their life in a series of conversations in which the therapist helps the client clarify the dominant story that drives their present behavior; helps identify the exceptions in the client's life that the dominant story discounts; helps develop an alternative plot derived from the exceptions; and helps recruit family and friends in support of the new narrative.

This is quite a lot of 'help'. In spirit, the approach favors the client's experience over the therapist's, but the actual behaviors involved in guiding, interpreting, initiating, and paraphrasing require the therapist to be an active director rather more than an attentive prompter of the performance. The narrative line must be constantly reshaped so that it builds to a therapeutic resolution in the final act. Yet recent research by Swedish psychologists suggests that accuracy and authenticity are not improved by persistent retelling. The risk of an incorrect account actually increases the more a story is told and retold.[6]

However, it may be that accuracy about the past is less important in 'de-centered' leading than the client's engagement in the present and their covenant with the future.

In another version of de-centering theory, South African psychotherapist Tim Barry uses video playback in an attempt "to offer the client more objective information about themselves" and "to democratize some aspects of the therapy relationship." We can infer from this that other aspects are not democratic. Barry suggests that moving clients between performing and observing roles helps them develop "a double self-description" in the same way that the brain perceives depth when it integrates right and left retinal images. Yet research into 'binocular rivalry' shows that when retinal images are observed as conflicting, one image is likely to be 'seen' and the other repressed or suppressed. The visual cortex not only interprets signals from the retina, it also sends feedback signals to the retina with information about what the brain *expects* to see, which shapes what the mind actually perceives.[7]

Applying this finding to the playback scenario would suggest that a client experiencing a conflict between what they experienced during the session and what they experience while viewing the recording might well repress or suppress one aspect and 'see' only the other. The "double self-description" would be incomplete.

Self-led

A 'self-led' approach called 'Focusing' was developed by philosopher-psychologist Eugene Gendlin in the United States in the nineteen-seventies. Clients make guided contact with a special kind of internal bodily awareness, which Gendlin calls a "felt sense". This is neither an emotion nor a symptom, but what he describes as "the many-stranded fabric of bodily awareness that guides golfers as they tee off." As the client focuses on this meaningful body sense, they are directing themselves inward to draw information "from the deeper, wiser self" in such a way that a "felt shift" or bodily release occurs. Gendlin believes that we are by our nature in charge of ourselves; that no external authority can resolve our problems for us or tell us how to live; that the main role of a 'focusing facilitator', who might even be a friend, is to observe; and that the best kind of observing is to stay out of the focuser's way.[8]

Information-led

Grovian practice has points of agreement with both de-centered and self-led approaches, but is able to draw the client's attention not only to a kinesthetic "felt sense" (as in focusing), or to an auditory "story" (as in narrative therapy), or to a "view" of themselves (as in video playback), but also to any linguistic or somatic signal – sound, symbol, symptom, picture, word, gesture, eye cue, movement, aroma, or flavor – originating in any representational system or combination of systems – visual, auditory, kinesthetic, proprioceptive (position and movement related), gustatory (taste), and olfactory (smell). Attention may also be drawn by the Clean facilitator to signals that a 'self-led' client might be tempted to avoid or ignore because they seemed too difficult or trivial.

Absolute acceptance of the client's world as perceived and relayed by the client is one of the underlying principles of information-led work. It can take a leap of imagination to realize that a client's inner world is complex enough without adding our own variables; to realize that genuine information emerges not as a result of external suggestion or installation, but through self-regeneration; and to realize, above all, that the information the client requires is already present. Plato believed that what we perceive as learning is in fact the recovery of what we have forgotten. Given what we know about psychology today, I would expand that to include what we have censored or suppressed.

If we already have the information we need, the appearance of change will merely be the result of a rearrangement of its parts.

Peter and the red balloon

> *It's like I'm two or three and I'm terrified.*
> And where is that terrified?

> *In my heart.*
> And does that terrified in your heart have a size or a shape?

> *(Gestures) It's about this big.*
> And when terrified is in your heart and it's about this big, that is terrified like what?

Like a balloon about to burst.
And what kind of balloon could that balloon be, before it was about to burst?

It's beautiful, red, light, and firm, and I'm having fun with it.

If an over-inflated balloon is Peter's deeply felt metaphor for a heart about to burst, it might in time be transformed into the lighter, firmer heart that it was when Peter was at one with the world and the world was at one with him. Terrified heart can become lighter heart again because it already *is* lighter heart. No Clean question itself could contain such an astonishing proposition, but the associations and connections a Clean question makes most certainly can.

The facilitator role

In his pioneering work *Against Therapy* (1988), former psychotherapist Jeffrey Masson advocated the abolition of the psychotherapies of the day. "No matter how kindly a person is," he wrote, "when that person becomes a therapist, he or she is engaged in acts that are bound to diminish the dignity, autonomy, and freedom of the person who comes for help." The Clean facilitator's job is not to diminish, but to enhance a client's dignity, autonomy, and freedom. An experienced Clean facilitator might have a shrewd idea about where to begin looking for the solution to a terrified heart, but will allow that only the client knows, exactly or tacitly, what the solution is, what the price of accessing it might be, and what kind of nurturing or maturing it needs in order to emerge freely and securely.

"The therapist's role," said the personal construct psychologist Jay Efran, and he could have been talking about any facilitator, "is not to treat people or heal them, but to encourage their curiosity about themselves." And the surest way of achieving that – simple in theory, exacting in practice – is to listen, really listen, to what clients say. The psychiatrist R.D. Laing was among the first to argue that doctors should really listen to their patients.[9] David Grove went significantly further: they should not only listen to, but also reflect, what their patients say, draw attention to it, and ask non-assumptive questions with the intention of eliciting more information. These are the skills of the good midwife.

In Part I, we considered how the singularity of our minds creates the world we inhabit. We saw how Clean Language and the new psychology of change prompt our unique perceptions to work for us by minimizing external influence and assisting us to know ourselves from within. More often than not, we will communicate what we know in symbolic or metaphorical terms. And these are the subject of Part II.

Notes to Chapter 6

1 The philosophy of 'humility'. Phil Swallow points out in his presentation, *The Tao of Clean,* that there is no precise word in English for a facilitator's refusal to 'take the lead' in changework while yet remaining instrumental. This was the synthesis sought by Lao Tzu and epitomized by the Tao ('path', 'way', or 'flow' of Nature).

The three treasures of Taoism, of which Lao Tzu is credited as founder, have been variously translated as charity, simplicity, and humility, or mercy, moderation, and modesty. It should be acknowledged that for some agents of change the loss of visibility involved in facilitating cleanly can be painful. I have no answer to this, other than for them to find a Clean facilitator and work on it.

2 Key elements of leadership: Barry Posner and James Kouzes, *The Leadership Challenge,* 1987, 2003.

3 The act of imagination: Arthur Koestler, *The Act of Creation,* 1976.

4 Influencing process, not content: thanks to James Lawley for his influence on the content of this paragraph.

5 De-centered leading: visit dulwichcentre.com.au for more on White and Epston's narrative therapy. An article on video playback by Tim Barry, *Screen Play,* appeared in the South African *New Therapist* magazine, July-August 2003.

6 Memory not improved by retelling. Research by psychologist Farhan Sarwar, Lund University, Sweden, reported in *Science Daily* February 2011.

7 Unreliability of eyewitness evidence: we see what we expect to see. Psychologist Tamara Watson, University of Sydney, in *Current Biology*, September 2004. Many other papers have been published on the subject.

8 'Self-led' approach to therapy: Eugene Gendlin, focusing.org

9 R.D. Laing further argued that not listening properly to the mentally ill led to classifying them schematically as psychotic, manic, schizophrenic, and so on, which discounted their individuality and stigmatized them in the eyes of the merely neurotic, i.e. the rest of us. He pointed out that labels could become self-fulfilling prophecies.

Part II

INSIDE INFORMATION
Symbol and Metaphor the Keys to the Unconscious

Introduction to Part II

A middle-aged woman weeps as she describes the "black cloud of despair" that has enveloped her for months. Angela has a sense that there is "light beyond the cloud," but that it is "too bright, too harsh" to venture into. I am tempted to come up with any number of suggestions in an attempt to move Angela on and to make something happen. Instead, I ask a question that in itself suggests nothing:

> And when black cloud of despair and light beyond that is too
> bright, too harsh, to enter into, what happens next?

There is a long pause. Again, I am tempted to intervene, to do or say something to 'help'. Angela has been here before, aware only of darkness and despair. Now something different happens. Her tears dry up and when she speaks, her voice has a quality, not of despair, but of curiosity.

> *I make a little hole in the cloud. It lets diffused light through*
> *and I see a little blue sky.*

It is at this moment that Angela brings symbol and reality together to create a new sense of herself. And she does so in a way that only she knows how. Without revisiting trauma, without years of analysis, without a single suggestion from the therapist, she has learned to trust her unconscious.

In Part II, we look at the significance and subjectivity of symbol (Chapter 7); at how our minds construct symbolic representations (Chapter 8); at the aggregation, interrelation, and implication of symbols in metaphor (Chapter 9); and at the ways in which metaphor can be utilized for good or ill (Chapter 10). You may never be wholly able to know what is right for another person – the everlasting struggle that is at the heart of being alive and in relationship – but in these chapters you will find the means for getting very close indeed.

Chapter 7
Light Beyond Angela's Cloud
The Significance of Symbol

I know what 'it' means well enough, when I find a thing, said the Duck: it's generally a frog, or a worm.

Lewis Carroll, *Alice in Wonderland*

Expressing the inexpressible – Jungian symbolism and its limits – Verbal and nonverbal symbolism – Ralph's rocky road – Functionality, structure, psychoactivity of symbol – Small changes, big difference – Involuntary symbolizing

When paleontologists announced the discovery of a stone axe-head among 350,000 year-old human remains excavated from a burial cave in the Sierra de Atapuerca, near the city of Burgos in northern Spain, they opened up a great scientific debate. If the placing of the axe were a deliberate act, as some believe, it would be the earliest evidence we have of symbolic thought in humankind – a defining moment when the mind first reached beyond the body's immediate needs into what would become a world of imagination, symbol, and language.

Today as we find new ways of exploring this world, the symbols that represent our internal experience are honored. We enter a secret garden of re-creation in which, sooner or later, there comes a moment when something unexpected, even magical, happens.

I make a little hole in the cloud.

Most of us express ourselves in symbol and metaphor constantly, yet most of the time we are hardly aware of it. If you were to say to me, "My heart is stirred," or "I am heavy with sorrow," or "I'm at my wits' end," the odds are that you would not find it helpful for me to use words of my own in an attempt to empathize. Your heart is not in fact "shaken", you are not "grief-stricken", "overwrought", or "out of sorts." These are my metaphors. For any friend or facilitator to paraphrase you and intervene on the assumption that they know what you mean supposes a kind of arrogance or innocence.

In this chapter, we dip a toe or two into the deep waters of the unconscious. We consider how it communicates via symbol and metaphor, and how these likenesses and signs can be tapped for the information they hold.

> *I try so hard but I come up against so many obstructions.*
> Obstructions like what?

> *Like stone walls.*
> How many stone walls?

> *Three.*
> And is there anything else about those three stone walls?

> *Well, I can climb over the first one, and get round the second, and the third I see now has a gateway.*

Objects, images, and ideas have symbolic value for their owners and creators when they contain something more than their common or immediate meaning. Korzybski and others suggested that we evolved as human beings because of our capacity for symbolism; that human knowledge is conditioned by the properties of symbolism; that all human achievement rests upon our use of symbolism; and that the solution to every human problem depends on our enquiries into it, because we are conditioned by its limitations and may be misled by their misuse.[1]

The danger, as Korzybski said of the rise of Nazism in the nineteen-thirties, is that those who rule the symbols, rule us. Understanding symbols and how they can be used and abused is as important to the principles and practice of self-determination as Clean Language itself.

A symbol is a thing that gives expression to the inexpressible. It is a coded message from the unconscious, which suggests that it is not a simple thing. The word first appeared at a time when money had been established as an agent of human agreement. It derives from the Greek *sym*, 'together', and *ballein*, 'to fit', and was first used in reference to the practice of breaking a coin or other small object in half when friends parted. Each half of the coin served as a token of the friendship: the visible sign of an invisible connection. When the halves were fitted together again after an absence, expression was given to the inexpressible again.

A symbol no longer needs to have visible or material form. The link with the storage of information, however, remains.

> A token of reality
> A sign of the times
> A badge of honor
> A mark of respect

Our ability to see one thing in terms of another is fundamental to our understanding of ourselves and the world. Angela's "black cloud" *is* her despair. Invited to consider the image she has created, she realizes intuitively that she can do something about what it represents.

> *I make a little hole in the cloud. It lets diffused light through and I see a little blue sky.*

As Angela modifies the form of her symbol, the shadow of despair it signifies is lit by the appearance of hope.

A symbol can be very different in form from the thing it represents. An atomic 'particle' is symbolic; a quantum 'wave' is symbolic. What we generally think of as particles (of dust, say) and waves (of water) differ considerably from atomic particles and quantum waves, but one prompts us into finding common ground with the other. Everyday objects like 'cloud' and 'wall' may be far removed in kind from the imaginative associations they give rise to, but they are the means we use to acknowledge the presence of what would otherwise be invisible and give expression to what would otherwise be inexpressible.

Among the objects I keep in my study is a statuette of St. George and the Dragon, which for me represents the victory of the human spirit over forces of fear and oppression. I keep such quasi-religious objects out of my consulting room (and such high-faluting explanations to myself), because I know how we all interpret these things differently. In this, I confess, I differ from Freud, who surrounded his patients with the accumulated clutter of his own inner life – masks, figurines, votive objects from around the world – because he believed that his personal symbolism reflected a typical and universal view of humanity. I prefer to keep my client space relatively free of clutter. Pictures and artifacts have a distinctive presence and mine have an emblematic significance that is unlikely to be shared by my clients.

What coins, masks, and statuettes have in common is that they are not only what they seem, but also what they 'mean'. Meaning is a profoundly private conversation. The content of a concept such as a holiday or a belief in fairies, or the content of an object such as a watch or a mobile phone, derives from the personal meaning we attach to them allied to the use we make of them. The more neural connections they make in the brain, the greater the meaning our minds will assign to them.

Jungian symbolism and its limits

Jung recognized several kinds of symbolism. One was created, spontaneously in the unconscious through the medium of dreams, which, if interpreted 'correctly' – that is to say, by the therapist himself – were the great guide and adviser to the conscious self. Jung proposed that everyone had within their psychic depths something corresponding to a mountain (a symbol he characterized as "an obstacle"); a meadow ("a garden of possibilities"); a river ("a flow of energy"); a path; a cave; and so on. Some of his followers still use these symbols to guide clients through journeys of the soul on the presumption that everyone experiences dreamful or mystical states in a similar way. In my experience of working with metaphor landscapes, the imaginative mental domains clients conceive to contain and connect their symbols, this is manifestly untrue. In facilitating many thousands of client metaphors, I have learned never to take the universality of symbolism for granted. Not every client who comes across a meadow in their mental landscape will view it as a garden of possibilities. It may equally be perceived as a field of frustration prone to periodic flooding. Caves contain wise old women or monsters; paths lead to heaven or oblivion.

Jung derived another kind of symbolism from his notion of a 'collective unconscious' in the form of archetypal images. Archetypes are recurrent patterns we share because of our common ancestry, but they are impossible to fully comprehend, define, or apply at the individual level because, as Jung himself admitted:

> they lead to ideas that lie beyond the grasp of reason. The wheel may lead our thoughts toward the concept of a divine sun, but at this point reason must admit its incompetence; man is unable to define a divine being.[2]

The wheel may have led Jung toward an indefinable divinity, but it leads some of my clients to symbolic encounters with bicycles, roulette, or hamsters in cages. In *Spiritualism and the Foundations of C.G. Jung's Psychology* (1993), psychologist Francis Charet speculates that Jung's break with Freud stemmed from the fact that Freud was not prepared to consider mystical or magical data as raw material on which to build a psychology.

Jung saw a third kind of symbolism in a version of the material and metaphysical mix he called 'synchronicity', a conjecture that certain of the everyday coincidences we notice are imbued with deep meaning. He thought of them as brief encounters between matter and spirit in regions of human experience he characterized as "dark, dubious, and hedged about with prejudice." One such was the entertaining phenomenon he called *Die Verpflichtung des Namens*, 'the compulsion of the name', in which a person's surname came to represent their nature or profession. One of Jung's patients, *Herr Gross* (Mr. Large), suffered, said Jung, from delusions of grandeur, while another, *Herr Kleiner* (Mr. Smaller), had an inferiority complex. Predisposed to notice these things, I see in the news today that one I. Judge has been appointed Lord Chief Justice of England and Wales and that a certain Dr. Carver is a plastic surgeon in Hertfordshire. "Are these the whimsicalities of chance," Jung would ask, "the suggestive effects of the name, or meaningful coincidences?" He inclined to the meaningful. My money is on the whimsicalities of chance. I wager there are many more plastic surgeons called Smith or Jones than Carver or Chiseler, and that a Frenchman called Petit will be found to hold a position of responsibility on the board of a large corporation.[3]

The auto-suggestive effects of the name may have a part to play on occasion. Amongst all the warm Winterbottoms in the world, there are sure to be a few with poor circulation. If a synchronistic perception is meaningful, we might ask wherein lies the meaning and find with some certainty that it resides in the bosom of the perceiver. Ultimately, Jung acknowledged that the significance of all dreamful, archetypal, and synchronistic symbolism came down to its meaning to the patient alone. After his death, his collaborator Marie-Louise von Franz pointed out that there was no such thing as a typical Jungian interpretation. All dreams, she said, were private and individual communications, and no two people used the symbolism of the unconscious in the same way.

A Jungian brought up in a western cultural tradition would probably identify my statuette of St. George and the Dragon as an archetype of the hero slaying his shadow, but in the Far East dragons are revered as benevolent forces of nature and for many millions of people that would make St. George the bad guy.

Verbal and nonverbal symbolism

Language is a limited system of symbols representing the tiniest tip of the iceberg of experience. The most it can do is hint at the extent and density of what lies beneath. Word-symbols in particular can evoke phobic responses over which we have little or no control. In his 1933-1945 diaries, the German philologist Victor Klemperer noted that

> Words can be like tiny doses of arsenic. They are swallowed unnoticed, appear to have no effect, and then after a little time the toxic reaction sets in after all.[4]

Around the same time, Korzybski was warning the world of "the structural semantic bondage of words," and the psycho-physiological disasters that words and their consequences could produce in the human organism at sub-microscopic levels. David Grove would later characterize these as "words that wound": signals in the present that evoke trauma from the past.

Such signals can appear without warning and in any form – a word, a snarl, the slamming of a door, the ringing of a bell. We learn from Pavlov's work on conditioned responses that it is not the signal itself that produces the response, but the meaning the signal evokes in the mind of the receiver. A client's sniff may be as symbolic as a sigh, as rich in information as a phrase, a pause, a stutter, a move, a doodle, or a few lines painted on the walls of a cave. The springboks depicted in early Namibian rock art may have stood for a spiritual quest, the abundance of nature, the next good meal, or perhaps all three.

Today's equivalent is the client's 'metaphor map', in which internally sourced information is represented externally and can be utilized therapeutically.

Ralph's rocky road

Ralph states his problem:

My life is like a rocky road with obstacles blocking my path.

He draws it.

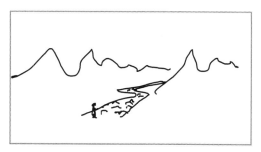

Figure 8 Ralph's rocky road. A drawn metaphor map,
but could be a collage, an arrangement of objects, etc.

I make no attempt to interpret Ralph's drawing or to ask him what
it means. I simply draw his attention to it:

And is there anything else about that rocky road?
I need to change it to a river, which can flow around the rocks.

And can you change it to river which can flow around rocks?
I can try.

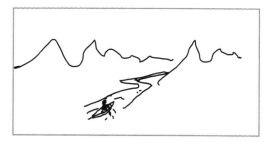

Figure 9 Ralph's river

And then what happens?
*Life flows on. The rocks are no longer obstacles, just interesting
features on the way.*

Mapping these symbols and their relationship to one another allows
Ralph to illuminate his thinking and feeling; to determine what is
going on for him by means other than strict 'reason'; to decipher his
unconscious processes and make them available to consciousness;
and to better understand – and potentially transform – his problem.
How do symbols work in this way?

Functionality, structure, psychoactivity of symbol

Symbols have functionality. A *cloud* may darken your internal landscape, you may come up against a *barrier* to progress, or feel a *knot* of anxiety in the pit of your stomach. Those rocks, locks, knots, and balloons about to burst all have a function related to their purpose. They are there for a reason. They may have appeared as emotional anti-bodies, formed to fight a perpetrator of abuse during childhood or to bring comfort to a part of the self that dissociated during trauma, neglect, or coercion. Questioning can elicit their existence and invite them to convey what they know, so that as their creator and owner you may determine their source and discover their purpose.

Symbols have structure. A symbolic cloud will have *size* and *substance* in your metaphor landscape; a symbolic barrier, *dimensions, location,* and *shape*; a symbolic knot, *ends* and *length*. These are not just any old rocks, locks, strings, and balloons. As manifestations of the unconscious, they may contain a fragment of the self that once sought protection, or needed to separate or suppress itself in order to survive. They may be sheltering the resources of a younger, more pristine self. Clean questioning will elicit their characteristics and explore their relation to the system as a whole.

Symbols have psychoactivity. A cloud may generate *rain* that brings *sustenance, new life,* or *healing*. A barrier may be *breached, lowered,* or *surmounted*. A knot may be *cut* or *unraveled*. Clean questioning can encourage the conditions for their transformation from static, repetitive pattern to dynamic, resolution related activity.

Small changes, big difference

Systems become unstable or disordered because, as playwright Michael Frayn has said:

> the events that constitute them are so completely interconnected – and so often feed back into themselves – that very small differences in initial conditions produce very large differences in outcome.[5]

In the classic stage farces – Frayn's *Noises Off*, Feydeau's *Hotel Paradiso*, Philip King's *See How They Run* – we witness how quickly a single event – a name misheard, a lost pair of trousers, a tipsy vicar – can escalate and turn a relatively stable system chaotic. Cosmologists point to the growth of a hugely complex universe from the simplest primordial beginnings. The British scientist Stephen Wolfram spent twenty years studying the way that minimal programs generate immense complexity. He discovered that only a few simple elements and a few simple rules were required for behavior that was far from simple to emerge. It is a finding that many believe to underlie every activity in the universe, on stage or off.[6]

The complexity of much of the phobic, neurotic, and irrational states we construct for ourselves emerges from the basic fear and anxiety we experience in the face of such threats to our well-being as the withdrawal or thwarting of attention and affection. In addressing the symbolic construction, rather than the real-life consequences, of Ralph's rocky road, the clarity of Clean Language speaks directly to the simple rules that set up his original program.

What kind of rocky could that road be?
How many obstacles blocking your path?

Involuntary symbolizing

How do we go about the ingenious job of constructing our internal worlds in the first place? If we return for a moment to the placing of the axe alongside its owner at Atapuerca 350,000 years ago, we may suppose that the symbolism of the act was instinctive. Most of our symbolizing is instinctive to this day. When I came across my statuette of St. George and the Dragon, I wasn't knowingly seeking a representation of good over evil. Involuntary symbolizing is a function of our cognition (how we think and feel), and of our speech and movement (how we communicate). It is an intrinsic outcome of the information-processing function of the mind, a complex program derived from elementary rules.

How does the mind create symbol and metaphor? It is an aspect of our mental make-up with particular implications for changework.

Notes to Chapter 7

1 We are conditioned by symbolism: Alfred Korzybski, *Science and Sanity*, op. cit..

2 Archetypes beyond the grasp of reason: Carl G. Jung, *Man and His Symbols*, 1964.

3 At the time of writing, I find that one Jean-Pierre Petit ('Mr. Small') is Executive Vice-President of McDonald's Worldwide and Henri-Dominique Petit is Senior Vice-President of Eastman-Kodak. The idea of 'nominative determinism' seems to work just as well, or as badly, in reverse, which suggests that neither determinism nor indeterminism can be relied on for the whole truth. My own name is a contraction of 'hard land', but I'm really quite accommodating. Make of all this what you will. In the philosophy of Clean, it is the individual client's perceptions – skeptical or mystical – that count.

4 "Words can be like tiny doses of arsenic." Victor Klemperer, *The Language of the Third Reich*, 1957.

5 Small changes, big difference: Michael Frayn, *The Human Touch,* 2006.

6 Simple rules, complex systems: Stephen Wolfram, *A New Kind of Science*, 2002.

Chapter 8
Drama Behind The Scenes
The Making of Metaphor

We shall all be chaunged and that in a moment and in the twincklynge of an eye. William Tyndale

In an instant – Ruth ambushed – An epic half-second – Infinite input – Serial selection – Involuntary association – Symbolic output – Moment of choice – Nina and Olympic gold – Summary of the process

The 16th century reformist priest William Tyndale challenged the orthodoxy of his day by translating the Bible into English for the first time. His motivation was political: to take this key instrument of ecclesiastical authority out of the hands of priests and scholars and make it available to all. As agents of change in positions of some authority, real or imagined, we have a political choice to make every time we intervene: does power derive from ourselves or from the people we serve?

The choice we make will affect every question we ask. Deeply sourced intentions take on a special significance when everything we are aware of, every sound and sight and thought and feeling, originates out of our awareness. And it happens in an instant. Every twinkle, every blink, every second of our lives has the potential for learning and change.

Ruth ambushed

It is not the past that keeps us from having what we want, but the way our perceptions are organized in the present moment. Ruth is a highly intellectual woman who has spent the greater part of her academic career trying to eliminate inconsistency in her thinking. She is finding herself more than usually anxious and uncertain about her present research project. In her first session of psychotherapy, she is at first discomfited, then delighted, to be expressing her reservations metaphorically rather than, as she calls it, "rationally".

> *There seem to be two kinds of 'fuzziness' that cloud my vision.* And is there anything else about those two kinds of fuzziness?

> *Well, one seems to be turquoise and matted in the shape of a ball. The other is purple and smoky like a forest fire.* Where did all that come from?

Ruth realizes that for once she is responding involuntarily. "It's strange," she says. "It's as though I have been ambushed by my own mind."

Our cognitive functioning actually derives from our physical and emotional relationship with the world and Clean questioning intervenes precisely at the point where sensory experience becomes speech, or "where sense becomes sentences," as linguistics researcher Maurice Brasher puts it. Ruth is signaling two kinds of fuzziness that appeared from nowhere to cloud her vision. And they appeared in a trice, in the twinkling of an eye.

An epic half-second

In this chapter, we take a trip into the inner life of the mind: into that epic, hectic, dramatic fraction of a second that it takes the microprocessors of the unconscious to sort, rank, and co-ordinate billions of bits of information and make them available with some kind of cohesion to consciousness. As the minutiae of our experience transmute into everyday perception, we consider the part these momentous events play in the making of symbol and metaphor, key players in the unfolding human drama.

Symbol and metaphor are not independent, exceptional phenomena, but the nuts and bolts of our mental constructions. Every word we utter and gesture we make are envoys on a special mission, recruited to represent vast numbers of sub-symbolic events in half a second or less of internal processing.

Half a second might not seem very long in the scheme of things, but as science author Steven Pinker memorably pointed out:

> A housefly dodging a crazed human can decelerate from rapid flight, hover, turn in its own length, fly upside down, loop, roll, and land on the ceiling all in less than a second.[1]

My aim here is to expand the moment it takes client and facilitator to process information; to suspend this barely perceptible fragment long enough to examine what happens in the minds of both parties; and to consider how that informs us as facilitators at the moment of our next intervention.

How do unconscious computations manifest as conscious information? It is a process involving an exceedingly large number of extremely small events.[2]

Infinite input

As you read this, many billions of light waves, pressure ripples, and chemosensory signals are crossing your physical threshold via many millions of sensory receptors to trigger electrical impulses that travel to your sensory cortices for sorting. For your mind to make any kind of sense of this continuous onslaught, a huge amount of preliminary processing has to take place, involving billions of simultaneous computations: sensory processors, language processors, and spacetime processors all working in parallel to sort and assemble the impulses that will become your perceptions, emotions, and decisions. And your conscious mind tells you next to nothing of this remarkable activity, just as the audience for a film we have little idea of the behind-the-scenes drama and technical know-how that went into producing what we see on the screen.

Those billions of impulses from the sensory cortices are not only involved in conveying new information, but also in physically interacting with existing information, or memory, carried by a ready-made store of neural circuits predisposed for activation across a large number of different levels of organization. Thus the present prompts the past and the past affects the present, and the mind does its best to make sense.

It is not the actual past that is evoked by the present, of course. Memory is a capricious mix of reconstructions (impressions from available evidence) and potentiations (nerve impulses enhanced by prior use).[3] I see a tree outside. I don't just see 'tree' in general. I see a particular configuration whose patterns of light and shade, shape and color, remind me almost simultaneously of other light, other leaves, thoughts of childhood, a mixture of feelings, all the attendant connections my mind cannot help but make in the moment. And this conscious content, whether it be a sensory representation of external reality or a sensory representation of internal imagining, is a result of a process of 'serial selection' in my brain.

Serial selection

The complex coded output of parallel processing generates a simpler coded output in a continuous process that allows me to see the tree or identify a feeling. I can only do so because my brain is forming representations. Correspondences. Billions of computations are being translated into symbolic forms that *betoken* the elaborate organization of the relationships between their component parts. As a result I can form and express feelings and concepts with relative ease.

The serial selector acts rather like a coordinating committee that examines resolutions from all around the country and cobbles them into a composite motion to put before annual conference. It is the coded information output of extremely complex input. Aldous Huxley described what happens in *The Doors of Perception* (1954):

> The function of the brain and nervous system is to protect us from being overwhelmed and confused by this mass of largely useless and irrelevant knowledge, by shutting out most of what we should otherwise perceive or remember at any given moment, and leaving only that very small and special selection which is likely to be practically useful.

Unfortunately, the workings of serial selection cannot be trusted implicitly. The mechanisms of mental association are subject to the same neurological processing that Ivan Petrovich Pavlov discovered in his work on conditioned responses.

Involuntary association

A dog salivates at the sound of a bell, which has previously been associated with the arrival of meat. A human reacts with high anxiety to the sight of an otherwise harmless spider, or responds with fear and alarm to the sudden slamming of a door. Language itself is an endless source of affective stimuli. Not many words come to us indifferent to the context in which we first experienced them. When a word comes with a bad feeling attached and nothing is done to detach it, the word can be highly charged forever.

Symbolic output

The effect of parallel processing, serial selection, and involuntary association means we are only conscious of information that has been constructed selectively and represented symbolically. This explains how we can be aware of the outcome of mental computations, but not of the computations themselves. The operations of unconscious processing work sub-symbolically, whereas the processors for consciousness can only work at a symbolic level. There is no actual picture of a tree in my brain. What I perceive after a few hundred milliseconds of processing is a coded representation to which I ascribe tree-like meaning.

The brain does not differentiate between 'real' and 'imaginary' representations, by the way. The mental image that drives Therapeutic Metaphor process (what neuroscientist Joseph LeDoux calls "that most ghostly of cognitions") is the product of a series of events very similar to those that result in the perception of actual objects. If we look at a scan of someone's brain while they create an internal picture of a room they know well, we will see activity in the same vision and recognition areas that are activated when they look at the actual room. The two acts make use of similar neural networks. There is, it seems, a small but significant difference in the resulting image, in that more sensory neurons will be activated in response to external stimuli than to self-generated experience, which would account for the fact that the symbols we imagine internally tend to be fuzzier and less well defined than the objects we see out there in the world.

To summarize what happens in the four stages of information processing:

1 *Infinite input.* The unconscious mind works like a series of parallel processors, constantly computing a limitless number of information inputs sub-symbolically in codes neither accessible to, nor decipherable in, consciousness.

2 *Serial selection.* A secondary process generalizes the coded output of parallel processing to create representations of experience in a way that is neither *directly* accessible to, nor *directly* decipherable in, consciousness.

3 *Involuntary association.* Memory circuits are prompted that affect both the selection and the meaning of what is selected. As the threshold to the conscious mind is crossed, we become introspectively aware of our representations and in some cases of the associations they have made. A stage that *is* accessible to, and *may* be decipherable in, consciousness.

4 *Symbolic output.* Thereafter we give utterance and credence to our internal representations: we think, feel, gesture, and speak. A stage that is clearly accessible and decipherable, if not always readily, in consciousness.

Moment of choice

Immediately following unconscious computation and conscious introspection (stages 1, 2, and 3) is a moment that deserves our special attention. It is the moment just before we speak (stage 4). In that instant, we can remind ourselves as facilitators that the same mental activity going on for the client as they process information is going on for us as we listen. *Exactly the same.* Serial selection, involuntary association, and the rest. Nothing can prevent these meaning-making procedures being activated in us as the client speaks. And this making of meaning is happening so fast and is so out of our awareness that we can have no idea of what is happening until we have already made ostensible 'sense' of what we have seen and heard.

The nonverbal and verbal language of the client is crossing our physical thresholds as visual and auditory input and over the next few hundred milliseconds many millions of neural firings are making electro-chemical connections to existing memory circuits evoking internal representations which are uniquely and irreducibly our own. Only a microscopically small proportion of these activities will be in our awareness, yet the *whole* of our reaction, not just the conscious part, is shaping our response.

Here, then, is our first moment of choice. We can choose to pursue a relationship with the client or to further the cause of their autonomy. In every moment before every intervention, we have a responsibility for making this choice.

Client *I'm so tense, I don't know if I'm coming or going.*

What would you say in response? You have barely a second or two in which to make a decision. If you resort to everyday language, every choice you make will be 'analogy making' – relating the client's words to your own experience and seeking some kind of commonality between the two, even if it is only to disagree with what you believe the client to mean.

This is a seductive time in a significant relationship, a moment when a facilitator can allow their language and the client's to become hopelessly entangled. In the case of the client who says, "I'm so tense," we might be tempted to nod and murmur, "I'm really sorry to hear that," in the hope that they will feel comforted, or to come up with a less than reassuring, "It does suggest you are still quite vulnerable."

The immeasurable importance of David Grove's contribution to the science and politics of psychotherapy is that for the first time we have a methodology that allows the conscious and unconscious sub-divisions of a facilitator's mind to operate without cross-contamination. Clean questioning minimizes the risks of casual assumption and involuntary association, equalizes the balance of power between client and facilitator, and reduces the confusion of negotiating between two sets of perceptions. The disciplines of the Clean syntax (Chapters 13 to 15) oblige the learned facilitator to listen very carefully indeed to the lay client and in doing so to cede authority where it rightly belongs. I think William Tyndale would have approved.

Nina and Olympic gold

Thirty-three year-old Nina has been talking anxiously about her infidelities. She concludes:

> *I need to be able to stop.*
> And you need to be able to stop. And when you need to be able to stop, what kind of able is that able?

> *It's when my head and heart work together I'm able to decide.*

What was going on consciously and unconsciously for client and facilitator in the few seconds of that exchange? How do the choices a facilitator makes map onto a client's actual processing?

> *I need to be able to stop*

is Nina's coded output of an unconscious computation of countless aspects of her life and psychopathology. Every one of her words is a symbol selected to represent a massive amount of information input and parallel processing.

The output of this computation becomes input into the facilitator's system, where it is processed unconsciously, represented symbolically, and becomes introspectively accessible as conscious information, by which time it has taken on all kinds of unconsciously derived subjective associations. We can convince ourselves that, despite all this, we know what Nina means. Or we can engage with her conversationally about what she means and have some influence on it. Or we can simply reflect her exact words:

> And you need to be able to stop ...

The verbatim reflection re-enters and re-informs Nina's system as *enhanced input*. Now what? The last thing adult Nina wants is to be challenged about what she has said and thrown back into some childhood related anxiety state. Every word other than the client's that the facilitator uses at this point has to be evaluated by Nina separately.

> And when you need to be able to stop ...

confirms to the client that these are her words and that this is her process. A minimal pause now allows the facilitator another moment of choice, this time about what question to ask.

> ... what kind of able is that able?

The most basic of Clean questions invites Nina to move into a part of her mind that she may have been ignoring, avoiding, or neglecting for years. It can be exhilarating to discover that there are important parts of the self that the everyday experiencing self knew nothing about.

The question sets up a 'systemic feedback loop' between Nina and her perceptions: sub-symbolic computation leading to unconscious symbol formation, introspective representation, and conscious articulation – at which point new information emerges:

> *It's when my head and heart work together I'm able to decide.*

Nina is exploring her anxiety without having to re-experience the trauma that caused it. Her output is now the facilitator's input and results in another moment of choice: whether to speculate on what Nina has said or simply to reflect it and draw her attention to it.

> And it's when your head and heart work together you're able to decide. And when your head and heart work together ...

The enhanced input into Nina's system is followed by a pause that invites her head and heart to do just that – work together – and gives the facilitator a moment to decide on the next question:

> ... that is work together like what?

The effect of the Clean question is twofold. It reserves political power for Nina and at the same time invites her to embark on a search for a personal resource. The question enters her system and sets up a feedback loop that gives rise to enhanced computation.

And what emerges is a metaphor with redemptive potential:

Oh, like Olympic gold.

Two Clean questions only ("What kind of?" and "Like what?") have encouraged the conditions for transformative change.

Summary of the process

During the fraction of a second it takes the brain to process new information, we make a multiplicity of unconscious connections. The traditional therapeutic exchange becomes hostage to a negotiation between two sets of symbolic perceptions, with all the potential for misunderstanding and distortion that entails. In comparison, a Clean exchange keeps the client's and the facilitator's language unentangled and focuses the client's attention on their internal processing.

The response to a Clean question tells client and facilitator not *what* is happening in the client's unconscious, but what it is *like*. The subject of this likeness cannot be modeled directly. It *can* be modeled via its symbols and the aggregation of those symbols in metaphor.

These backstage events are of critical importance in setting the scene for the on-stage spectacular that is to follow.

Notes to Chapter 8

1 All in less than a second: cognitive scientist and author Steven Pinker in *How The Mind Works*, 1997.

2 References for symbolizing as a fundamental function of the mind include Mark Johnson, *The Body in The Mind*, 1987; P.N. Johnson-Laird, *The Computer and The Mind: An Introduction to Cognitive Science,* Harvard 1989; A. Newell et al, *Symbolic Architecture for Cognition*, in *Foundations of Cognitive Science*, 1989; George Lakoff, *The Neurocognitive Self*, in *The Science of The Mind*, ed. Ralph Solso and Dominic Massaro, 1995; Colin McGinn, *Mind and Reality*, Chapter 4 of *The Making of a Philosopher*, 2003; and Vilayanur Ramachandran in *Conversations on Consciousness*, ed. Susan Blackmore, 2005.

3 Memory: it is not the actual past that is evoked by the present. Recent research by neurobiologists at Rockefeller University in New York suggests that brain synapses (the junctions between brain cells) change constantly. In a mouse cortex, they have been found to turn over at the rate of seven per cent per week ('The Greatest Map of All', *New Scientist*, 15 February 2011). These replacement patterns cannot help but have an effect on memory circuits.

Chapter 9
Metaphor and Meaning

I'm the only one who can walk through the door. Other people can take me up to the door, but I have to go through and face my future.   Dwain Chambers, 100 m. athlete

Conveying information − Figuring of speech − Embodied cognition − Containing chaos, engaging the emotions − Isomorphism: Clare and the hamster, Hans-Peter's arrows − Idiom and cliché − Mixed metaphors − Ambiguity and multiple meaning: the boy in the woods, Richard III, the Two Ronnies, abandoned Ellen − Puns and wordplay

Metaphor is a higher order courier for conveying information from the unconscious into consciousness. Its importance for health and well-being lies in the fact that it mediates the boundary between what is known through the senses and what is imagined by the mind. Metaphor reaches and reconciles both sides of that critical frontier, and therein lies its power and potential. Metaphor informs us in a way that simile, with its simpler, more transparent comparisons, does not.[1] Ralph's "rocky road", as we saw in Chapter 7, *is* the way he sees his life; Angela's "black cloud" *is* her despair.

"Other people can take me up to the door," says Dwain, "but I have to go through and face my future." Somehow the patterns of organization of Dwain's unconscious processing have produced this compelling metaphor. He is communicating something of importance about himself that at a superficial level we have to take for granted, because its deeper structure − the means by which he put together the many billions of bits of information that went into producing these words − is not directly accessible to us. In the normal course of events, it may not need to be. But what if Dwain were asking for help with a block to improved performance whose origins were more mental than physical? What would you say to him? "I've taken you this far, Dwain, the rest is up to you." I think he knows this already. Or "There's a great future on the other side of the door, Dwain, that's got to be all the motivation you need." That might reassure him for a nanosecond, but will it help him move on? It might be time to find a new coach.

Figuring of speech

Metaphor is an essential ingredient of human cognition and communication. It is what philosopher Mark L. Johnson calls:

> one of the chief cognitive structures by which we are able to have coherent, ordered experiences that we can reason about and make sense of.[2]

It is a continual 'semantic mapping' from one mental domain to another, a ceaseless figuring of speech going on in the mind as we apply one kind of object or idea to another in order to describe a subjective mental state, or to articulate something more readily, or to convey information in a concentrated or more colorful form.

I'm the only one who can walk through the door.

Metaphor is the creative end product of the human intuitive-cognitive-linguistic mix. The word comes from the Greek *metaphorein*, to 'carry over' or 'transfer'. Dwain's "walk through the door" is a message from the unconscious. Every neurologically intact person has the capacity for ordering their experience, perceptions, and feelings this way.

Embodied cognition

The universality of metaphor may well derive from its embodiment, its 'in-corporation' (Latin *corpus* = 'body') of ideas into physical form. Dwain's metaphor centers on his need to "walk through" and "face" his future. Related primary metaphors that associate affection with physical "warmth" or equate help with physical "support" probably came from our experience as infants. The data from the experience of being looked after physically became 'embodied cognition' and our neurology continues to use it in metaphors such as "a warm greeting" or "being given the cold shoulder". "Feeling tense" derives from the experience of physical stretching until strain is evident; "depressed" from physically pressing down and weakening: a depressor is a muscle that pulls down the part to which it is attached. The metaphor-making bodymind makes no distinction between these ideas and their physiological equivalents.[3]

The beauty of Dwain's "walk through the door" – an imaginative representation of what is certainly a highly complex, intensely felt perception – is that it is entirely accessible and decipherable in consciousness. What does this metaphor represent for Dwain? An opportunity to redeem himself? The possibility of knocking a tenth of a second off his best time? He will have a better idea of how to go about it when he finds out more about the door itself. Is it unlocked, ajar, or firmly closed? What is it made of? What is on the other side? The differences between Dwain's door and your door or mine will lie in the details. Only Dwain will know the characteristics and purpose of this particular door. And only Dwain will know what is meant by "go through and face my future" and what needs to happen to fulfill that intention. He may not know explicitly. He will know at some level. This will be tacit knowledge: information he does not know that he knows until it pops into consciousness.

How Clean Language facilitates the information incorporated into metaphor to pop into consciousness is the subject of Part III, Chapters 11–15. The rest of this chapter looks at the varied roles of metaphor in changework, and explains why metaphor is such a key ingredient of the therapeutic mix.

Containing chaos, engaging the emotions

Metaphors appear in many forms with diverse functions. "For my days are consumed like smoke [...] I am as a sparrow alone on the housetop" wrote the poet.[4] One role of metaphor is to offer a creative constraint to the wandering mind. It provides a structure in which chaos is contained.

Metaphor frees us from emotional immobility. "Shall I compare thee to a summer's day?" asks Shakespeare's lover of his mistress. Clients who have never written a line of poetry in their lives find it coming up unannounced to describe their deepest feelings, frailties, difficulties, and dilemmas at moments when ordinary language is inadequate.

> *I'm a dormant volcano about to explode.*
> *I want to come out of the dark corner of my life.*
> *I'm like a hamster in a cage on a wheel going nowhere.*

Lyrical language is a means of heightening awareness and engaging the emotions. Every day I hear clients using this kind of imagery entirely intuitively. Dorothea imagines herself as "a house in need of a makeover," a figure of speech that helps her familiarize herself creatively with her depression. "It makes the mess manageable," she says as she finds a way to moderate her anxieties and fears by "adapting and remodeling" the structure of the house, creating "new views", "freshening up old rooms," "cleaning out the loft," and so on.

Isomorphism

The structure of Dorothea's metaphor is isomorphic, alike in form, to the structure of both her problem and its solution. Every structural adjustment she makes to her metaphor will be echoed in a parallel change to the configuration of her condition.

Kevin is an IT consultant who suffers from a lack of confidence when meeting new clients. At home after his first session of therapy, he finds himself writing

> *I begin as a mushroom –*
> *A rounded hump sheltering from the wind –*
> *Moving air leaves me untouched*

Kevin has difficulty relating to people who do not warm to him readily and he has traced this back to the lack of physical contact he experienced as a child. In his therapy, he makes use of a capacity almost all of us share, the ability to communicate difficult feelings by analogy. "A rounded hump sheltering from the wind" is alike in form to Kevin's feelings of coldness and loneliness.

The meaning he assigns to the symbols "mushroom", "hump", and "wind" lies in the patterns of neural associations his mind makes around them. Feeling cold and lonely has evoked memories, which create representations, which feed back into the present to reinforce his discomfort.

Joanna is a 25-year old nurse, tired of taking responsibility for a younger brother and a mentally ill parent while struggling to hold down a demanding job.

> *I want to manage my family relationships better. It's like a sewing box that has lots of different stuff in it, some useful, some not. I want to compartmentalize it, to make it more manageable.*

The significance of the sewing box lies in its role as a container that keeps things separate but accessible. Form follows function. The metaphor is isomorphic with Joanna's wish to be helpful while having her boundaries respected.

Colin is depressed as he approaches his fiftieth birthday:

*I want to come out of the dark corner of my life into open sunshine
and see the road ahead as sunny and bright.*

Paula is a menopausal client graphically describing her physical
distress:

*These hot flushes are like a thousand red ants marching up
my body.*

Kevin, Joanna, Colin, and Paula have no idea what is happening in
their unconscious processing to create these images, but now that
the images have an appropriate form, they can make alike-in-form
meaning of them.

Clare and the hamster

Clare is a 22-year old graduate who suffers from claustrophobia
while driving on the highway where there are few places to turn off.
She expresses her fears of being trapped as

Like a hamster in a cage on a wheel going nowhere.

The metaphor is isomorphic with her feeling of being condemned to
remain trapped in the phobia. She feels as imprisoned in her car on
the highway as the hamster is in its cage.

And is there anything else about that hamster in a cage on a
wheel going nowhere?
It can't get off. It's going over and over again in a cycle of fear.

Clean questioning facilitates Clare to decode the alike-in-form
relationship between the hamster and herself. She goes on to
develop a metaphor that matches the structure of her solution.

And when [summary of current situation] what would you like to
have happen?
*To find some way of lubricating the cycle of activity in my brain so
that it runs more smoothly and I don't panic.*

And what kind of lubricating could that lubricating be?
A solution of, oh, gold liquid!

"Gold liquid" is an intuitive resource that Clare uses to "lubricate
the cycle of activity" in her brain. The cycle developed from the
original "wheel going nowhere," while the lubricant is a "solution"

(an intuitive double meaning) that serves to first ease, then free, the mental stuckness associated with the original phobia.

Hans-Peter's arrows

The isomorphic potential of therapeutic metaphor was dramatically demonstrated in the late nineteen-nineties by the experience of a young Stuttgart lawyer, Hans-Peter Salzmann, who had contracted amyotrophic lateral sclerosis, the disease that paralyzed Stephen Hawking. Hans-Peter had no speech or voluntary physical movement, but his mind remained alert. He learned to communicate using a device inspired by research that shows us using the same area of the brain to imagine making a movement as actually to make it. Electrodes attached to Hans-Peter's forehead measured electrical signals produced in the cortex by *thoughts* of moving and these signals fed to a computer, which activated a cursor on the screen. By directing his thoughts, Hans-Peter was able to induce changes in the amplitude of the signals that caused the cursor to move to letters of the alphabet as they appeared on the screen. The electrodes were only able to measure the average activity of a large number of neurons with different functions, however, so moving the cursor to build up sentences was an arduous exercise requiring immense control.

Hans-Peter needed a technique for marshalling and maximizing these 'slow cortical potentials'. To do this he enlisted a skill that most of us have in abundance, an innate ability to tap unconscious resource through self-generated metaphor.

> *To move the cursor I build up tension with the help of certain images, like a bow being drawn or traffic lights changing from red to yellow. I use the tension built up and kind of make it explode by imagining the arrow shooting from the bow or the traffic lights changing to green.*[5]

Metaphors have a way of holding the most information in the least space, which allowed Hans-Peter to facilitate his unconscious efficiently. He was also highly motivated; he knew what he wanted; and, crucially, the metaphors were his alone. They were not suggested by doctors, carers, or research psychologists. They had personal meaning and Hans-Peter controlled them himself.

Idiom and cliché [6]

A second-hand phrase can hold an original idea. Idiom, cliché, and slang are expedient ways to get across an idea or a feeling without thinking too much. "If there is light at the end of the tunnel," said the singer Mariah Carey, "hopefully it's not a freight train." It is tempting to suppose that the only function of popular idiom is to make 'run of the mill' communication easier. In fact, the Greek word *idioma* originally meant 'an uncommon construction, an individual peculiarity of language.' An uncommon peculiarity becomes popular in direct proportion to its fitness for purpose.

Idiom is always metaphorical. 'A weight off my shoulders', 'fit as a fiddle', 'down in the dumps' have meaning that cannot be derived from the literal meaning of their individual elements. The more useful the idiom, the more likely it is to cross over into cliché. "This is a blind alley," said a Whitehall source when journalists were trying to implicate 10 Downing Street in the 2011 phone hacking scandal. "It's a red herring. There's no smoking gun." Overworked expressions are as easily undervalued in the context of counseling as they are in everyday speech. I have facilitated countless clients who saw light at the end of the tunnel, yet each of them saw a particular kind of light in a different kind of tunnel as a result of working on a unique problem in a distinctive way to every other client. Clare's hamster is so obviously not a real rodent on an actual wheel in a physical cage that it may be tempting to dismiss it as a mere turn of phrase. And yet our personal tunnels, hamsters, chips on the shoulder, knots of pain, and so on are descriptions of unique psychosomatic states. They can be easily overlooked in therapeutic process or dismissed as throwaway remarks of no real significance.

> Is there anything else about that overlooked / dismissed / throwaway?

Each of these commonplace expressions is a mapping of one semantic circumstance (a complexity of emotion and cognition) across to another (a physical action). We don't literally look over a remark, or order it to leave the room, or physically discard it, but the metaphorical implications of these literal behaviors may resonate helpfully in the client whose attention is drawn to them. I am as sure as night follows day that you are up to scratch now with the way figures of speech turn up in every nook and cranny. You can ferret them out and reflect on them for yourself.

Mixed metaphors
Is it possible to have too much of a good thing? Soccer coach Glen Roeder apologizes at a post-match press conference for his team's poor start to the season:

> *The way forward now is to stand up and be counted, and this clean sheet hopefully gives us something to build on now we have got our hands full and we have a major fight on our hands.*

Even if you have no interest in sport, you might feel sorry for a coach attempting to make up for a no-score draw with seven metaphors a minute. Here is a man under stress. A mixed metaphor could be an indicator that the speaker is confused or that the brain is running ahead of itself. A while ago I overheard a young man in the City sharing his thoughts with a colleague about imminent redundancy:

> *The blanket's going to be ripped from under my feet and I'm going to hit the ground running. Either I jump onto the top rung of the ladder or take a step backwards.*

The speaker has come up with a succession of vivid images signaling what seems to be a mixture of optimism and anxiety. And yet his "blanket", "hit the ground", "top rung", etc. may all be turned to advantage. Problem-related metaphors convey latent solution-related potential. They carry little parcels of history back and forth between the conscious and the unconscious so that, properly unwrapped, layers of learning will be revealed.

There is a way of doing this in style. It is by conveying two or more meanings at once.

Ambiguity and multiple meaning

As I was printing a draft of this chapter, the paper in the printer jammed. I tried all the usual things and ended up phoning a technician. I described the problem and my attempts to solve it. He speculated that the paper censor may have failed. I was puzzled. Had I left in something rude or politically incorrect? How would he know? He repeated what he had said and this time I heard it differently. The paper sensor had malfunctioned.

One of the tricks of the unconscious is to throw up linguistic encryptions and contradictions without the least warning. A client's double meaning will as often as not be a mental contrivance that conceals or reveals an unresolved conflict.

Alan is a sports psychologist in his forties. When he was seven, his father gambled away the family home, leaving Alan, his mother, and sister to move into a caravan in the woods. Alan was sent to a boarding school financed by an aunt. His mother told him later that he changed at this time. This is no surprise to him now. He had bad school reports, he tells me. They were waved in his face.

> *I was no good at exams. I was very poor at Latin. I only remember* puer in silva, *'boy in the woods'.*
> And you were very 'poor' at Latin. And you only remember *'puer in silva'* ...

Noticing this kind of linguistic ambiguity gets easier with practice. I have only to hint at the double meaning for Alan to translate it as the boy in the woods who was 'poor in silver'. It wasn't much fun for him attending a private school surrounded by the sons of the wealthy. It had a traumatic effect on the seven-year-old that has echoed to this day.

As the audience for a mystery play, we pay equal attention to every character who appears on stage. We speculate about everyone with an obvious motive for the crime while keeping a mental note of the rest who have no obvious motive. In the theater of the mind, an ancillary meaning that emerges as a result of attending to the supposed primary meaning of a word or phrase may turn out to be the prime suspect after all.

"If I asked for a cup of coffee, someone would search for the double meaning," said Mae West. The English language is full of double meanings, homophones, nouns masquerading as verbs, and so on. A word can contain a whole world. Given the poet Milton's failing eyesight and generally dismal disposition, we can speculate about his use of the word "dark" in this line from the poem *Comus*:

> *He that hides a dark soul and foul thoughts benighted walks*
> *under the mid-day sun.*

Dark can mean not only lack of light, but also secret, angry, sad, and remote, all of which may have applied to Milton personally.

Shakespeare brought a studied ambiguity to the opening lines of *King Richard the Third*:

> *Now is the winter of our discontent*
> *Made glorious summer by this sonne of York*

The ambiguity in question is printed as "sonne" (sun) in the First Quarto (1597) and "son" in the First Folio (1623). There are scholarly disputes over which version is correct, but they don't in the least matter because the play was written for performance and if the double meaning is played as the playwright certainly intended, the audience will hear it. Laurence Olivier would look suddenly upwards on the word "sonne", hinting that not only was he an eminent scion of the House of York, but also something more than a mere mortal.[7] We might have asked Richard:

And what kind of son could that sun be?

And he might have replied:

The incomparable kind.

Double meanings and puns are more often than not coded messages from the unconscious and should be honored as such until the code can be cracked. Facilitators unattuned to phonetic ambiguity will tend not to hear it, yet in a quirk of the English language about eighty per cent of words in common use have more than one meaning. Look no further than the last sentence. A "quirk" can be a peculiar trait, a chance occurrence, an abrupt twist, or a groove separating architectural moldings. "Yet", "about", "per", "cent", "have", "more", and "one" all have more than one meaning waiting to trip you, trap you, or snap at your ankles. The less obviously multivalent words in the sentence – "in", "a", "of", "English", "language", "word" and, yes, "meaning" – also have different values, connotations, sense, or significance. Even "the" is a less definite article than one might suppose. The Shorter Oxford Dictionary lists no less than fourteen uses for the word.

In the classic BBC television sketch, hardware store assistant Ronnie Corbett comes to the counter.

There you are, four candles.

The customer, Ronnie Barker, responds:

No. Fork 'andles. 'Andles for forks.

The English language is so flexible that we can easily find ourselves saying things we don't really mean. We can also find ourselves saying things we really do mean, but wish we hadn't said. I can still see the blush on politician Chris Smith's face after his unscripted contribution to 'Question Time', a television discussion program:

Gays and lesbians should be welcomed into the armed forces with open arms.

This sign at an Ontario lakeside:

WARNING: NO WAKE ZONE

is clearly intended to alert motor boat owners of the need of others who live there for uninterrupted sleep. Or is it?

Ambigu is an Old French word for 'a medieval banquet at which a medley of dishes is set upon together,' which perfectly describes the feast of possibilities clients serve up in the form of:

Homophones: words with the same sound but different meanings or spellings. "New" and "knew" are homophones of each other.

Homonyms: words with the same sound and spelling but different meanings. The noun "bear" and the verb to "bear" are homonyms of each other.

Homographs: words with the same spelling, but different meanings or inflexions. The noun "conduct" and the verb to "conduct" are homographs of each other.

While recognizing the risk of guessing wrongly and distorting the exchange, a facilitator could choose to go for one of a client's possible meanings explicitly and hope to be lucky –

And when right, where is left?

– or devise a Clean question that retained the ambiguity while freeing the client to make explicit any meaning they choose:

And when right, what kind of write could that rite be?

The client's response will usually make the sense clearer, though the appearance of a pun, an ambiguity, or a homophone could mean that the speaker is conveying two equally valid meanings at once.

Ellen is an articulate, middle-aged executive who thinks of herself as being rather too prudish. She would like to be able "to act with more abandon," as she puts it. I ask:

What kind of abandon could that abandon be?

Ellen is silent for several seconds.

I keep getting a picture of a little girl in a hole in the ground.
And is there anything else about that picture of a little girl
in a hole in the ground?

Ellen comes up with another sense of "abandon". As a child, she had
been left by her mother when her parents divorced. She felt at the
time as if the earth were swallowing her up. Ellen links the feeling
now with having lost her sense of playfulness – abandon – at the
same time. She has been inhibited as an adult as a result of
unresolved feelings around her insecurity as a child.

Puns and wordplay

No matter how much you push the envelope, it will still be stationery.

Language by its nature is as pliant and resilient as play dough. We
are constantly entertaining ourselves by extending its boundaries
and changing its shape. Plays on words are not always to be taken
lightly, however. An unintentional pun may be telling the
unintentional truth.

A client reports on his drawing of a metaphorical prison in which
he has incarcerated himself:

The prison walls are not drawn to scale.

Which could mean either that he will have some difficulty scaling
them, or that he has drawn them so small as to be easily scalable.

Irony is a different kind of *jeu de mots*. It allows us to express
meaning wholly at odds with literal meaning. When Richard of
York speaks of glorious summer, we should not assume that all is
well with him. Or when a few lines later, he declares:

I am determined to prove a villain,
And hate the idle pleasure of these days

he may simply be playing with the language, confident that he is a
jolly good fellow who intends to enjoy these days to the full. Or he
may be expressing ambivalence: at one moment certain that he is a
villain and resolved ("determined") to prove that he is, and at the
next moment uncertain, having not yet made up his mind
("determined") whether he is a villain or not. Here is a monarch
with conflicts who should be in therapy.

Ambiguity and equivocation lurk in every line of the English language, which is one of the reasons Shakespeare's characters, like the rest of us, make such compelling clients.

The possibility of multiple meaning points to the necessity of responding to a client's words with questions that make no assumptions.

> *And what kind of thick could that thick be?
> *I wathn't feeling very well.*

In every example in this chapter, the metaphor itself is the message. The message is not in the meaning an outsider makes of it. The message is in what the metaphor means to its maker. There are important differences in both intention and viability between a genuinely self-made metaphor and one shaped elsewhere, as we shall see.

Notes to Chapter 9

1 Difference between metaphor and simile: a simile is an explicit comparison of two separate unalike things: 'cheeks like roses' and 'as white as snow' are similes. A metaphor implies the comparison, incorporates it, and identifies with it: 'rosy cheeks' and 'snow-white' are metaphors.

2 Metaphor one of our chief cognitive structures: Mark L. Johnson, *The Body in the Mind*, 1987.

3 'Being given the cold shoulder', 'icy stare', etc: research subjects made to feel socially excluded reported feeling physically colder (*Let Your Body Do The Thinking*, New Scientist 27 March 2010). As the human brain evolved, more complex emotions may simply have hitch-hiked a lift onto circuits that were already handling basic sensory experience. Thus our metaphors of 'tension', 'depression', 'heartache', 'buoyancy', 'warmth', 'attraction', and so on.

4 "For my days are consumed like smoke": the Bible, Psalm 102, which is sub-titled, "A Prayer of the Afflicted, when he is Overwhelmed, and Poureth out his Complaint before the Lord."

5 Metaphors in the mind: these days brain implants can permit thought alone to move a computer cursor to read emails, change TV channels, and turn lights on or off. Before long, it is said, a brain implant will make it possible for thoughts to be turned into human speech.

6 In printing, a cliché (from the French *un clicher*, 'a stereotype') was a plate cast from movable type. At a time when every letter had to be set separately, it made sense to cast a repeated phrase as a single slug of metal. Cliché came to mean a ready-made phrase. All such conversational short-cuts ('bite the bullet', 'ride roughshod', 'don't hold your breath', etc.) were once originals. Clean facilitators should continue to treat them as such. Writers, of course, should avoid clichés like the plague.

7 'Sun/son of York'. The actor Geoffrey Rush, who plays speech therapist and amateur Shakespearean actor Lionel Logue in the film *The King's Speech* (2011), recites these lines and pays homage to Olivier by rolling his eyes melodramatically upwards.

Chapter 10
Abuses and Uses of Metaphor

Metaphors can kill. George Lakoff

I felt I was on the Titanic, literally. Sherron Watkins

I tell my patients to imagine their fear as a big baby crying in a crib. U.S. physician turned therapist

Euphemism – Limitations of metaphor – Systemic metaphor – Potential of metaphor – Taking metaphor literally

The goddesses of the Greek underworld who ascended to earth to pursue and punish the wicked were known as *The Erinyes* ('The Avengers'), but those who feared to speak their name directly would call them *The Eumenides* ('The Kind Ones') instead. It was an early instance of *euphemismos* – the use of favorable words to represent ideas that we feared. Euphemism has its origins in our dread of divine wrath and is still at the root of our present-day sexual, anatomical, political, sporting, and corporate circumlocutions. 'Life insurance' is really death insurance; a 'professional foul' is cheating; 'downsizing' and 'resource reduction' are dismal alternatives for depriving people of their jobs; politicians refer to controversial changes as 'reforms' in order to reframe the debate to their own ends. All are instances of fear of one kind or another prompting manipulation, avoidance, or denial. (See the shame » denial loop in the Introduction to the book).

A well-worn Whitehall euphemism is "the prevailing wisdom", a phrase that appears six times in the Butler Report into the British government's over-assessment of the threat posed by Saddam Hussein in the run-up to the war in Iraq. "The prevailing wisdom" is a civil service synonym for 'doing things our way because we have the power to do so.' Thus the caveats and cautions of outside experts did not became part of Whitehall's prevailing wisdom in the

Butler Report, whereas the lapses, exaggerations, and mistakes of establishment officials and politicians did. Lord Butler classed these coyly as "understandable" or, at the worst, "unsafe". The government's dossier did not lie about the key claim it made, he suggested, but "stretched it to its outer limits." He castigated officials mildly for "placing more weight on the intelligence than it could bear." Metaphors like these are designed to anaesthetize a part of the brain. Butler was a master of the humbug of which he almost, but not quite, accused officials.[1]

Euphemism is metaphor contrived to condition our thinking. "Metaphors can kill," linguistics professor George Lakoff pointed out in a 1991 paper drawing attention to the terminology used by U.S. politicians to justify the Gulf War.[2] Military metaphors employed by service personnel during the wars in Iraq and Afghanistan diverted the public from the full implications of what was actually happening. "Spraying and praying" brought an air of amateur gardening to the reality of indiscriminate killing. "Friendly fire" and "blue on blue" reduced death by incompetence to a kind of benign game. "Collateral damage" and "operational accident" are the latest genteelisms. It may not be long before we simply say "Oops". Orwell's 'double-speak' and its contemporary equivalent, 'spin', are powerful vehicles for avoiding personal and political responsibility.[3]

Like all vernacular, euphemism can be wild and untameable. At best, it entertains while it shies away from reality. "Pointing Percy at the porcelain" is one of many expressions for which we have to thank Australian sensibilities. It takes a special creativity to come up with a euphemism arguably ruder than the plain speech it replaces.

Limitations of metaphor

Metaphor is more than a means of denial or avoidance, or a bit of linguistic fun we can have now and again. It indicates bias. It shapes our beliefs. 2,500 years ago, philosopher Lao Tzu came up with this aphorism:

> *A tower nine stories high is built from a small heap of earth.*
> *A journey of a thousand miles starts in front of your feet.*

A construction that was intended to help his pupils think differently about ambition and learning at a time when teachers were required to demonstrate the correct way of thinking rather than to facilitate a pupil's own way.

Some teachers complain that not a great deal has changed since. Consider this presentation from a training course for police witnesses:

> Your evidence represents just one brick in the wall. It's your job to supply that brick. It's your counsel's job to put all the bricks together and to fill any spaces between. If you pass comment on any brick other than your own, you could open up a gap that could undermine the whole wall.[4]

An entertaining analogy, though perhaps less than helpful if your metaphorical mind runs on different lines, or sings to a different tune, or happens not to like bricks. Educationalist and mother of three Caitlin Walker speaks passionately about the missed opportunities for self-generated metaphor in British primary schools as a result of what she describes as a huge failing of the SEAL [Social and Emotional Aspects of Learning] initiative:

> My daughter is being told to imagine herself as made up of a bouncy dog, an aggressive bear, and a depressed donkey, and to control these metaphors as a means of controlling herself. It would be far more effective and less confusing to ask pupils, "When you are having fun / feeling angry / sad, you are like what?"[5]

Walker argues that the self-awareness the initiative is supposed to promote would then be genuine rather than teacher-imposed. Schools would also get – when relevant – the behavioral changes they sought, while at the same time they would be helping pupils develop their capacity for lyrical and self-directed language. And all through the use of pupils' own metaphors.

In sensitive situations, there are few things as toxic as a bad metaphor. Here is a television reporter interviewing a foster mother who has been obliged to give up the children she has been looking after for seven years.

> Reporter   Lump in the throat, eh?
> Foster mother   *It's a pain in the chest, actually.*

Oops. A number of books have been written about how to generate allegory, analogy, and anecdote – how in effect to tell fictions – for the purpose of guiding the listener's response. The listener is invited to incorporate an alien metaphor into their personal narrative while being denied the opportunity to originate and develop their own. The intention of the speaker is to obtain or retain political influence in the relationship. It is misleading to call this practice 'therapeutic metaphor'. Grove's use of the term applied specifically to client-generated material. It would be more scrupulous to call it 'therapist metaphor' and for storytellers to come clean about the lesson they draw for themselves. Here is the boast of one new age physician, who shall remain anonymous:

> I tell my patients to imagine their fear as a big baby crying in a crib. I tell them to pick up the baby, caress him [sic], and see what happens.

What happens, of course, is that his patients are obliged to channel their energy into imagining themselves as the kind of person who would picture their fear as a big baby crying in a crib, or a rabbit caught in the headlights, or whatever is taking the physician's fancy that day. It may work for a while for highly suggestible clients who have been coerced into ceding ownership of their process to the therapist. I suspect it will not work for long. Either way, it is rather different to the experience of being asked:

> And your 'fear' [if that is the actual word they have used] is like what?

A question that empowers the client to characterize their fear as their unconscious dictates.

> *It's like a dark cold cloud swirling around my head.*
> *Like the steel walls of an elevator closing in on me.*
> *Like every sense is suddenly alert.*

The inferential logic of therapist metaphor can have a profound effect on a patient's psyche. Mentally ill patients reading an information leaflet put out by a counseling agency in the South of England are expected to ponder the necessity of "fighting those fractured parts" of themselves that are, they are told, "responsible for all their anxieties and obsessive-compulsive disorders." Fighting a part of oneself, fractured or not, may not be the best thing to suggest to a mentally ill patient who is at the mercy of more than enough conflict already. The symptoms presented by so-called "fractured parts" are signals of the presence of some older, deeper pattern. They will have information about what the pattern is, what it needs in order to heal, and how that might be achieved, quite possibly by means other than "fighting".

Research into autism that focused on parental attitudes reported that parents typically saw themselves as "battling against autism" rather than "embracing" it, which is what new approaches advocate. Autistic children whose parents learned to pace and embrace their behaviors have, it seems, made remarkable improvements and in some cases a complete recovery.[6]

Therapist-originated metaphor can be a compelling diversion from a client's own path, because metaphor is such a familiar way mark. It has always been the means by which innovative ideas were indicated by reference to well-known domains. The physicist Ernest Rutherford described his discoveries about the structure of the atom by drawing an analogy with the solar system. His account of electrons circling the nucleus much as planets circle the sun did not require the two domains to be alike in every particular – the nucleus of the atom was not required to be hot or bright – but it did require the structure of the two domains to be similar enough for key properties of the less familiar, the atomic, to be explicit in terms of key properties of the more familiar, the solar system. Rutherford's metaphor helped non-scientists to follow the logic of his theory. If we apply the principle to a therapist attempting to explain a client's inner life to them, however –

Imagine your fear as a big baby crying in a crib
Think of your depression as a giant wall around you

– it falls at the first hurdle. Symbols with meaning for the therapist – big baby, giant wall – may have little relevance to the client and nothing in common with their feeling of fear or depression. A client's fear may feel more like a knot in the stomach or the rattle of Jacob Marley's chains. Meanwhile the big baby they have been instructed to imagine could be growing into a monster, while the giant wall is collapsing under the weight of the therapist's expectations. At best, clients have limited control of therapist metaphors; at worst, none at all.

I have heard it argued that therapist-generated metaphor is a good thing if it shocks a client's system into recognizing something new about itself. It can equally be a bad thing if it leads to client/therapist co-dependence. The client comes to depend on the therapist for ideas and on the therapist's approval for getting the analogy 'right', while the therapist comes to depend on the client's gratitude and respect. The emotional needs of both parties are engaged. Shocks to the system can have unpredictable effects.

Systemic metaphor
When therapist metaphor is out in the open, it is at least available for scrutiny. And if a client is smart enough, it may even prompt a

correction ("Actually, my fear is more like a roomful of rats"). If a therapist-generated metaphor has any legitimacy, it derives from a highly questionable systemic metaphor that goes 'doctor/teacher/ priest knows best.' While a metaphor like "fighting those fractured parts of yourself" is born of a larger systemic metaphor, 'therapy is war', which sets the self against itself and implicitly demonizes all a patient's unwanted feelings and behaviors. Systemic metaphors of the sort that hold therapist metaphors in place are generally so all-pervasive that we are quite unaware of living in their shadow.

American philosopher Stephen C. Pepper pointed to the difference between regular metaphors and systemic (or what he called 'permeating' or 'ritualized') metaphors:

> Usually metaphor is used to vivify an unusual concept, then drop out when the concept is grasped. But when the metaphor's use is permeating, it may never completely disappear even after it gets ritualized.[7]

Metaphor is not only about comparing two things, but also about hitching a ride on one aspect of experience in order to access another. Permeating or systemic metaphors like 'therapy is war' are demonstrably false if taken literally, just as a regular metaphor like 'Juliet is the sun' is false. Juliet may radiate warmth and vitality, but she isn't the sun. Yet the regular metaphor can help us shift information from one domain to another and see things in a way that the systemic metaphor, being implicit and inconspicuous, cannot. Systemic, permeating, or ritualized metaphors like 'doctor knows best,' 'juries decide the facts of a case,' and 'society consists of winners and losers' conspire to keep a complete apparatus of dependency and co-dependency in working order, whether we subscribe to them knowingly or not. Juries do not get to know all the facts, so cannot 'decide' them. Doctors may have a great deal of technical knowledge and be generally helpful, but do not always know what is right for individual patients.[8]

Potential of metaphor

> And your fear is like what?
> *A cold dark cloud.*

Intuitive metaphor pops up from a mind that is not at the mercy of politicians, clairvoyants, or medieval healers, but one that is attempting to heal itself. "In the paradigm of the presentation of the problem," said Grove, "lies also its solution." A client may induce the cold dark cloud in their metaphor landscape to condense into refreshing rain or to diminish and disappear. Autogenic metaphors reflect not only the limitations of the perceptions that formed them, but also their potential.

The constraints in Clare's "I'm like a hamster in a cage on a wheel going nowhere" are obvious. She is trapped in a repeating pattern with no resolution in sight. But the cage may be opened; the hamster may venture out to graze or escape altogether.

Nothing we believe to be fixed or irrevocable is beyond revision. Old metaphors make way for new ones. Theoretical physicists are currently revisiting their work on black holes. Stephen Hawking has suggested that black holes do not, after all, absorb and destroy the matter they attract; the information in the matter may return in some way or travel to another universe. Even constants like the speed of light are under scrutiny. Self-discovery, like scientific discovery, progresses by trial and error, by continually updating itself. It is the essential condition of all knowledge and learning.

Clare's cage is only a prison if Clare continues to identify herself as prisoner rather than keeper, designer, or destroyer. The wheel in the cage will only go nowhere if its axis remains fixed. The bars will only contain Clare if they are made of steel rather than chocolate or Styrofoam. Modifications like these may not be installed by an outside contractor. Structural or functional faults will show up sooner or later. Clare must devise and deliver the alterations herself. In overseeing the safety and quality of her work, however, there is one sure thing her facilitator can do. And that is to take her metaphors literally.

Taking metaphor literally

> *I want to come out of the dark corner of my life into open sunshine and see the road ahead as sunny and bright.*

To take Colin's metaphor literally, I simply have to question him as if he were in a real dark corner with a real road ahead of him.

> And is there anything else about that dark corner?
> And where is that road ahead?

As Colin processes the questions, the figurative meaning of the words is incorporated into their literal meaning, and *vice versa*, to become the default language of the unconscious. "I'm on the road to recovery," said the injured road-racer Nicole Cooke. "It's a big weight off my shoulders," said the light-welterweight boxer Bradley Saunders after beating a heavier opponent. Literal normally means strict adherence to straightforward sense, but in the light trance state of Therapeutic Metaphor process (Chapter 16), the literal and metaphorical combine. There is no distinction.

It comes as no surprise, therefore, to find the word 'literally' being used to amplify metaphorical meaning. Here is *Coronation Street*'s Archie Butterworth making a metaphorical promise to his bride-to-be:

The world will be our oyster, literally.

Enron whistleblower Sherron Watkins anticipates metaphorical disaster:

I felt I was on the Titanic, literally.

Southampton football club's manager claims that his players

literally gave blood

in losing the game against Newcastle.[9] Taking these literallys literally would be absurd in real terms – Archie's world is not an oyster, Ms. Watkins was not on the Titanic, the Southampton players had no more than a bruise or two – but may well be justifiable emotionally. And this is, literally, what happens in Clean Language when we treat symbols *as if they are real*.

And what kind of road could that road ahead be?

The conscious mind can tell the difference between a physical/literal road and an emotional/metaphorical one, at least when sober, but the unconscious cannot. It is only at the very last stage of cognitive processing that the brain signals a distinction between the real and the imagined. Clean Language psychotherapist Richard Siegel describes it this way:

I treat the [client's] black cloud like it is literal because the subconscious mind sees it as real. In the subconscious mind, these figures are as real as the concrete you stand on in a dream. The subconscious world has physicality as far as the subconscious is concerned, so treating it as such opens that world to us.[10]

In using Clean Language to bypass the border patrols of consciousness, we have readier access to the hidden information the metaphor holds. Metaphors are not real. We know this intuitively.

Not many of us respond in strict accordance with the physical sense of the everyday language of others. If you tell me you are "down in the dumps," or "on cloud nine," I would be foolish to expect to find you in these places. An exception to the rule might be made in the case of the client who says, "My smoking and drinking go hand in hand," which is both figurative and literal. In Therapeutic Metaphor process, statements like this make perfect sense either way.

When we call upon metaphor – literally, lyrically, conceptually, or intuitively – to express ourselves, we are making use of a unique aid to self-understanding. As clients, we do not need to be aware of our metaphors as such in order to put them to use, but it can be handy for a facilitator to be able to identify one when it appears. A few years ago, U.S. soccer coach Bob Bradley was studying with the Italian manager Fabio Capello. "When you make wine," Capello would say, "the grapes are not always the same." After a while, the American realized that his mentor was telling him something about team selection and management. "At first," says Bradley, "I thought he was on about wine."

I thought I'd put the past behind me.

Is there a metaphor here? To be certain one way or the other, we can ask ourselves, "Could this happen literally? Could my client have physically taken hold of something called "the past" and placed it "behind" them? Well, no. But the client who has put the past behind them metaphorically might well benefit from being asked how far behind, in what direction, and what happens as a result.

In Part II, we looked at the way we represent our perceptions via self-generated symbol and at the aggregation of those symbols in metaphor. We assessed the information content of client metaphor and, in this last chapter, its limitations and inherent potential.

Almost all of us use metaphor to describe those aspects of our perceptions and problems that are complex, emotionally driven, or unresolved. The metaphors will contain coded intelligence about both the problem and its resolution. The "door to the future" that Dwain identified in Chapter 9 is a symbol in which two discrete notions, a conceptual threshold and a physical doorway, are thrown together. The potential for change Dwain anticipates in this way calls for him "to go through" the door. At the moment, he does not know if such a move is possible and, if possible, whether it will be simple or difficult. Much will depend on whether he perceives the door as an obstacle or an opportunity.

In Part III, we consider how potential of this kind can be activated.

Notes to Chapter 10

1 Whitehall euphemism: acknowledgments to Andy Barkham, *Lord Butler's Language*, The Guardian 15 July 2004.

2 Metaphors can kill: George Lakoff, *Metaphors and War: the Metaphor System Used to Justify War in the Gulf*, 1991.

3 Double-speak and spin. George Orwell wrote, "political language is designed to make lies sound truthful and murder respectable, and to give an appearance of solidity to pure wind." *Politics and the English Language*,1946.

4 Evidence as "just one brick in the wall": London Metropolitan Police trainer quoted by Christopher Middleton in *How to Survive in the Box*, The Guardian 22 July 2003.

5 Misuse of metaphor in primary schools: Caitlin Walker, director of Training Attention Ltd., personal communication.

6 "Embracing" rather than "battling" autism: see autismtreatment.com. A remarkable instance of the difference a small change can make.

7 Permeating or ritualized metaphor: Stephen C. Pepper, *World Hypotheses: A Study in Evidence*, 1942. Pepper argued that our conceptual systems evolved from 'root' metaphors such as 'ideas are more real than perceptions' (at the root of formism), 'living things are machines' (mechanism), 'communion with God' (mysticism), and 'the spirit of the river' etc. (animism).

8 Doctors' knowledge of drugs is typically based on the results of drug/placebo trials. In *The Emperor's New Drugs* (2009), emeritus professor of psychology Irving Kirsch shows that in trials in which the drug produces noticeable side effects, patients who notice the side effects realize they are taking the real drug, not the placebo, and are more likely to report an improvement. Kirsch questions the validity of all such trials, believes that the efficacy of many prescription drugs is questionable, and concludes that we may be wasting billions on worthless medication. The key to healing, he reckons, is patients having something to believe in.

9 Metaphorical blood: Newcastle United fan Richard Brenchley comments: "If the Southampton players did give blood – at half-time, say – it might be the reason they ran out of steam in the second half. Perhaps next time they should wait until the end of the game, admirable though giving blood is at any time. The supporters, I feel, are entitled to a full eight pints per player over the entire ninety minutes."

10 Dr. Siegel's use of "subconscious" is probably an unconscious tribute to Freud and Jung and not all that different to my use of "unconscious". Freud and Jung's notion that 'subconscious' wishes and fears affect the conscious mind from below the threshold of consciousness is a little different from the current neurological view that most physiological processing is 'unconscious'. If you want to go further into this, see *The Unconscious and The Explanation of Behavior*, in John R. Searle, *Mind,* 2004, Chapter 9. Searle identifies four types of unconsciousness: the preconscious, the repressed unconscious, the deep unconscious, and the 'non-conscious'. He accepts the generalized notion of 'the unconscious' as legitimate if it is recognized as "dispositional", which I take to mean how the term is used in relation to other things.

Part III

SYMPTOMS AND SOLUTIONS
Propositions and Practice of Clean Language and Therapeutic Metaphor

---

Full wys is he that kan hymselven know.
Geoffrey Chaucer, *The Monk's Tale*

Chapter 11   Propositions of Clean Language

Chapter 12   A Clean Start

Chapter 13   Clean Reflection
Part 1 of the Clean Language Syntax

Chapter 14   Clean Attention
Part 2 of the Clean Language Syntax

Chapter 15   Clean Questioning
Part 3 of the Clean Language Syntax

Introduction to Part III

How do the symbolic and metaphorical indicators of trauma and hurt (Part II) relate structurally to the healing art of Clean Language (Part III)? If we suppose

> *metaphor* to be the coded message and
> *symbol* the code in which it is written, then
> *Clean Language* is a formula for deciphering the code.

That in itself is a metaphor, of course; a figure of speech drawing a comparison between two differing domains. Every client metaphor for anxiety, illness, or injury contains a number of symbols that make a contribution to the history and composition of the problem and to the overall meaning of the metaphor. Clean Language provides a set of keys for unlocking the subjective sense of the symbolism and making it available to the client for healing and change.

The philosopher Benedict de Spinoza believed that our nature was to "strive to achieve a greater perfection of function."[1] Charles Darwin came to the same conclusion. He concluded *On the Origin of Species* with the proposition that

> as natural selection works solely by and for the good of each being,
> all corporeal and mental endowments will tend to progress towards
> perfection.

We are driven by the need, and have inherited the capacity, to persevere and to prosper. Darwin deduced that from as simple a beginning as the requirement to survive, endless self-improving forms evolved:

> Natural selection is [...] silently and insensibly working, whenever
> and wherever opportunity offers, at the improvement of each
> organic being.[2]

To make the most of this 'silent and insensible' tendency, we need access to the workings of the unconscious. Some of the principal procedures by which we can gain and maintain access are considered in Part III, a 'what' and 'how to' of Clean questioning, healing, and change.

Chapter 11, *Symptoms and Solutions*, considers the reasoning behind Clean procedures: six propositions indispensable to keeping the channels open.

Chapter 12, *A Clean Start*, examines what is involved in setting up a psychoactive space for a Clean Language process.

Chapters 13, 14, and 15, *Clean Reflection, Clean Attention,* and *Clean Questioning*, deconstruct the syntax of Clean Language into its three interdependent, indispensible parts and explain how they work separately (one at a time), severally (in turn), and serially (in sequence).

Notes to the Introduction to Part III

1 "Greater perfection of function": Spinoza quoted by neuroscientist Antonio Domasio in *Looking for Spinoza: Joy, Sorrow, and The Feeling Brain*, 2003. Three hundred and fifty years ago, Spinoza was opposing the idea of mind-body dualism espoused by Descartes and arguing that mind and matter were composed of a single infinite substance: mind and matter were two incommensurable (not comparable by a common standard) ways of conceiving the one reality.

2 "Progress towards perfection" and "The improvement of each organic being": from Darwin's conclusion to *On the Origin of Species*, 1859 .

Chapter 11
Propositions of Clean Language

We all have within ourselves the ability to heal the psychological and somatic wounds of the biographical, ancestral, and cultural past.   David Grove

The ability to heal – Symptoms as signals: the pain in Elaine's finger – Coded solutions: Vicky's way – Creating the conditions for healing – Self-decoding – Utilizing every kind of information

As Clean procedures feed into the psychological mainstream, they meet resistance from some professionals. Questions are raised: how can the troubled or the mentally ill be trusted to know what is good for them? How can highly trained agents of change admit to ignorance about what is best for their clients? Only with an about-turn in our antiquated authority-driven belief systems do questions like these to begin to answer themselves.

The chief propositions of Grovian Clean Language can be summarized as:

1 We all have within ourselves the ability to heal

2 Symptoms are unsuccessful attempts by the bodymind to heal itself

3 Every symptom contains a coded solution

4 The facilitator's role is to create the conditions for successful decoding

5 Clean Language speaks to a self-decoding process

6 The process utilizes every kind of client information

Six articles in a systemic relationship with one another.[1] Understanding how they operate and interact will enhance your ability to facilitate others in ways aligned with their natural development.

1 The ability to heal

We grow up in the certainty that the bodymind heals itself. Aches and pains are relieved, spots and scratches fade, the concerns of the day self-repair in the night. But what happens to the deeper traumas, the psychological wounds we are heir to or acquire that fail to get better of themselves?

It was not so long ago that damage to the matter of the mind, the brain, was thought to be irreversible. As recently as the end of the twentieth century, neuroscientists believed that brains impaired by accident, stroke, and degenerative disease were untreatable. It is well understood now that the brain continually and dynamically reconfigures itself, even in adulthood, even after trauma.[2] Neurons in the vicinity of traumatized tissue make new connections and take over some of the functions lost. Scans have shown that many of the functions of the brain are organized differently *each time they are examined*, which suggests that every region of the brain adapts itself continually. Neurons themselves may be grown from stem cells and potentially even from glial cells, the worker cells that support and sustain neurons. It is as certain as it can be that repair to the neural networks of the brain will soon be as commonplace as the restoration of normal functioning to the heart, liver, and other organs. We may then be more able to accept that psychological damage, which has a necessary bearing on the way our neural networks are organized, is reparable too. Psychological change is implicated in neuronal reorganization just as neuronal reorganization is implicated in psychological change.

A key feature of self-organizing systems is their propensity for homeostasis, or stability, for the purpose of continuity and self-preservation in response to the threat of disruption. We achieve stability by the autonomous process of remaking ourselves. In *The Web of Life,* systems theorist Fritjof Capra notes that "we are produced by our components, and in turn we produce those components which produce us."

This continual remaking, this physio-, psycho-, and neuro-plasticity, is a prerequisite for mental and physical health. Remarkably, the ability to heal is not confined to our immediate selves. It can be extended back through the generations in a fundamental reversal of the classical Freudian notion, which supposed that the present would be automatically repaired by healing the past. In fact, healing the past results from the attention we give *to the present* (there is more on this in Chapter 16). Each of us has a rich genealogical inheritance that is as much a part of us as the foundations of a house. It allows us to build on the work of earlier ages and to repair their upheavals. In healing the present within us, we heal the past that is a part of it.

It is in this debt to our forebears, this duty to the future, that our capacity for self-regeneration lies. And common sense, not witchery or ideology, tells us that we do it ourselves.

2 Symptoms as signals

The main function of the nervous system is to co-ordinate the activities of the organism for its preservation. Some painful or distressing signals will be successful – a twisted ankle or nervous exhaustion indicate rest – while others will go unacknowledged or ignored, because the signals come so deeply encoded that we misconstrue them or surrender ourselves unquestioningly to the confusion they cause.

It has taken us a long, long time to accept that 'physical' symptoms like rashes, aches, and pains are more often than not coded signals to something going on in the mind as much as 'mental' symptoms like phobia, obsession, and depression. Most health professionals now accept that body and mind are not separate systems; they are not even conjoined or adjacent; the words 'mind' and 'body' describe different levels of the same system.[4]

"Symptoms are unsuccessful attempts by the bodymind to heal itself," said Grove. "Our job is to create a context in which they can be encouraged to be successful." However distressing a symptom may be, it signals the potential for healing.

The pain in Elaine's finger

Elaine is talking about the problems she is experiencing in her marriage. I notice the way she is holding her hands.

> And what do those hands know?
> *Well, they know I have arthritis in this finger.*

> And arthritis in that finger is like what?
> *It's like a tightly wrapped band.*

And is there anything else about that tightly wrapped band?
(Pauses) *It's like a band of tarnished gold.*

And is there anything else about that band of tarnished gold?
It reaches out from here [indicates ring finger] *to every extremity.*

And when it reaches out from here to every extremity, what
would you like to have happen?
Oh, to polish it and enjoy it again!

Every unwanted symptom has within itself the coded potential not
only to transform or relieve the negative effects of the symptom, but
also to contribute a compensatory resource. Elaine's arthritic finger
had given her the attention of others: she had a story to tell.
Healing the condition will mean the loss of this outlet. The
compensation might be obvious or not, but the choice will be hers.
As Elaine learns to ease the metaphorical band and to polish its
neglected metal, her problems in the marriage begin to ameliorate.

Countless clients have traced their aches and pains in the heart,
gut, and other organs to stresses and strains at work, at home, or in
themselves. As the anxieties abated, the pains have subsided.

There are many examples of unsuccessful symptoms surfacing later
in life in the form of anxiety, addiction, anger, and so on.
Earthquakes appear suddenly, but result from deep stress built up
over years. A classic example of a deeply coded symptom is the
onset of adult depression as a result of childhood abuse. In the
desire for sanity and stability, the child has suppressed or
minimized its confusion in order to survive at a time of
unprecedented threat to its well-being. Subsequent signals of the
need for healing – physical symptoms, antisocial behavior, an
excessive need for attention, and so on – have been ignored or
misunderstood by the child's carers and the child has adjusted to
the vicissitudes of life as best it could. And years, sometimes many
years, later, those parts of the child-adult whose needs were
deferred will make themselves known in a distorted or perverted
way through perpetuating the abuse or in mental breakdown.[3]

These *cris de coeur* are upsetting for the victim, but their intentions
are intelligible and honorable: to alert the organism to the need for
repair. Only when this need is acknowledged and embraced can the
symptom be treated and healed.

3 Every symptom contains a coded solution

The remedy that will moderate a presenting symptom or contribute a compensatory resource is not always apparent. Indeed, it may be very well disguised.

> *My heart is aching.*
> *I'm up against a stone wall.*
> *There's a dense fog around me.*

As often as not, the symptom will present itself in autogenic metaphor, an unmediated construct of the client's unconscious. Metaphors like these compress large amounts of data into very small files. They have to be unzipped and given time and space to reveal both the source- and resource-related information they hold. An inherited ache in the heart may be a neglected signpost to the redemptive love it contains. A self-erected stone wall may have retained the warmth of the sun. A dense fog may be swept away by spring winds.

The concept of 'illness' has always contained its antithesis, 'wellness'. "In poison there is physick," wrote Shakespeare. Injury and trauma do not in themselves cause beneficial effects; they induce symptoms which in the right circumstances encourage the organism to produce reactive conditions for a return to stability.

Vicky's way

The source of Vicky's bipolar and dual identity problem (Chapter 5) turned out to be the extreme conflict she experienced as a child, veering wildly between obedience to her parents' rules and the will to be herself. "All sensible people are selfish," wrote Emerson, "and nature is tugging at every contract to make the terms of it fair." Deep within Vicky is a belief that the terms of her relationship with her parents were unfairly skewed in their favor.

> *When I was a kid my parents always said there was a right way of*
> *doing things, but I always thought I should do things my way.*
> And a right way and your way are like what?
>
> *A right way is like a dense vibrating nut. My way is like a warm*
> *soft peach.*

Coded within Vicky's fluctuating symptoms of euphoria and despair are compensatory resources – warmth and comfort in the peach (her way) and vibrancy in the nut (her parents' way). She goes on:

> *The problem is that the nut sucks energy from the peach, leaving it cold and angry, and the vibrating energy of the nut gets over-excited and goes haywire.*
> And what would vibrating over-excited nut and cold angry peach like to have happen?
>
> (Pauses) *To come together.*

Once Vicky has represented the qualities of her conflict symbolically, she is able to identify more readily what needs to happen to resolve it: nut and peach must combine in some way. As she continues her work, they manage to do just that. She calls the resulting resource "a vibrating peach".

It is doubtful whether even the most imaginative of therapists could have created such a scenario on the client's behalf. Even if they had, it is extremely unlikely that Vicky would have taken it on as her own and put her name to the credits. Vicky's vibrating peach is entirely self-derived. It generates sufficient warmth to moderate her hyperactive public persona and enough dynamism to energize her passive private persona, without either feeling deprived.

4 The facilitator's role is to create the right conditions for successful decoding

Most therapies treat client symptoms as negative and needing to be confronted, buried, disrupted, or denounced. The Clean facilitator's job is to create a safe environment in which they can be identified and engaged.

In the following extract from a television program about psychoanalysis, a female therapist in her early thirties is conducting an exploratory session with a male patient in his mid-twenties. At the end of the session, there is an exchange that goes:

> Analyst Do you have any questions for me?
> Patient *Yes, I was wondering how long you have been doing this kind of work.*
>
> Analyst Are you coming on to me?
> Patient *I'm sorry?*

Analyst I'm suggesting you are coming on to me sexually.
Patient (Embarrassed) *No no no.*

Analyst Now you are resisting.

The analyst goes on to talk about 'resistance' and 'emotional transference', while the young man looks increasingly dismayed. He has been placed in an impossible bind. If he disagrees with the analyst ("No, I am *not* resisting you"), he will have fallen for an old trick and suffer a technical knock-out. If he comes out fighting ("Yes, I *am* resisting you"), he will have set himself up for losing on points. A relationship in which his real symptoms could have been engaged and decoded has been compromised.

The content-free nature of Clean questioning does not require the client to respond to a therapist's fantasies, or to accept or reject a therapist's reasoning. The risk of being drawn into a Byzantine emotional relationship with the therapist is thereby greatly reduced.

5 Clean Language speaks to a self-decoding process

The Grovian reliance on self-determination is not to deny the existence of a relationship between facilitator and client, but to de-emphasize it. In Clean process, the primary therapeutic relationship is between the client and their perceptions. Clean Language is employed, as Grove has said:

> so that a person can understand their perspective internally, in their own matrix. Our questions will have given a form to, and made manifest, a particular aspect of the person's experience in a way that they have not experienced before.

A different kind of facilitator-client relationship is thus established. Clean Language is neither client-centered nor therapist-centered, but client information-centered.

Client-centered interventions may be experienced by the client as supportive, but are likely to be pre-loaded with assumption ("That must have made you feel awful"), presumption ("Why do you put yourself down?"), and suggestion ("You might want to consider ..."). The ensuing conversation is not so much a dialogue as a 'dualogue', an exchange with two sets of intentions pitched one against the other. A key intention of the client is to be 'understood' and the anticipated benefit is having someone who 'understands'. A key intention of the agent of change is to 'understand' and the anticipated pay-off is a grateful client who gets what they want. The road to understanding follows a tortuous route pitted with semantic potholes and having no certain end.

Therapist-centered interventions tap into reserves of speculation based on the therapist's theoretical school of thought. In the 'sexual transference' example above, what to many would be a negligible issue has been inflated to fit a catch-all thesis. Even if the therapist's fantasy does not match the young man's internal experience, his contribution to the exchange ("I was wondering how long you have been doing this kind of work") will still be interpreted according to the theory. And what happens next is that patients, unless they are independently minded and smart enough to pick and choose from what is on offer, find themselves joining the therapist's world. They begin to have the 'right' responses. Freudian patients have Freudian dreams; Jungian patients draw on Jungian archetypes. What started out as a symmetrical relationship becomes heavily skewed to one side.

Information-centered exchanges are geared to self-psychoactivity. The facilitator does not introduce ideas to the client, or speculate about their motivation, or voice opinions about anything they say. There can be no debatable answers to Clean questions. A client's apparent resistance to, inability to answer, or problem understanding, a Clean question would derive either from the client's unfamiliarity with their internal experience or from the facilitator's inept or inelegant construction, timing, or delivery of the question. In such a case, the facilitator's response is not complicated: it is to ask another, usually simpler, question based on what the client has actually said. A Clean question properly put will almost always be answerable.

6 The process utilizes every kind of client information
Each of us assimilates and generates an extraordinary amount of semantic, somatic, graphic, energetic, perceptual, locational, spatial, temporal, cosmological, and metaphysical data every moment of the day. Information-centered facilitation thrives on this abundance. The semantic, somatic, and graphic information Vicky came up with earlier prompted a certain line of questioning, but it is not the only line the facilitator could have taken. There are a variety of ways to harvest the wealth of potential in a client's

language. Different kinds of verbal and nonverbal information prompt different kinds of question. The following exchanges (some real, others marked * are imagined) are intended to be illustrative rather than typical.

Semantic information
Deriving from the client's words, sounds, and linguistic constructions.

> *When I was a kid my parents always said there was a right way of doing things, but I always thought I should do things my way.*
> And a right way and your way are like what?

Somatic information
From the client's physical memory, including feeling, gesture, posture, and pre-conscious micro-movements:

> *When I was a kid my parents always said there was a right way of doing things* (gestures with left hand), *but I always thought I should do things my way* (gestures with right hand).
> And what does that hand (nods to client's right hand) know about your way?

> *It knows it's a real feeling.*
> And where is that real feeling?

Graphic information
From a client's drawings, metaphor maps, doodles, glyphs, etc.

> And is there anything else about that (indicates object on left)?
> *It vibrates, it has to move, it needs to work hard.*

Energetic information
Found in references to volition, force, motion, energy, agency, or causation in the client's verbal and nonverbal constructions.

> *And when it vibrates, what happens next?
> *There's a kind of rush of energy, then it explodes into a force for good.*

Perceptual information
The client's perceptual relationship with their information may be clearly indicated or not at all obvious. What is the perceptual sense involved? Where is the perceiver's point of view?

> *The problem is that the nut sucks energy from the peach.*
> And how do you know that nut sucks energy from peach?

> **I watch it happen, I can see it and feel it.*
> And when you can see it, where are you?

> *Over here, too far to do anything about it.*

Locational information
From the placing and positioning of symptoms and symbols in the metaphor landscape.

> *And when you are too far, where is nut?
> *Way over there, outside the window.*

> And when way over there, where is peach?
> *Right here, floating in a warm bath.*

Spatial information
Derived from the psychoactive physical spaces in which clients locate their symbols or themselves.

> *And when peach is right here and nut is way over there, what is between?
> *An unploughed field stretching as far as I can see.*

The metaphor has taken on a life of its own. Grove coined the term 'psychoactive space' to describe the means by which a person comes to live in their metaphor (see Clean Space, Appendix C). James Lawley describes how a space becomes psychoactive "when the spatial relations of the physical objects and imaginative symbols in it invoke an extra significance over and above their everyday meaning."[5] It is this extra significance to our perceptions – when they seem to take on a life of their own – that is at the heart of psychoactivity.

A subset of spatial/locational information I call 'horizonal' derives from the client's awareness of what might lie beyond the ostensible limits of their current perceptions.[6]

> *And when unploughed field stretching as far as you can see ...

what is beyond?
My silent father, working the farm.

Temporal information

From the coding of biographical, ancestral, and even geological time in the metaphor landscape:

> *And where could silent father working the farm come from?
> *From his father before him and from the earth they shared.*

Cosmological and metaphysical information

Sourced in the client's sense of distant origins or a further dimension.

> *And where could the earth they shared come from?
> *From the energy of a distant star.*

Clean procedures are as simple in practice as they are in principle. The less attempt there is by the facilitator to change the client's model of the world, the more the client will get to know it for themself. Power returns where it rightly belongs. And what happens next is inevitable and compelling: the self-system learns from itself.

Notes to Chapter 11

1 These six propositions were developed from a seminar led by David Grove in London in 1996. Six has been calculated as the optimum number of elements needed to interact and integrate to form an emergent system. More on emergence in Appendix C and at powersofsix.com

2 Neuronal repair: the University of Cambridge Centre for Brain Repair, brc.cam.ac.uk

3 Onset of adult depression. In 2011, researchers at the Institute of Psychiatry at King's College, London, published a meta-analysis of 26 studies of 26,000 people. They concluded that people who suffer abuse during childhood are *twice* as likely to suffer depression in adulthood. Classic indicators are maternal rejection; harsh discipline by either parent; unstable primary care arrangements; and physical or sexual maltreatment.

4 The term 'bodymind' is widely used in other languages. The equivalent in French is 'psychocorporelle', in German 'Körpergeist', and in Italian 'corpo-mente'.

5 Psychoactive space: James Lawley, *Where Where Matters: How Psychoactive Space is Created and Utilised*, article in *The Model*, January 2006.

6 'Horizonal' information: acknowledgments to Clive Bach for introducing the 'What is beyond?' question to the Clean Practise Group some years ago. There is more about it in Chapter 18 under *Specialist locating* questions.

Chapter 12
A Clean Start

We are here and it is now. Further than that, all knowledge is moonshine. H. L. Mencken

A present breath – Lorraine at the gate of change – Clean positioning, attending, listening, observing

There are few preconditions for a Clean exchange. One is the premise that every breath we take is a present breath; every moment is a place we have never been. We can draw from what has happened and anticipate what is to come, but we can only do so here and now. As the moral philosopher Blaise Pascal observed:

> We anticipate the future as if we found it too slow in coming and were trying to hurry it up, or we recall the past as if to stay its too rapid flight. We are so unwise that we wander about in times that are not ours and blindly flee the only one that is.[1]

The combination of intense focus and genial detachment that I saw in David Grove came from his capacity to readily disengage from the client's story and personality while engaging to the greatest possible degree in their process *in the moment.*

A volunteer client approaches him at a public seminar. As she steps onto the platform, she touches the lapel of her jacket.

> David   And what kind of (indicates gesture) could that be?
> Client   *Er, sadness, anxiety.*
>
> David   And is there anything else about that 'er'?

The client's hesitation and sadness may be a response to a reminder of her past, her anxiety may be a projection into the future, but only now does she feel them. Even deeply neurotic or mentally ill patients who perceive themselves as living wholly in the past, whose personalities are mediated by everything terrible that ever happened to them, can only experience the past as a present (re)construction. Their memories will seem real enough, but at the time they were stored would have been subject to strong emotional affect, and since then the neural networks involved will have been subject to countless other influences, good and bad, relevant and peripheral. The reconstruction may be authentic or not, but it has a genuine and present effect.

Lorraine at the gate of change

The ability to recognize the present and be in it is a major component of mental wellness. Here is Lorraine, diagnosed elsewhere as depressive and paranoid. She struggles to answer my first question:

What would you like to have happen?

She makes no reply. I wait for a moment, then ask:

And what is happening now?
I'm having a problem focusing on my goals.

And when you're having a problem focusing on your goals,
what would you like to have happen?
To focus on my goals.

What Lorraine wants to happen is actually happening. She is focusing on her goals, though she is, as she says, "having a problem" doing so. It is the problem of focusing, not the goals, that is the subject of her present attention. Her knowledge of what she would like to have happen does not therefore lie ahead. She is stumbling across it right now.

Before long, Lorraine is deeply into Therapeutic Metaphor process and finding herself confronted by two "guardians of the gate", who are conspiring to prevent her entry into what she calls "the gilded mansion" of her dreams..

And they won't allow me in.
And when they won't allow you in, how old could you be?

Six or seven.

Lorraine is re-creating some kind of symbolic event from the past.

And when six or seven, what kind of guardians could those guardians be?
My foster parents.

What Lorraine is experiencing is a 'remembered present'. Authentic up to a point, but not the real thing, like any contemporary re-enactment of an historical event. To learn from re-enactments of the past rather than simply continuing to repeat them, we need to ask the right questions in the present. As we only exist in the moment, the present is the only time that change can happen. And for change to happen, the brain must be in the right frame of mind. Clean Language is ideally suited to the learning brain, because it maximizes psychoactivity while minimizing discomfort and distraction.

The Clean facilitator sets up the optimum conditions for psychoactivity from the start with a combination of

Clean positioning
    attending
    listening
    and observing

The behaviors related to these will be revisited throughout every session and serve to vitalize every exchange. Taken together, they create a special kind of intercession, an *easing between* the client and their unconscious.

Clean positioning

Two basic starting points for a Clean process are the questions

Where would you like to be in the space?
And where would you like me to be?

which invite the client to position themself and the facilitator physically in relation to each other. In doing so, they encourage both parties to take another kind of position about the power relationship implied.

A traditional counselor's first intervention will normally be to usher the client to a chair designated for visitors; the next, to sit in a chair they have reserved for themself. It might be hard to think of these conventional moves as meaningful interventions, but they constitute a clear *mise-en-scène*, an artful disposition of elements necessary for telling the story. In setting out a Clean space, the client is required to take these initiatives for themself. The facilitator's first question:

Where would you like to be in the space?

subverts any expectation the client may have had that the facilitator would be taking lead role in the drama. The question can have a mildly unsettling effect or it can be experienced as no more than a passing curiosity; either way, it obliges the client to seek out a psychoactive space that intuitively mirrors something of significance to their internal landscape. All a facilitator has to do at that point is to honor the choice without attempting to influence, second-guess, interrupt, or interpret it.

The client is then invited to position the facilitator, who asks:

And where would you like me to be?

Not every client wants to be seated at a 135-degree angle to their interlocutor or to lie on a *chaise longue* with a view of the ceiling, yet many clients (and therapists) believe these to be 'correct' positions, particularly if they have seen them on television. The only correct alignment of client and facilitator is one that, given the freedom to choose, the client freely chooses. Inviting the client to make this choice is a first step in helping them adjust to the idea that responsibility for what happens thereafter is theirs. It also serves as a reminder to the facilitator that this is now *the client's space.*

Relative positioning may change as the work develops. A client may instinctively modify their distance from, or angle to, the facilitator to reflect an internal change. One of my clients moved his chair progressively nearer a fireplace over the course of his work because, he said, it symbolized the warmth and energy he was rediscovering in himself.

If a facilitator asks these positioning questions at the start of every session, the client is obliged to continue monitoring their internal configuration of the problem while at the same time renewing their responsibility to themself.

Attending cleanly

Willie Loman's wife in the Arthur Miller play *Death of a Salesman* longs for her thoughtless son to respect his self-deluding father for doing the best he can in a harsh world. "Attention – attention must be paid to such a person!" she cries.

Respect is the parent of attention and sister to curiosity. They require a facilitator to focus on the big close-up at times and zoom out to the big picture at others, and occasionally do both together. To improve the concentration needed to do this well, facilitators have to maintain their dopamine levels – to sleep well, eat sensibly, and take plenty of exercise. At the same time, the intention to attend to whatever the client comes up with has to allow for what Dutch psychologist Victor Lamme calls "attentional selection", the process by which our sensory processing is modified by current state as shaped by genetic factors, memory, beliefs, and recent events. We select for attention those things we consider to be important. Selected inputs are processed faster or deeper than inputs related to things we consider less important and thus make a correspondingly greater contribution to our conscious awareness. We can't help it: we notice some things more than others.[2]

The Clean Research Group explored ways in which facilitators could improve their attentiveness. One thing we did was analyze the metaphors we used in "paying", "giving", or "focusing" attention. Attenders for whom vision was the lead sensory system did something like concentrate their inner eye on an image projected onto an internal screen. Beams of light were popular with our visualizers. Focusing attention for them was like

> a beam of light from Lord of the Rings
> a beam of light, a stream of particles in a magnetic field
> a spotlight that can be moved, widened, or narrowed.

Kinesthetically inclined attenders performed an imaginary physical act like focusing the lens of a camera, or concentrated on an internal sensation of intense connection via the heart or gut. Some "directed", "summoned", or "shifted" their attention to their clients. Others represented the process in terms of

> a kitten ready to pounce on a ball of wool
> a tube of clarity through miasma
> a railway on which I need to stay on track.

Attention extends into listening. Clean facilitators are not passive listeners.

Learning to listen
'Giving ear' is an intentional act. But there can be conflicts between aural and visual input that cause us to hear unreliably. Sighted

facilitators have to concentrate more if they cannot see the client, but it means they hear them more acutely and accurately. This may be a self-evident effect (concentrate more, hear better), but is supported by research that shows visual signals arriving at the brain slightly earlier than auditory signals.[3] As we observe clients, we are already narrowing down the range of possible interpretations of what we are about to hear by the time the sound actually arrives. Fewer choices allow faster responses – a useful skill on the African savannah, but not quite so necessary in the consulting room. It will not normally be helpful to have instant responses to what we see before considering what we hear.

Clean listening involves a ceding of personal territory by the facilitator in an act of linkage between the client and their unconscious. The client and their unconscious may wish to come together, but are often under constraints of ignorance or timidity. The Clean listener intercedes between them on behalf of both.

It is 100,000 years or so since we made the change from gesture to speech as a primary means of communication; more than enough for words and their associations to have become capable of representing infinite possibilities and endless ambiguities. To avoid being overwhelmed with alternatives, we take an enormous amount for granted when we listen to others. Inevitably, miscalculation and distortion abound.

> "You should say what you mean," the March Hare said.
> "I do," Alice hastily replied; "at least – at least I mean what I say – that's the same thing, you know."
> "Not the same thing a bit!" said the Mad Hatter. "Why, you might just as well say that 'I see what I eat' is the same thing as 'I eat what I see'! [4]

To cope with the immense imprecision of my client Colin's

> *I have to get out of this state, this space, I'm stuck in this dark corner ...*

I latch on to one or two familiar words, note what sounds to be an identifiable emphasis, and lump them together with a ragbag of memory and imagination in order to come up with some kind of sense. "He means what he says," I tell myself, meaning, "He means what I believe him to mean." This is not Clean listening.

Clean listening ensures that we hear the specifics, not the gist, of what clients say. It frees us from the shackles of conventional understanding. Energy saved on attempting to decipher what the client means is released for paying keener attention to their actual words and to those subtle moderators of sound that contain as much information as the words: the sighs, clicks, and coughs; the silences, stalls, and pauses; all the unconsciously derived phonic punctuations we use to indicate emotion, accentuate sense, or designate value.

Clean listening is related to, but is not, *empathy* or *impartiality*. It is related to, but is not, *hearing*.

Listening and empathy

Empathy is not sympathy. Sympathy is a feeling of pity for the misfortunes of others. Empathy is the name we tend to give to 'sharing and understanding' the feelings of others. In the nineteen-fifties, one of the leaders of the humanistic psychology movement, Carl Rogers, defined empathy as "the ability to feel what the client feels." We know now that this is really not possible. Neurological research using magnetic resonance scanning shows that when we receive a painful stimulus, signals travel from the site of the stimulus to the brain and result in both sensory and emotional areas lighting up.[5] Similar sensory and emotional areas are activated when we observe someone else's pain, which can lead us to believe that we are both observing *and feeling* their pain. Yet the emotional areas of the brain consist of subjectively reconstructed neural networks activated by memories exclusive to ourselves. They light up with our own emotional associations, which activate our own sensory areas. A feeling of 'empathy' can divert us down a path of our own making, believing we are actually treading the client's path. In fact, we can as little know the painful feelings of others as we can jointly possess them.

Even so, it can take very little to get emotionally entangled in a someone else's distress and feel compelled to offer advice. As Clean listeners, we will have feelings of compassion, sadness, and so on, and they are useful for doing the job, but we will acknowledge them as *our* feelings: sourced locally, experienced internally. We will not claim to feel what the other fellow feels. If the other fellow so desires, however, we will help them transform it.

Listening and impartiality

Alfred Korzybski asks readers of *Science and Sanity* to place themselves in a state of emotional impassivity. Whatever he declares to be so, he writes, is neither the truth nor the totality.

He asks readers to detach themselves from identification with the author, from believing they know what he means. Equally, whatever a client expresses to a counselor or coach is not 'it'. It will be some part of it, it will represent it in some way, but it will be not be the whole of it.

Of course, as facilitators we cannot always be impartial about what our clients present. It would be impossible to check in our emotional responses like umbrellas at an exhibition in case we were tempted to misuse them. It would require a complete reversal of our habitual modes of being to separate ourselves from our humanity in this way. But it is precisely because such a separation is impossible that the ritual, the rigor, the benevolent precision of Clean listening and questioning exist. They are a means of achieving detachment while remaining in rapport. If we cannot be impartial, we can act with impartiality.

Listening and hearing

The responsibility of the Clean listener is to really hear what the client says – and not just the words, but the sounds echoing in, around, and between them. That isn't easy. Our capacity for hearing has been tuned by natural selection to hear human speech more acutely than the other properties of sound.

MRI scans show the brain separating auditory input into two streams: words are moved to the left temporal lobes for processing, while the acoustic patterns the voice makes are channeled to the right, a region more stimulated by music.[6]

> *I have to get out of this state, this space, I'm stuck in this dark corner ...*

The client's word-stream is differentiated into primary, secondary, and occasionally tertiary and further *meanings* in our minds, while the sound-stream is differentiated into variations of *volume, pitch, emphasis, rhythm, and musicality.*

> *Volume.* High volume may be coded by facilitator or client for strength or lack of control, just as low volume may signal anything from diffidence, fear, and anger to confidence, arrogance, and self-reliance. It will partly depend on the association of volume with:

> *Pitch or tone.* The low or high acoustic frequency of the sound is a qualitative indicator. It might be characterized as 'thin', 'hushed', 'colorful', 'rich', etc.

Emphasis is about the stress given to a word or sound in order to indicate its comparative value in a sentence. "I *have* to get out of this state" and "I have to get *out* of this state" signal the need for a different approach to reflecting the client and preparing to intercede.

Rhythm applies to the pattern of the client's words and sounds. A regular, irregular, or metronomic rhythm is likely to be an indicator of the feeling behind the sounds.

Musicality or melody applies to the 'tunefulness' or lack of it in a sequence.

As the client's word-stream and sound-stream re-combine after being processed separately, our minds have to make sense of several different things. They don't always get it right. It is common for the volume or pitch of a person's anger, for example, to drown out our attention to what they are actually saying. Or we may hear a person's words well enough, but misinterpret their emotional significance.

Sue wants to find out more about the origins of the arthritis in her feet. She identifies the pain, unusually, by its tonal qualities. In her right foot, it is

like the soft twang of elastic

while in her left foot it is more like

a sharp rattle of beads.

"Soft" has implications for volume and pitch, and perhaps in this case for touch; "twang" and "rattle" offer tone and movement related information. By differentiating and exploring the auditory and kinesthetic qualities of her arthritis, Sue is able to trace antecedent influences that identify not only the sources of her pain, but also a remedy incorporating the potential for healing the metaphors represent.

Sensitivity to sound is an essential requisite for Clean facilitation. Hearing volume, pitch, emphasis, rhythm, and musicality accurately is an obvious prerequisite for reflecting them faithfully. It needs practice, but is not as difficult as it may sound.

Observing cleanly

Attention extends into observation. There may be as much information in the involuntary raising of an eyebrow or the tapping of a foot in relation to a phrase or a pause as there is in a wholesale shift of position. A facilitator concentrating on verbal information may fail to spot the nonverbal signals. These may be conspicuous or barely discernible, but their significance is not a function of size. A fleeting glance may be a random occurrence or an unconscious 'line of sight' to the location of new information. The twitch of a muscle could be the result of a fortuitous event or the appearance of emotional information in the bodymind a split second before cognition intervenes.

Observing, like listening, is driven by intention; intention by what we believe to be important. We readily disregard items in the visual field unless we have sufficient reason for paying attention to them.[7] You may have seen a video of the experiment in which a person stops another in the street to ask for directions. While the two are talking, workmen carrying a large screen walk between them and after they have crossed, the person who was asking for directions has changed. Half the people who have been stopped do not notice the substitution. Interviewed a few minutes later, they have noticed nothing strange.

Experiments like these have far-reaching implications for the recall of traumatic incidents from childhood. It is not unusual for clients to have a detailed memory of a non-existent event and a corrupted memory or no memory at all of an event that actually took place. We know that imagining a scene activates the same parts of the visual cortex that actually seeing it does.[8] The brain does not distinguish between the two. Only the mind can do that. It is inevitable, therefore, that clients, like the people in the street giving directions, will fill in gaps in their memory by remembering not only what they were actually attending to at the time, but also what they have filled in since, and in retrospect *be unable to make a distinction between the two.*

Given the incessant bombardment of parts to which our brains are subjected, our minds cannot help but make convincing wholes. The Guardian newspaper's 'Bad Science' correspondent, Ben Goldacre, put it like this:

> We have an innate human ability to make something out of nothing. We see shapes in the clouds and a man on the moon [...]

Our ability to spot patterns is what allows us to make sense of the world but sometimes, in our eagerness, we can mistakenly spot patterns where none exist.[9]

Why is this so important for therapists, coaches, and other agents of change? Because if we know that our vision and hearing are at best partial and at worst deeply flawed, we have no excuse (though some would say we have every excuse) for misreading our clients and deceiving ourselves. If we are taking in no more than a few items of information and relying on imagination and memory for the rest, we are, not to put too fine a point on it, making our clients up.

There is a remedy. It requires an elementary but exacting condition to be met.

Notes to Chapter 12

1 Blaise Pascal, French mathematician, physicist, and moralist; *Pensées*, 1660. We "blindly flee" the present, he pointed out, yet the present is the only time that is truly ours.

2 Attentional selection: neuroscientist Victor Lamme, *Why Visual Attention and Awareness Are Different*, in *Trends in Cognitive Science* January 2003.

3 Visual signals processed more quickly than auditory: Virginie van Wassenhove and colleagues, *Visual Speech Speeds Up Neural Processing of Auditory Speech* in *Proceedings of the National Academy of Sciences* 102(4) 2005.

4 "You should say what you mean." Lewis Carroll, *Alice's Adventures in Wonderland*, 1865.

5 *Empathy for Pain Involves the Affective but not Sensory Components of Pain*. Tania Singer and colleagues at the Institute of Neurology, University of London, reporting in *Science* 303 2004.

6 How the brain sorts auditory input: *The Neuroanatomical and Functional Organization of Speech Perception*, Sophie Scott and Ingrid Johnsrude, *Trends in Neuroscience* 26 (2) 2003.

7 What we see depends on our intention at the time: Laura Spinney, *New Scientist*, 18 November 2000, reporting on research into vision, attention, and awareness by experimental psychologists at the Universities of Derby, Harvard, and British Columbia, the French National Center for Scientific Research (CNRS), and others.

8 Seeing or imagining activates the visual cortex similarly: psychologist Stephen Kosslyn, Harvard 1999.

9 Making something out of nothing: Dr. Ben Goldacre, *The Guardian* 21 April 2007.

Chapter 13
Clean Reflection
Part 1 of the Clean Language Syntax

Why did we invent mirrors? Because everything that can be seen can be seen except ourselves. Jonathan Miller

1 And X ...
2 And when X ...
3 Question about X ...

Suspending judgment – Secrets of the syntax – Accurate reflection: Kay and the child within – Use of the word 'and': emphasis, addition, consequence – Reflecting lines of attention, nonverbal language – Hazel's unexpected move

The Skeptical ('Inquiring') school of Greek philosophers held that a suspension of judgment was the only sensible attitude to pretty much anything. Seventeen centuries later, the German philosopher Schopenhauer went some way to agreeing:

> Everything we perceive is merely phenomenon; we do not know what things are like in themselves, that is independently of our perception of them.[1]

The positioning, listening, and observing demands of a Clean Start oblige the Clean facilitator to train their perception to note as much as possible of what seems to be, knowing that one cannot take in everything that is, and to clear the mind of all certainty about what any slice or scrap of it means. The result of this suspension of certainty is the requirement to keep on looking and listening, and never to claim to have discovered the truth.

Some Clean trainees experience considerable anxiety when for perhaps the first time in their lives they are obliged to keep their beliefs and speculations about clients to themselves. Some despair as they remember the unnecessary calculations they have brought to the therapeutic equation in the past. Some suffer withdrawal symptoms as they find themselves deprived of the familiar burden of responsibility for making the 'correct' intervention. One psychoanalyst I trained was happy not to bear this cross any longer, but privately admitted to mourning the loss of his favorite chair, a symbol of status that had marked the reality boundary between himself and his patients for over thirty years.

In the experience of being facilitated cleanly during their training, facilitators get added value: they get to know themselves better. This has a knock-on effect. In every training I have led or attended, I have seen that when a facilitator's own way of knowing is respected without challenge, they are more disposed to respect the knowing of others in turn. Clean Language encourages this exchange of value. Neither party to a Clean exchange needs to be at pains to explain themself. The facilitator is concerned only with establishing a context for the exploration and resolution of whatever is taking the client's attention, and not with analyzing or interpreting it. The client is concerned only with expressing what is taking their attention, and not with explaining, excusing, or defending it.

For the facilitator, this means disengaging from conventional relationship and attending scrupulously to the other person instead: observing without interpreting and listening without judgment. Some agents of change find this disagreeable in principle and difficult to realize in practice. Yet the impulse to engage cleanly has to be activated before the client comes through the door. The client may already be organizing their unconscious defenses against the possibility of challenge or intrusion. What historic patterns may be playing at this time?

During the Second World War, the British learned to recognize the signature of enemy Morse code operators by the way they spaced their dots and dashes. Every operator had a distinctive pattern that would reveal itself in the smallest sample. Experienced interceptors had only to listen for a few seconds to pick out the individual responsible for the transmission. Knowing who was where in this way contributed in no small way to the larger intelligence.[2] Counselors who forswear judgment and conventional relationship from the start find it easier to attend to the smallest specifics of what their clients express.

Alex gives a little cough as he enters the room. What is he signaling? I draw his attention to it gently:

And [cough]. And when [cough], what kind of [cough] could that be? (Surprised) *Embarrassment. Apology. I'm in the spotlight and I don't deserve to be. I suppose that's really why I'm here.*

A single question can get to the heart of the matter, so a facilitator has to be more than ordinarily prepared.

Secrets of the syntax
The performance of Clean Language has a simple three-part syntax:

1 Reflecting the client's words
2 Selecting what to attend to
3 Questioning what is selected

The power of this pared-down format lies in its coherence and elegance. It welcomes wherever the client is at and simply invites them to go further. First, I respectfully reflect what Alex has said:

1 And embarrassment. Apology. You're in the spotlight and you don't deserve to be.

Next, I invite him to attend to (the whole or a part of) it:

2 And when you're in the spotlight and don't deserve to be ...

Then I question what I have selected:

3 Is there anything else about that spotlight?

The purity and precision of the formula:

1 And X ...
2 And when X ...
3 [Question about X]

has several effects. It maintains the client in their perceptual present while freeing them to be as coherent or as complex as they wish. It deters the facilitator from adding extraneous words of their own which might misrepresent the client's perception. And because the structure of the syntax repeats predictably, it creates what Grove called "a protective temporal and spatial womb or matrix" around the perception.

The facilitator's role is to be midwife to the information contained therein and to assist in its birthing.

Accurate reflection

I have to get out of this state, this space, I'm stuck in this dark
corner ...
And you have to get out of this state, this space, you're stuck
in this dark corner ...

Reflecting the client in their own words is an exceptional act to which we apply two exacting conditions: accuracy and immediacy. Meticulous reflection is the supreme test of Clean listening. Some counselors find it difficult to repeat exactly what their clients have said because they have been too intent on processing it – attempting to figure it out in personal or global terms ("Does he mean what I think he means?" "Is she depressed?" "How does this fit what I know about psychosexual development?") – and become so disorientated by the twists and turns of their own reasoning that they ignore or forget what triggered their figuring out.

Conventional understanding is not as important as many listeners or agents of change suppose. At a basic procedural level, the Clean response to what a client presents is simply a matter of acknowledging it accurately. Facilitators with poor attention skills or the ingenuous, if understandable, desire to make their clients feel better can make this essentially straightforward act of reflection unnecessarily difficult for themselves.

After a holistic holiday on the Greek island of Skyros, the journalist Sandra Deeble reported on the challenge of participating in a psycho-educational exercise that required her to listen to someone else without interruption and to repeat exactly what they had said. Deeble confessed that "it proved impossible to repeat what the other had said without your own spin, adding anecdotes, emphasizing, or even getting it completely wrong."[3] She admitted that all too often while the other person was speaking she was thinking about how her tan was progressing or planning what to say next. And she learned an important lesson: experienced listeners do not say, "I know just how you feel."

"How can you possibly know how I feel?" the Samaritans ask their volunteers. "It may sound empathic, but it's very presumptuous and can be demeaning." According to Deeble's tutor, the experienced listener responds instead with, "Let me say this back to you, just to be sure I've completely understood what you mean." Acceptable enough on a Greek island holiday, perhaps, but this is not a Clean response. To put someone's words in the context of a need to "completely understand" them is to shift the spotlight from the performer onto the audience, from the speaker to the listener. The drama has taken a gratuitous twist.

The intention of *immediate and literal* repetition is to keep the client center stage: to maintain them in their present perception; to affirm what they have said without distortion; and to embrace their experience without reservation. "We cannot change anything until we accept it," said Jung. Analytical or critical responses, however well intended, do not liberate clients; they hold them in check. While a response such as "I know exactly what you mean/ how you feel/where you are coming from" would simply be untrue and leave any self-respecting client supposing that you do not.

Accurate and prompt reflection conveys affirmation and encourages the client to accept themself *just as they are at that time.*

Experienced facilitators can pat their head and rub their tummy at the same time — have fantasies about what the client means while repeating exactly what they have said at the same time as working through a standard Clean procedure. The rest of us cannot go wrong if we simply repeat the client's words, preferably in the order in which they have used them, for it is not only the words themselves but also the way they are organized and presented that can contain valuable information.

> *I find myself confronted by two guardians of the gate who won't let me in.*

How has Lorraine constructed this perception? There are three principal episodes to her little parable. First, she finds herself; then she is confronted; then she isn't let in.

> *I find myself*
> *I am confronted by two guardians of the gate*
> *I am not let in*

In addition to these three obvious opportunities for intervention, there are at least five more: one before Lorraine finds herself, another after she is confronted; and several more in-between. A lot could be happening in any one of them. Given the amount of potential packed into a statement like this, the conventional counselor will not always find it easy to have a simple response ("What do you mean? Who are these guardians? Your parents? Yourself? Is there some mythical reference here?"). The Clean facilitator's initial response is simplicity itself:

> And you find yourself confronted by two guardians at the gate
> who won't let you in.

It could be even simpler:

> And who won't let you in ...

The last phrase is frequently a summation of what went before and
will often do perfectly well on its own.

Kay and the child within

Kay is a clinical psychologist who came for a session of supervision.

> *I've been working with this girl with multiple personalities. A few
> sessions ago, we started a Grovian process and after a couple of
> sessions, she got to a 'child within'. Suddenly her eyes filled, she
> stopped and said, "I'm not going to continue." I felt terrible, like a
> little sister again, I had no confidence. A few sessions later, the
> same thing happened. She got to her 'child within' again and said,
> "I can't cope any more." I came away totally unhappy, I don't know
> why.*

By the time Kay has finished what she has to say, I have forgotten
how she began. I remember her last words, however:

> And she got to her child within again and said, "I can't cope any
> more." And you came away totally unhappy, you don't know why.

Deciding what to select for Kay's attention in the next stage of the
syntax suddenly becomes easier. Whether I repeat everything she
has said or only a part of it, reflection triggers a process in which
Kay's inner world becomes privy to its own inherent logic. The
client may be hearing themself for the first time. This perhaps more
than any other factor is the *sine qua non* of the syntax. A Clean
reflection that acknowledges the client's perceptions without
challenge is an essential condition of the facilitator's response. It
encourages clients to hear – to really hear – themselves.

Use of the word 'and': emphasis, addition, consequence

'And' prefaces every reflection, irrespective of what the client has
said. It is a servant with multiple roles. It signals that what is to
come will neither be a quibble nor a counter-argument. It operates
as a gentle connective, linking the logic of the client's narrative to
the facilitator's. And it helps maintain the client in their present
state with the linguistic equivalent of a regular breath.

And you felt like the little sister again ...
And when you felt like little sister again ...

'And' has no absolute meaning in itself, but in its relationship to the client's material it acquires several ancillary meanings. As the facilitator repeats what the client has said, 'and' offers undertones of *emphasis* ('nota bene'), *addition* ('plus'), or *consequence* ('as'), any of which could be relevant as the client's unconscious determines.

'Nota bene' you're stuck ..

would be a self-reminder that this kind of thing could have happened before. Stuck may be a pattern.

'Plus' you're stuck ..

In addition to, or perhaps as a result of, everything else. Your stuckness is not a thing on its own.

'So' you're stuck ..

There are causes and consequences to your stuckness. How did you arrive at this state? Now what happens?
"When I make a word do a lot of work like that," said Humpty Dumpty, "I always pay it extra." 'And' has a rich ambiguity. It encourages the client to incorporate whatever nuance of emphasis, addition, or consequence might be appropriate to their process at the time. Each meaning of 'and' already inhabits the parallel worlds of the client's reality, so if the client attends to any one of them, the others are not excluded.
In most models of therapy, clients are likely to have notes of emphasis, addition, or consequence made on their behalf. "Bear in mind that this kind of thing has happened before," says the therapist in a supposedly helpful observation that points up the difference between inviting and directing attention. Repeating the client's exact words ("And you felt like the little sister again ...") *invites* attention in that it adds nothing to what has already been said. "Bear in mind that this kind of thing has happened before" crudely *directs* attention, in this case to an external perception.

There is more value yet in our little friend 'and'. Its ritual repetition helps induce a mildly altered state in the client, which allows them readier access to unconsciously stored information ... and helps them remain rooted in their own process ... and temporarily suspends any concern they might have about the external world.

Not everything a facilitator reflects will be verbal.

Reflecting lines of attention

We can suppose two lines of attention a client might follow: a 'line of sight' or a 'line of listening'. I first learned the value of a line of sight as a source of information while waiting to work with David Grove during one of his seminars and gazing – idly, as I thought – at the pattern in a Persian carpet. Rather than asking me what I was thinking about or what I would like to have happen, he simply reflected the direction of my gaze:

> And [looks to where I am looking] ...

A client's unconscious line of sight may be directed to a memory in the metaphor landscape or to an item in the real world that holds symbolic information.[4] David's simple reflection set me off on a journey into patterns deeper than those in the carpet.

The original 'Horse Listener', Monty Roberts, discovered a more elusive line of attention – a 'line of listening' – in his studies of wild mustangs. He studied their body language and noticed in particular how they angled their ears towards the source of a sound. In humans, the source of an imagined or a remembered sound may be indicated by nothing more than a slight inclination of the head or a micro-movement of the eyes. Humans can, however, be invited to reflect on what they do. Here is Matt:

> *My mum was angry* (angles head slightly to one side).
> And your mum was angry (facilitator hints at angling of head) ...
>
> *Yes.* (Pause. Younger voice tone) *I hear her slamming the door as she leaves the house and I think she may never come back.*

I *mirror* Matt's line of attention. My head and eyes are angled in the same direction as his. I would not mirror him exactly if he were indicating the existence of something behind him. True mirroring by me (turning to look behind me) would be indicating something behind me, which would clearly be false and likely to be misleading. Instead, I would look towards the place that Matt had mapped out in the metaphor landscape behind him. Only a slight glance or nod would be required, sufficient to orient Matt to the location or direction of the symbol in question.

Reflecting nonverbal language

Movements of the hands, feet, head, and trunk help organize our thoughts as we speak and free up working memory for other tasks. Hand gestures in particular are tools for complementing speech that lighten the burden on working memory. They are sometimes called 'iconic' from the Greek for 'likeness'. They symbolize something of significance unsaid.

The French essayist Montaigne was rather taken by the eloquent potential of gesture. "What of the hands?" he asks.

> We request,
>   we promise,
>   call,
>   dismiss,
>   menace,
>   pray,
>   supplicate,
>   deny,
>   refuse,
>   interrogate,
>   admire,
>   count,
>   confess,
>   repent,
>   fear ...[5]

Hands can convey every one of these feelings and behaviors without the aid of a single sound. Neuroscientists have discovered that the hand and mouth areas of the brain are located next to each other, which has led to speculation that there might be a spillover of signals between them that date from a time when our ancestors were evolving a system of gestures for silent communication while hunting. The body learned to express itself independently of speech.

I suggest that it is not a good idea to mirror a client's every move. People soon realize that their body language is less amenable to conscious control than their speech. Those twitches, touches, tics, licks, glints, and squints have bypassed the mill of the mind and appear in a coded flow direct from the unconscious. Clients made to feel self-conscious about the way they express themselves might be tempted to control the flow and a valuable source of information would be compromised.

Hazel's unexpected move

Hazel is a designer in her early forties. "I need to get more business oriented," she tells me. I invite her to write this up, place it where it needs to be, and position herself where she is now in relation to it. She writes:

I need to get more businesslike and marketing oriented.

She tacks the paper to the wall, stands facing it from a few feet away, and reads it aloud. Suddenly her mouth contorts, she twists away from the statement, and looks over her shoulder. I have no idea what the move means. Should I reflect it with the same degree of accuracy that I reflect her words? Generally, no. In most cases, it is better to allude to physical cues rather than attempting to duplicate them. But there are no hard and fast rules. A few kinesthetically sensitive clients are very particular about the way they express themselves physically, and unless mirrored precisely will shift their attention critically to the facilitator rather than maintaining it on themselves. Other clients will hardly notice. Most come between these extremes and will only be distracted if a facilitator is perceived to be mimicking a gesture, or over-dramatizing it, or getting it manifestly wrong.

I learn later that what Hazel means by her unexpected move is that she doesn't want to get businesslike at all. She feels pulled in another direction. I am reminded that a client's psychoactive space may extend some way beyond their physical position. If I am unsure how far Hazel's active landscape extends, the reflective gestures I make will be small. I do not wish to intrude with a move that could change the shape of her perceptions or distract her from her purpose in any way.

All right, you may say, I have been patient. I have attended with curiosity, I have listened with care, I have accurately reflected what my client has said, and I have mirrored discreetly what my client has shown. Now it's my turn. Well, yes and no. This is not the time to be introducing new ideas, or making up metaphors, or trotting out perceptive suggestions. Having reflected what the client has said or expressed, we must now simply invite them to attend to it.

How do we do that cleanly, and why?

Notes to Chapter 13

1 Suspension of certainty: Arthur Schopenhauer, *Parerga and Paralipomena*, 1850, translated by R. J. Hollingdale in *On the Suffering of the World*, Penguin 2004.

2 Identifying the Morse code patterns of individual operators: Malcolm Gladwell, *Blink: The Power of Thinking Without Thinking*, 2005.

3 Difficulties of repeating exactly what someone has said: Sandra Deeble, *Lend Them Your Ears*, article in *The Guardian* 20 March 2004.

4 "There is a content-rich significance to Grovian 'lines of sight' that distinguishes them from the systemic, content-free patterns of NLP 'eye accessing cues'." James Lawley.

5 "What of the hands?" French courtier and philosopher Michel de Montaigne, *Essays*, 1580 (my layout).

Chapter 14
Clean Attention
Part 2 of the Clean Language Syntax

I earned all the attention I'm getting.

Anna Kournikova, tennis player

1   And X ...
2   **And when X ...**
3   Question about X

Kay's little sister – Use of 'And when': presence, importance, immediacy – Jenny talks to her father – Abusive M – Re-associating into the perceptual present – Avoiding re-traumatization – Special attention to summaries and repetitions, ambiguities and unusual constructions, gesture and posture, micro-movements

To attend to another person is to be fully present with them. It may be the deepest form of care one can give. In Chapter 13, my psychologist client Kay had a lot to say about herself and her multiple personality client. Kay's last words were:

> *She got to her 'child within' again and said, "I can't cope any more." I came away totally unhappy, I don't know why.*

In the first part of the Clean syntax, I simply reflect this back to Kay so that she can hear her own words – a rare enough experience for anyone.

> And she got to her child within again and said "I can't cope any more." And you came away totally unhappy, you don't know why.

This is still a tightly wrapped bundle with at least seven separate observations. I can reselect the lot for Kay to make of it what she will or I can simplify things by unbundling a part of it for her selective attention.

That "again" ("she got to her child within again") points to a pattern. Whether it is Kay's pattern as well as her client's is a moot point at this moment. A repeating pattern will invariably hold the problem. How and why should I draw her attention to it?

Use of 'and when'

We are at a critical watershed from which the course of Clean Language flows. The two words

And when ..

are followed by a further repetition of the client's exact words. It is an invitation to the client to *re-associate* into their perceptions and to be entirely present in them.

And when she got to her 'child within' again ...

The second repetition induces increased activity in the neurons processing the attendant stimuli. The aim is to heighten both conscious and unconscious awareness in the client and thereby increase the likelihood of related information not yet in consciousness appearing. The invitation has a number of effects. It

- identifies specific perceptions
- embraces them
- re-associates the client into their perceptual present
- primes the client to relate what they have said to the question that will follow
- allows the facilitator breathing space to decide on a follow-up question

The discipline of the structure of this stage of the syntax minimizes the risk of the facilitator intruding with personal opinions and suggestions. This is a crucial restraint. Most facilitators would otherwise find it very difficult to keep their own ideas and interpretations out of the client's way.

And when she got to her child within again ...
I felt like the little sister again, insecure, inferior, frustrated.

Kay's insight into herself is a thousand times more useful to her than any conjecture you or I might have made.

The word "when" in "And when ..." is a prodigiously gifted figure of speech. It adds to the utility of "and" by encouraging the client to take their unconscious pick of a number of simple and compound, relative, correlative, and conjunctive nuances – all of them senses of "when" – including:

And 'at the time' that you felt ...
And 'in view of the fact' that you felt ...
And 'in the circumstances in which' you felt ...
And 'given' that you felt ...
And 'although' you felt ...
And 'after' you felt ...
And 'whenever' you felt ...

A collection of niceties wrapped in a very plain parcel. Any one of these meanings of "when" could relate to Kay's particular perception, but only she will have a sense, almost certainly unconscious, of which fits best. My initial repetition:

And you felt like the little sister again ...

is simply witness to what Kay has said. It acknowledges and confirms it clearly. My second repetition:

And when [at the time that/given that/whenever, etc.] you felt like the little sister again ...

honors the information. "And when ..." has a quasi-ceremonial role. It brings presence to the proceedings.

Presence, importance, immediacy

Presence confers importance with immediacy. It is an endorsement of value in the therapeutic exchange. It signals to Kay that these disagreeable, perhaps even shameful, feelings of hers are not to be derided or deplored, but embraced and cherished. I believe that clients are more open to learning when the means they choose to express themselves are accepted in their totality.

And when you felt like the little sister again, insecure, inferior, frustrated ...

The syntax is the same whether the client's language is conceptual, emotional, metaphorical, or nonverbal:

[Conceptual] *It brings up unresolved issues related to my family history.*
And it brings up unresolved issues relating to your family history.
And when it brings up unresolved issues relating to your family history ...

[Emotional] *I'm sad and angry.*
And you're sad and angry. *And when* you're sad and angry ...

[Metaphorical] *I feel like a mouse in striking distance of a cat. And you feel like a mouse in striking distance of a cat. And when you feel like a mouse in striking distance of a cat ...

[Nonverbal] *(Cough, shift, gesture, etc.)
And (cough, shift, gesture, etc.). And when (cough, shift, gesture) ... ..

Up until now, Kay has chosen not to explore the feelings that came up for her when she was working with her multiple personality client. "I came away totally unhappy," she said, "I don't know why." This might be a prime case of a symptom ("unhappy") with a positive intent – to signal something that requires attention – seeming to make the problem worse by denying or disguising it. "Unhappy" had become Kay's focus, rather than what the feeling of unhappy was signaling: that she felt insecure, inferior, and frustrated. These feelings only agreed to show up once "unhappy" had been acknowledged and accepted.

Over the course of the session, Kay comes to understand that her feelings are not figments of an over-heated imagination, but somatic realities with an identifiable bodily location and an accessible neuro-linguistic construction. She can locate them, discover their characteristics and provenance, and do something about them.

The predetermined reflecting and attending stages of the syntax allow little room for symptoms like Kay's to be denied by the therapist as phantoms of the mind or challenged as absurd. Some therapies would define Kay's symptoms as negative or destructive, the cause of the problem rather than its effect, and therefore needing to be exorcised. Clean Language embraces them without reservation. They hold essential information about how Kay's personal epistemology – what she knows or believes and how she came to know or believe it – has been configured and how it can be resolved. The facilitator's job is gently to interrogate her symptoms until, as Grove would say, "they confess their strengths."

Twofold repetition also helps patients who have lost some of their normal cognitive, emotional, or behavioral functions. The syntax echoes the routinely duplicated processing that people suffering from brain dysfunctions, particularly those with prefrontal disturbances, normally have to do for themselves. And it respects their need to do it at their own pace.

Here are two cases where simple reflection and attention brought their own reward without the need for a single question. Jenny's father is declining mentally and she is finding it difficult to communicate with him. M is an abusive mental patient who has been unable to get the help he needs.

Jenny talks to her father

Jim's short-term memory loss means he has difficulty piecing his life together, which makes communication with him laborious. When his daughter uses Clean Language conversationally with him, he is able to orientate into his experiences more fully. He tells Jenny about a day out from his care home in Ontario:

> *I went out with my friend Leonard today.*
> And you went out with your friend Leonard today.
>
> *And I visited somewhere.*
> And when you went out with your friend Leonard today and you visited somewhere ...
>
> *Yes, somewhere where I could see Oshawa from the window ...*
> And somewhere where you could see Oshawa from the window. And when you could see Oshawa from the window ...
>
> *There was the baker that sells those butter tarts I like.*

The reiterative nature of the syntax allows Jenny to take on the role of repetition that her father normally has to do for himself. It frees him to notice or remember new things, to piece together his experiences with greater coherence, and to relate to his daughter directly once more. They have a formula for sharing experience that is practical and respectful.

Abusive M

I am confronted by a belligerent patient who turns up at the mental health center where I am working and insists on being seen. He shouts at the receptionist. I try to reason with him. He shouts at me. I show him into a consulting room. He says:

> *I know, I've been told I'm aggressive and abusive and I almost feel the need to be.*

I now fall back on the Clean Language protocol that I could have employed from the start:

> And you've been told you're aggressive and abusive and you almost feel the need to be ...
> *That's right.*

At this point, the second stage of the syntax kicks in automatically.

> And when you've been told you're aggressive and abusive and you almost feel the need to be ...

Two things happen. M calms down and I become curious. The ritual of the syntax has given us the space to separate emotionally from any threat the situation might have presented. M no longer feels challenged or denied and I feel free to wonder about him. Who told him he was aggressive and abusive, I ask myself. What is this need to be so that he "almost" feels? The question I ask M, however, is simply:

> ... what happens next?

Clean Language – in common, it has to be said, with most other therapies – does not seek to approve or disapprove of what clients present. The difference with Clean Language is that *it has no means* of approving or disapproving. Respect for self-process is woven inextricably into the fabric of the syntax. M's next response:

> *I've tried overdosing and jumping in front of buses as if my father was saying from another world, 'kill yourself'*

is spoken matter-of-factly. What in other circumstances might have been a terrible threat or a plea for intervention is simply new information. M is not seeking solace or reassurance. He is offering his perceptions and I can acknowledge them without over-dramatizing them or being drawn into them.

> And you've tried overdosing and jumping in front of buses as if your father was saying from another world, 'kill yourself'. And when you've tried [etc.], then what happens?
> *I suppose it isn't the answer.*

Every perception, every reflection, every repetition, is an opportunity for the client to find out more.

Re-associating into the perceptual present
Schopenhauer pointed out that every moment of our lives belongs to the present – but only for the moment! Perhaps the most important role "And when" has to play is to re-orient the client into the present timespace of their perception, whether that be a memory, a fantasy, or a feeling.

Let us say that Kay, while hearing my initial reflection, "And you felt like the little sister again ..." has had a second or two in which to be distracted by a car alarm outside, or by thinking about the meaning of existence, or planning tonight's supper. By following up with "*And when* you felt like the little sister again ..." I invite her to re-contemplate the feeling and associate into it. This "when" breathes new life into the memory and shepherds it gently into the present, the only time in which more information is available and in which change can happen.

In the general flow of spacetime, the time indicator 'when' includes the space indicator 'where'. Where = here and when. Here and when = now. I am saying to Kay, in effect:

*And *here and now as you feel like* the little sister again ...

The words I actually use – "*And when* you felt like the little sister again" – do not re-associate Kay into a time of potential trauma, because they are significantly less direct than 'And here and now as you feel...' and also contain the ancillary meanings of 'whenever you felt' or 'at the time that you felt', etc (see the list on page 157). They permit Kay to contemplate the memory from half a step away.

Avoiding re-traumatization
Kay is associated *with* the feeling rather than associating *into* it. She is adjacently placed. Even if this is not an altogether comfortable place, she has been here or hereabouts repeatedly over the last forty years and shows every sign of having survived. The difference now is that she can begin to attend to her discomfiting feelings of insecurity, inferiority, and frustration in safety rather than avoiding them, reliving them, or biting her lip. She can discover where her insecure little sister feeling resides, how she has constructed it, and what needs to happen to resolve it.

Some therapies encourage clients to re-associate fully into past trauma in order to 'work through' it. I believe this increases the possibility of re-traumatization by inviting the victim to replicate a situation over which they had no control. Trauma is to all intents and purposes a close encounter with death. Whether Kay's was the result of a single high impact experience or an accumulation of lower level suffering over a period of time, her mental or physical integrity were at stake. Obliging a client to relive such a deeply distressing experience is not in my view remotely justifiable.

Reliving it can also reinforce the belief, common among victims of abuse, that it was all their 'fault'.

Clean Language avoids re-traumatization, even in this second, re-associative stage of the syntax. How does it do that?

Firstly, because the facilitator is obliged to work with what the client has said and so can generally go no further or faster than the client is going already.[1] The construction of the syntax obliges the intercessions of the facilitator to be at the same level as the client's perceptions, which means that Clean questioning can only accompany or follow the client's self-process rather than deliberately lead it (see Chapter 6, *The Good Midwife*).

Secondly, because a client's intuitive use of metaphor enables them to pack difficult or complex perceptions into simpler, safer forms, which can be safely unpacked in a manner and at the pace that the client desires (Chapters 7 and 9 on symbol and metaphor).

Thus most client perceptions will pop into consciousness when they are good and ready to pop, and healing will take place when the time is right. In the unlikely event of associated trauma returning, I can invite Kay to step back from the brink with a simple dissociative question, "And what happens *just before* X [the traumatic moment]?" Alternatively, I can invite her to "*Find a space that knows about X*," which will take her out of the spacetime of the trauma into one with a different perspective.[2]

Special attention

Given that every part of a client's statement will have an isomorphic relationship with the whole, we can select any part for the client's attention and never be entirely wrong. The roof will not collapse if we examine the detail in a doorway.

When faced with multiple choices, a facilitator can look and listen out in particular for the psychoactive possibilities of

- symbols and metaphors
- lines of attention
- client summaries
- repeated themes
- ambiguities and unusual constructions
- gesture and posture
- micro-movements

We considered symbols and metaphors in Part II and lines of attention in Chapter 13. I have more to say here about summaries and repetitions, ambiguities and unusual constructions, gesture and posture, and micro-movements.

Summaries and repetitions

I drew Kay's attention to her "little sister again" for several reasons. In placing it towards the end of her statement, she was probably summarizing what went before. Final phrases often encapsulate much of the content of the earlier material. "Little sister again" also happens to be a repeated phrase, which gives it greater presence in the client's mind. And there is a possible correlation between the "child within" that Kay noticed in her client and Kay's own 'child within'. Again, the phrase is repeated:

> *After a couple of sessions, she got to a child within ...*
> *A few sessions later, the same thing happened. She got to her child*
> *within again ...*

If there is a hidden correlation, my repetition of something Kay attributes to her client might help blow its cover in herself. One way of repeating the two perceptions would be to combine them:

> *And when a little sister again and a child within again ...

This juxtaposes two things that the client has offered separately. It is arguably Clean, because these are the client's own words, but comes perilously close to the conflation I argued against earlier. A cleaner way of drawing Kay's attention to elements that appeared at different times and might or might not be connected would be to recapitulate them towards the end of a session in the form of a summary:

> And you were working with this girl with multiple personalities ...
> and she got to a child within ... and you felt terrible, like a little
> sister again ... and the same thing happened ... she got to her child
> within again ... and you ...

The conjunctions and pauses indicate that these are different perceptions which manifested over time.

Ambiguities and unusual constructions

Caterina is a graphic artist from Italy. She writes up her mission statement on the flipchart:

> *To connect to heart. To feel less fearful. To loose the 'shoulds'.*

Caterina's English is normally very good, so it is possible that her use of the word 'loose' (a near-homophone of 'lose') is more than a simple mistake. I draw her attention to what she has written.

> And loose the shoulds. And when 'loose' the shoulds ...
> *Ah, I mean 'lose', but maybe I only want to loosen some of them rather than lose the whole lot. I guess some of them are too difficult to lose just yet, but maybe I can loosen them!*

Gary from Iowa emails to arrange a phone session. His first words to me on the phone are:

> *I feel like I am being guided by the Holy Spirit in speaking to you – some other force that I cannot control. If I accept it, I am filled with love, peace, and understanding and the future looks bright.*

I have several puzzles. What does Gary want? What part of what he has said should I reflect and invite him to attend to? I have made a verbatim note as he spoke, so I decide to reflect the lot. And as I do so, I begin to notice its little infelicities. Gary's language is as riddled with ambiguity as a church roof with woodworm. His use of the word "like", for example, in "I feel *like* I am being guided by the Holy Spirit." Does he feel that he *is* being guided by the Holy Spirit or *as if* he is being guided by the Holy Spirit? Is this Holy Spirit guiding him or is there something even more elusive? As each equivocation sails by, it leaves a riddle in its wake. When he says, "some other force that I cannot control," is the Holy Spirit this other force, or is there some force "other" than the Holy Spirit? He goes on: "If I accept it ..." Is this a genuine reservation or unconsciously cryptic? And given that the little word "it" has at least three meanings in this context, which is the correct one – the Holy Spirit, some other force, or the fact of speaking to me?

I have chosen Gary's case to illustrate the possibilities of ambiguity, but I could quote hundreds more. Where should I go with a statement like this? Initial reflection is relatively simple. I can choose any one of:

> And you feel like you are being guided by the Holy Spirit ...
> And some other force that you cannot control ...
> And if you accept it ...

I could then move on to the selective second stage of the syntax with any one of the following (my emphasis would be on the word in inverted commas):

And when you feel 'like' you are being guided by ...
And when some 'other' force ...
And when 'if' you accept it ...
And when if you accept 'it' ...

Problems of paradox and internal contradiction often contain a number of solutions and in that resides their purpose and promise: they can hold more than one truth at a time. The verdict must remain open until the evidence comes down unambiguously on one side or the other. I can draw Gary's attention to any one of the constructions that take my attention, but I can only do so one at a time. Ambiguity is not pressing for an instant decision.

Gesture and posture

Physically mirroring and matching the client is the somatic equivalent of semantic reflection, if not quite so exacting. (See *Reflecting nonverbal language* in Chapter 13.) Our aptitude for 'mirroring' behavior seems to be an inherited ability comparable to language, social intelligence, and tool use. Humans are natural mimics. It used to be thought that babies copied their parents until it was discovered that as often as not it was the other way round. Feedback and learning are mutual. Parent and baby teach each other to pay attention to the same smiles, frowns, signals, and gurgles.

The facilitator educates the client by drawing attention not only to their words, but also to their posture and gesture. The client educates the facilitator in a similar way, though not so deliberately. The way a client positions themself in relation to their environment can be a signal as informative as iconic movements of the hands and head. The challenge for the facilitator comes less in making meaning of what is observed than in deciding how much of it to reflect back that will have the effect of easing the client into their personal perceptual present rather than into the facilitator's.

Micro-movements

The dilemma is at its most acute when it comes to drawing attention to micro-movements, a special sub-set of nonverbal manifestations of feeling. These evolutionary-related reactions show up as twitches in the musculature within a few milliseconds of the event that triggers them, as the brain primes the body to confront discomfort or danger (fight), escape (flee), or consider things a while longer (freeze). The body produces these unconsciously derived physiological 'readiness potential' responses to external events well before the mind has appraised them.[3] Micro-movements thus make excellent indicators of real feeling. A problem would only arise if a facilitator told themself that they knew what the real feelings were.

Facial expressions normally last for two or three seconds, but micro-movements are very short-lived, as little as one-twentieth of a second, the lifetime of a blink. Noticing them calls for a facilitator's attention to be very highly focused indeed. Yet reflecting them accurately, even if that were possible, would mean that they would almost certainly go unnoticed by the client – it is not the client's job to study the facilitator's facial expressions minutely, after all – while exaggerating them to be sure the client noticed could amount to parody and wouldn't be the smartest thing a facilitator could do in a day. Incorporated discreetly into a verbal intercession, however, the merest hint of a tic, shrug, or twitch can subtly enhance what Grove called the '"physicality" of the question: its precise and appropriate 'placing'. (Chapter 19 has more on placing questions.)

Here is an example of drawing attention to micro-movements with a very expressive client, Hugh. It strays into the questioning stage of the syntax (next chapter), but illustrates the possibilities of highlighting verbal and nonverbal language together.[4]

And what would you like to have [client flinches almost
imperceptibly] happen?
I'm not sure.

And (subtly mirrors flinch) you're not sure. And when (mirrors the flinch again) you're not sure, what kind of (flinch) you're not sure could that be?
Hmm. It comes through my body.

And hmm it comes through your body [client makes same micro-movement]. And when hmm it comes through your body, it comes through your body like what?
Like a typhoon.

And like a typhoon. And when like a typhoon, what kind of typhoon could that typhoon be?
(Blinks) *It's quite striking.*

Indeed. Tiny movements can be pointers to great events. They can easily be dismissed by the casual observer, because they look no different to the succession of twitches and turns we make every moment we are alive. Yet it is in such here-and-now micro-moments, as much as in more obvious indicators – overt metaphors, unusual words, grand gestures – that new information manifests and change takes place.

Hugh's "typhoon", by the way, is an example of the kind of 'transport' symbol – cloud, stream, airplane, and so on – that can help convey the client from problem state to solution state in the metaphor landscape. Transport symbols have more attention given them in Chapter 17.

Having fulfilled its other functions, "And when X" has one last little task: to allow the facilitator a second or two in which to decide what question to ask. Our intercessions are about to become more intentional. Things will never be the same again.

Notes to Chapter 14

1 Questions based on what the client has said can generally go no further or faster than the client is going already. The exception to this would be if the client were in a vulnerable place just before a moment of remembered trauma and the facilitator were to ask – ill-advisedly – 'What happens next?' There is more on avoiding re-traumatization in *The physiological domain*, Chapter 16.

2 The invitation to "Find a space that knows about that" could also be a cue for a full Emergent Knowledge process. See Appendix C, part 3, and powersofsix.com

3 Unconsciously derived physiological responses: see also psychologist Daniel Wegner's work on "ideomotor automacity" in *The Illusion of Conscious Will*, MIT 2002. A mental event can prompt an unintentional bodily action while the owner remains oblivious to its causal relation.

4 Micro-movements: the example is from a Clean Practise Group exercise facilitated by Caitlin Walker. Caitlin and Dee Berridge ran the first Practise Group in London after Tompkins and Lawley's first Clean Language training in the UK, jointly with Grove, in 1995.

Chapter 15

Clean Questioning
Part 3 of the Clean Language Syntax

For your information, I would like to ask you a question.
Samuel Goldwyn

1   And X
2   And when X
3   **Question about X**

Sacred and profane questions – Two key Clean questions – A Four-Phase guide: opening, describing, locating, sequencing questions – M's tight fist – Popping into consciousness – The man who learned to fly

The Hollywood producer Sam Goldwyn ("Anyone who would go to a psychiatrist ought to have his head examined") was unintentionally right when he pointed out that the questions he asked were for the questionee's information and not for his own.

"Our questions are deliberate," said Grove, "and should be treated as hallowed and sacred."[1] 'Profane' questions, in comparison, have inbuilt assumption or bias ("Did that make you angry?"); or incorporate suggestion ("Why not tell him how you feel?"); or contaminate the client's metaphor landscape with the questioner's own metaphor ("Can you turn this around?"); or restrict the client to a particular representational system in which to process their response ("Can you see the other side?" "Are you able to hear that differently?"); or require the client to detach themself from the primacy of their experience in order to respond cognitively ("What do you think/feel about that?"). The intention of questions like these may be to ease clients into a state of objectivity about themself, but what they actually do is propel the client into the uncertain world of the questioner's perceptions.

Two key Clean questions
applicable to pretty much any client perception are:

> Is there anything else about that X?
> What kind of X could that X be?

where 'X' is a word, a phrase, or a gesture that the client themself has used. It is possible to repeatedly apply either of these questions to the result of the previous application in a series of iterations – and without recourse to any other question – until, as Grove once described it, "there is nothing left." It is unlikely to be desirable, as most clients would wilt very quickly, but it is certainly feasible, because these two quintessentially Clean questions make the least possible presumptions about the nature of the client's experience. They are 'sequential', in that they are closely coupled with the client's last statement. They reserve political power for the client. They are almost always answerable. And they set up a systemic loop between the client and their information that encourages new perceptions, choices, and solutions to emerge.

A Four-Phase guide
incorporates these two key questions with ten more in a basic model applicable to practically any client problem.

> Phase 1 *Entry point*. Three *Clean Start* questions leading to a client statement of their current perceptions.
>
> Phase 2 *Describing*. Four questions of *form* inviting the client to discover more about the characteristics of those perceptions.
>
> Phase 3 *Locating*. Two *space* questions to determine which perceptions are where in the metaphor landscape.
>
> Phase 4 *Sequencing*. Three *time* questions establishing what happens before and after the current perception, enabling the spacetime structure of the problem to emerge.

Phase 1 Opening questions
Three interdependent questions which allow facilitator and client to negotiate a mutual 'entry point' into the process. They are:

> Where would you like to be?
> And where would you like me to be?
> And what would you like to have happen?

The first two ("Where would you like to be?" and "Where would you like me to be?") were considered in detail in Chapter 12, *A Clean Start*. The third in the sequence secures the theme of self-determination that the first two imply.

What would you like to have happen?
We all have preferences and desires, and what results, inevitably, are feelings of deprivation and frustration. These may be mild and serve only to motivate our behavior, but in some cases they can be severe and debilitating, leading to a lack of action (depression, anxiety, agoraphobia, etc.) or to behaviors with undesirable wider effects (drug-taking, violence, abuse, etc.).

The standard entry point question "What would you like to have happen?" can be asked in all cases. It is an invitation to the client to embark on a personal journey. It holds no presumption that the pursuit of happiness and fulfillment is any more desirable than the pursuit of self-knowledge and understanding.

Here are some of the responses of patients who attended a psychotherapeutic clinic that Grove and I ran under the auspices of a community medical practice in New Zealand.

> What would you like to have happen?
> *I want things to be different.*
> *I want to sort my head out.*
> *My wife says I'm having a mid-life crisis.*
> *I'm having some problems with anger.*
> *I don't know, the doc persuaded me to come.*
> *I want the voices to stop, to feel normal again..*
> *I'm trying to come to terms with the pain.*
> *I'm always so anxious, why can't I live without fear?*
> *It's these panic attacks.*
> *I feel unsafe if anyone is behind me.*
> *I don't know what to do.*
> *I need to come off the drugs.*
> *There's like a wall around me.*
> *I'm not sleeping well.*
> *I'm depressed.*

The responses are not so different from what my private clients in London say or what patients attending the mental health clinics where I have worked say. They can be assigned to one of three categories: perceived problem, possible remedy, or desired solution.[2]

A *perceived problem* ("It's these panic attacks") is something unwanted or a state in which the client is currently stuck ("There's like a wall around me"), or simply an existential puzzle ("I don't know, the doc persuaded me to come"). The facilitator's response to a perceived problem might be to call for more detail or to ask the entry point question again.

> And when panic attacks, is there anything else about those panic attacks ?
>
> And when there's like a wall around you, what kind of wall could that wall be?
>
> And when the doc persuaded you to come, what would you like to have happen?

A *possible remedy* ("I'm trying to come to terms with the pain") is a means of counteracting or eliminating a problem without necessarily having any idea how to go about it or what the solution might be. The client might like to find out more about what it is they are proposing.

> And when you're trying to come to terms with the pain, what kind of terms could those terms be?

A *desired solution* ("I want the voices to stop, to feel normal again") is an idea of where the client wants to be. The facilitator might question their capacity, readiness, or willingness to change.

> And when you want the voices to stop, to feel normal again, what needs to happen for the voices to stop, to feel normal again?

The standard entry point question, "What would you like to have happen?" does not in itself imply that the client has a problem requiring a remedy or a solution. It is an inclusive question. It does not confront or challenge. It offers the client an opportunity to make a statement at any level of need or desire, coherence or complexity, that they wish.

First responses usually evolve as the work progresses. A puzzle, for example ("My wife tells me I'm having a mid-life crisis") is likely to unfold into a more specific problem, remedy, or potential solution as the client gets to know more about what is puzzling them.

Some therapists and coaches believe that every client should have an identifiable, well-formed outcome from the start, on the basis that everyone wants something and they are more likely to get it if they know what it is. In practice, many clients find it difficult to articulate an outcome without finding out more about themselves first. It is no coincidence, therefore, that the question is about preference: "What would you *like* to have happen?" The preferences that drive our fitness to reproduce have direct implications for self-determination and survival. The preference question invites us to pursue the variation best suited for prospering.

The question ends with "... *to have happen*", implying an obligation on the client to take ownership of both the intermediate means and the eventual outcome. Grove suggested that the adult client's acknowledgment of ownership freed their inner child from direct responsibility for achieving the adult outcome. 'Inner child' and 'child within' are metaphors for a fragment of the self that holds unresolved pain or trauma. It is for the adult client to take responsibility for identifying and deploying a resource that will resolve the inner child's lack of resource. This is not a 'take it or leave it' obligation on the client, but the start of a gradual process of learning.

The construction, "What would you like *to have* happen?" contains the slightest of hints that we are on the fringe of probability. The syntactical agent *"have"* has a useful ambiguity. It carries the meanings of both 'possess' and 'get done.' In *to have*'s meaning of 'possess', it obliges the subject of the question, 'you', to take ownership of the object, which is 'what like to happen'. In *to have*'s meaning of 'get done', it signals possession of another kind involving action and achievement. An internal shift may happen in the client in the moment that the impulses to ownership, action, and achievement register.

The apparently similar 'What would you like to happen?' is too timid. It maintains the facilitator, or even fate, in the lead by implying that responsibility for what follows belongs to something or someone other than the client.

'What do you want?' goes too far. Its global possibilities extend beyond the deliberate limits of the "What would you like to have happen?" frame. And it, too, places implicit responsibility for achieving the outcome on the shoulders of the facilitator-questioner rather than on the client-questionee.

"What would you like to have happen?" requires the client to attach personal value to one thing over another. "I would like my partner to stop drinking" would be a remedy beyond the limits of the client's (and the therapist's) competence, whereas an outcome such as

I would like to leave the party when my partner starts drinking

supposes the speaker to have a preference that stems from a unique account of their internal (and in this case, external) perceptions. It may relate to, but is not about, someone else.

Clients can only respond to the preference question from within the limits of their present perceptions. The factors that influence those perceptions, and the choices and decisions clients make as a result, are not directly available to either client or facilitator. Conscious preferences reflect attitudes, beliefs, and values that can be articulated explicitly. Unconscious, or implicit, preferences need a catalyst and a context in which to materialize.

A remedy or solution with which a client starts out is unlikely to be the one with which they end up. This being so, a facilitator may have to ask the preference eliciting question more than once. After a certain amount of information has emerged, for example:

And what would you like to have happen *now*?

Or as a reminder to get back on track after a lot of information has emerged or if the information that has emerged is confusing:

And *when all that,* what would you like to have happen?

Or to mark and mature a change, and take a step towards building on it:

And when [identify change], now what would you like to have happen?

Phase 2 Describing questions

What kind of X could that X be?
Is there anything else about that X?
Does that X have a size or a shape?
That is an X like what?

are all questions of *form*. They help the client elaborate on the characteristics and attributes of their symbols.

> And when there's a wall around you, what kind of wall could that
> wall be?
> *It's a garden wall of old yellow bricks.*

The questions can also help the client get a clearer picture of their
perceptions.

> And when panic attacks, is there anything else about those panic
> attacks?
> *Yes, I have weird thoughts, I feel light-headed, I start shaking.*

Clean questions of form respect the idiosyncrasy of the client's
perceptions and discourage the facilitator from introducing
assumptions or imposing suggestions of their own. They also help
shift the client's attention from their external perceptions – the
carpet, the view from the window, the state of the wallpaper – to
their internal processing.

Use of the demonstrative pronoun, "that" ("that wall" rather than
'a wall' or 'the wall') aligns the client to the particular wall that has
appeared in their landscape rather than to any other wall or to
walls in general. There is more on "that" and "the" in Chapter 19.

What kind of X could that X be?
is arguably the most undemanding of the descriptive questions and
as such could have a role to play at any stage of the process. It
invites the client to give the subject of the question their attention
in order for them to further define its characteristics. Every
characteristic that appears – every dimension, feature, and quality
– is grist to the therapeutic mill. The question can be asked of any
of the client's words or combinations of words.

> And when it's a garden wall of old yellow bricks ...
>   what kind of 'garden' could that garden be? /
>   what kind of 'wall' could that wall be? /
>   what kind of 'old' could that old be? /
>   what kind of 'yellow' could that yellow be?

"What kind of" is such a familiar phrase that even the most
hesitant or ambivalent of clients will be able to answer it without
any great heart-searching and as plainly or as profoundly as they
wish.

> *What kind of symbol / concept / feeling / behavior could that
> symbol / concept / feeling / behavior be?

The use of "could be" in the question is more politic than "is". This "could" does not raise the specter of obligation ('could you respond?') or mock-gentility ('could you do this for me'), but respectfully combines curiosity with possibility. It offers the client discretion.

Here again is M, the belligerent patient who eats therapists for breakfast. In response to my positioning questions ("Where would you like to be?" and "Where would you like me to be?"), he has placed us facing each other directly. This is unusual and slightly unnerves me, but it is his process. In response to "What would you like to have happen?" he says:

> *I know, I've been told I'm aggressive and abusive and I almost feel the need to be.*

As I reflect this back to him, I am struck by his use of the word "need". Compare two approaches I can take to my next question. The first is in the present tense:

> *What kind of need is that need?

At this early stage of the work, a client like M is likely to be feeling unsure of himself, suspicious of me, and dubious about the whole process. He could well experience the question as a challenge.

> *I don't know. What are you implying?*

His uncertainty about what he wants to have happen would be compounded by the likely inference ('What *is* that need?') that a correct answer existed. A more circumspect approach uses the conditional tense:

> What kind of need could that need be?

which makes time and space for M to sense what is really going on for him internally and to answer in any way that feels right to him. After a couple of seconds, he responds:

> *Well, it's like if I don't come up with the goods you'll give me a hard time.*

Still belligerent, but less so, and new information has appeared. "Could be" in the question is an indicator of both feasibility and opportunity when clients are learning to trust the often unfamiliar experience of being themselves. One of the unsung benefits of Clean questioning is that clients come to realize that they are free to report whatever they see, hear, or feel uninfluenced by the imagined expectations of the questioner. The benefit continues outside the consulting room. The imagined expectations of teachers, colleagues, partners, and friends tend not to loom so large once people learn to trust their own process and allow themselves to be who they are.

When a client is more sure of themself and has more trust in what comes up for them, I might use "is" more.

What kind of certainty is that certainty?

There is another question that can be asked of anything the client has said.

Is there anything else about that X?
has been called the Clean default question. A facilitator who can think of nothing else to ask can be confident there is always something else the client can add to what has already been said.

And when give you a hard time, is there anything else about that give you a hard time?
Yes, I was scared as a kid if I didn't say the right thing.

Another descriptive question has a special role to play in the transition from everyday narrative to the world of transcendent possibility.

Does X have a size or a shape?
invites a symbol to take a more specific form or a concept to take a more symbolic form.

And does that scared as a kid have a size or a shape?
It's kind of round and hard.

Some clients, like M, will readily picture a feeling as having size or shape, but others will not, at least on first acquaintance with the notion. It can be an odd kind of question for an overly cognitive client – a legitimate response might be "What do you mean?" – so timing is all. In such a situation, I would be more inclined to ask the question of a symbol that was likely to have dimensions or form.

*And does that box have a size or a shape?
It's about this long and this wide, like a shoe box.

The 'size or shape' question can often be followed with an even more powerfully descriptive question, one that is likely to take the client to another level entirely.

That is an X like what?
"Like what?" is an invitation to move into metaphor, the royal route to the unconscious.

> And that's kind of round and hard like what?
> *Like a tight fist.*

If M had already identified a metaphor for his scared feeling ('It's like a red mist' or 'Being under enemy fire') the "like what?" question would be redundant. 'A red mist like what?' would be inviting a metaphor for a metaphor. Like gilding the lily, it would be a superfluous act that could kill off the original.

Clean beginners sometimes find themselves asking, "What is that like?" instead of "That is like what?" What is the difference? The question "What is that like?" is almost guaranteed to evoke a cognitive evaluation by the client rather than a metaphor.

> *And what is that 'scared' like?
> *It's horrible. I think of all the things that could happen.*

Whereas:

> *And that 'scared' is like what?

is more likely to come up with a workable symbol or metaphor.

> *Like a rabbit caught in the headlights.*

Equally, some beginners find it difficult to distinguish between the description evoking "What kind of?" and the metaphor evoking "Like what?"

"What kind of?" is at the same level as the existing information. It simply invites more detail to appear. "Like what?" invites the client to take an imaginative leap into the parallel world of their symbolic perceptions. The question sends M on a search for higher organizational and deeper structural information about "kind of round and hard." His "tight fist" is likely to have every bit of information that has appeared so far packed into it.

Phase 3 Locating questions

> Where is X?
> Whereabouts is X?

One of the presuppositions of the Clean Language and Therapeutic Metaphor process is that everything has to be somewhere. Having elicited a name for the symbol in question ("tight fist"), we can now ask for an address. Like a baby joining the family, new information must first be honored and then given a name and a home.

Where is X?
Every 'X' will have a place in the client's metaphor landscape. The question "Where?" invites the symbol to reveal its general location:

> Where is that round and hard tight fist?
> (Placing his hand) *Here in my stomach.*

Establishing the location of symbols and feelings in the therapeutic landscape puts their existence beyond peradventure and makes access to the information they hold appreciably easier.

M has given his perception a name and a virtual postcode.

Whereabouts is X?
asks for the full address.

> And when in your stomach, whereabouts in your stomach?
> *Just here, in the middle, an inch or two in.*

Being asked for the specific location of the symbols and feelings that pop into consciousness is a good test for anyone skeptical about the existence of a metaphor landscape of the mind. Some clients need to clarify the locating questions, but I have never known a client who could not answer them. The more precise a client can be about the location of their symbol or symptom, the more amenable the symbol or symptom will be to revealing its history, purpose, and relationship to other elements in the landscape.

Phase 4 Sequencing questions

> What happens just before X?
> What happens next?
> Then what happens?

Having asked questions of *form* ("round and hard tight fist") and *space* ("in the stomach, in the middle, an inch or two in"), here now are questions of *time*: three questions aimed at giving M a sense of the sequencing of his perceptions and an idea of the pattern they create.

My strategy at this point stems more from where M's information itself is taking the questioning than from any conjectural or theoretical line of enquiry I might have. Every one of my questions takes its cue from M's last response. Whether his answers prompt me into pursuing a conscious strategy or not, I remind myself that any internal model I make of his patterns and processes will always be provisional (more on this in Chapter 19). It has to be open to updating by every new item that appears. I can be sure of one thing about M, as of any client: that any prototype model I make of his process will not be the real thing.

I am curious how M came to have this troublesome "tight fist" in the stomach, right there, in the middle, an inch or two in. What happened – and continues to happen, for this is a repeating pattern – to create the feeling, and what happens as a result of its appearance?

What happens just before X?
pulls time back to a previous event in the sequence.

> And when tight fist just there, in the middle, an inch or two in,
> what happens just before tight fist just there?
> *A hardening in my stomach like I'm expecting the worst.*

It may need perseverance to move time 'back' when most of us have a sense of it moving 'forward'. A special quality of vocal emphasis is required:

> What happens *just before* ...?

Another common sequencing question:

What happens next?
helps the client establish a context for their experience.

> And when a hardening in your stomach like you're expecting the
> worst, what happens next?
> *I start to sweat. I want to run away, but can't.*

If this is an indication of the imminent presence of early trauma, it calls for some sensitivity. A Grovian process does not require an unresourced client to revisit trauma in order to work through it. If I am in any doubt, I can ask "What happens just before X?" which invites the client to take a step back from the brink.

Then what happens?
allows time to evolve in a slightly different way. It offers M an opportunity to change tack to an event or a phase a little further down the timeline.

> And when you want to run away but can't, then what happens?
> *I stay and fight.*

Notice the difference a word makes. If I were to ask M simply "What happens?" or say, "Tell me what happens," he could easily become lost in possibility and drawn into believing that I am pressing him for an ultimate outcome. "*Then* what happens?" invites him to relate specifically to what he has just said. It allows events to unfold as they will.

Einstein likened time to a river that could slow down and speed up, but was never a constant. In the therapeutic universe, a patient's perception of time is a factor in a wide range of mental disorders. A bipolar patient may experience time as moving more slowly in the depressive phase and more quickly in the manic phase.[3] Psychotic patients have been known to experience time as standing still or divided into pieces and chaotically re-ordered.

If the client speaks of themself as "looking ahead to the future" or "putting the past behind" them, they are expressing time not only in terms of self-referential *space* – as somewhere metaphorically ahead of or behind them – but also as metaphorical *matter* and *form*: 'something' is ahead of them and 'something' is behind them.

It is virtually impossible for any of us to conceptualize and communicate our perception of time without recourse to metaphor. The members of one South American tribe gesture 'forward' when describing generations past, because their shared metaphor for the past is ahead of them, enabling the speaker to readily locate a place where the wisdom of the forebears is available for guidance.

The sequence of events in a client's metaphorical world may happen earlier or later than in the parallel physical world. Events may be closer together or further apart; they can be of longer or shorter duration; they can occur simultaneously or sequentially.

Jill is a mental patient suffering from hallucinations.

> There is so much going on, I'm very confused.

Most of us feel that time 'flows'. We experience things as happening in sequence and it is relatively easy to separate them out. In Jill's mind, a number of things appear to be happening at once. It could be supremely useful for her to be able to 'freeze time,' 'hold time still', or 'stretch time out' in order to identify the contribution various events are making to the overall problem.

> And when there is so much going on, what happens just before there is so much going on?
> *It's very quiet.*
>
> And when it's very quiet, what happens next?
> *Things start to appear.*
>
> And what kind of things start to appear?
> *Insects, mice, shoes.*
>
> And then what happens?
> *I get confused.*

Time-related questions may reference the past or the future, but in Clean Language are always submitted in the present –

> And what *happens* just before?
> And then what *happens*?

– the only time (forgive the repetition, but I believe it to be an important point) in which change can happen.

Time is as embodied, idiosyncratic, and symbolic as form and space in defining our experience. The sequencing questions help Jill suspend time, delay it, or curtail it in order to allow a detailed consideration of the information her perceptions contain.

Popping into consciousness

Jill's "insects, mice, shoes" came to her intuitively. Clients occasionally react with uncertainty to ideas and images that seem to appear out of nowhere, yet all that has happened is that unconscious (or 'non-conscious' or 'pre-conscious') perceptions have become conscious. Things that were amorphous have taken on form.

Shakespeare understood the power of sudden imagery. Alone for a moment, Macbeth has a vision:

> *Is this a dagger which I see before me,*
> *The handle toward my hand?*

The workings of the unconscious are dynamic, continuous, and responsible for every one of our everyday perceptions, feelings, decisions, and actions. Neurological research shows that two things are required for unconscious processing to become conscious: the stimulus must be strong enough and attention must be focused on it.[4] In Macbeth's case, the stimulus is already present: he has just been informed of the imminent arrival of the king. He passes the news on to Lady M: "Duncan comes here tonight." She responds in a flash: "And when goes hence?" The double-edged question focuses Macbeth's attention. His unconscious desire to dispatch Duncan becomes suddenly conscious.

The first two parts of the Clean syntax, reflection and selection, combine to orientate the client's attention to what is happening as their unconscious takes on the task of integrating an immense amount of information. The third part, the question, is the stimulus that brings an essential element of the information into foreground.

The three-part syntax focuses the client's attention in a way that prompts unconsciously derived items to cross the threshold into consciousness. 'Unconscious' and 'conscious' are not separate systems, but different levels of the same system. The item that comes into consciousness may still have to be decoded. And that too is the job of Clean questioning.

The man who learned to fly

It is possible to orchestrate an entire session with five or six or fewer of the twelve questions in the Four-Phase guide. Here is an example using seven. To follow the content, read the left-hand column. To follow what is happening at a process level, keep an eye on the right-hand column. For easier reading, the repetitive parts of the syntax ("And X ..." "And when X ...") are in the main omitted.

Neil is a corporate manager who is experiencing a lack of fulfillment in his work. He is considering whether to set up in business for himself.

What would you like to have happen?	Phase 1 opening question
I want to be myself freely.	Client current perception
That is be yourself freely like what?	Phase 2 form question
Like a bird.	Client moves from conceptual to symbolic description (NB this is a likely 'transport' symbol, Ch. 17)

What kind of bird could that bird be? *A red cardinal.*	Form question invites attribute
Where is red cardinal? *On my shoulder.*	Phase 3 space question seeks general location
Whereabouts on your shoulder? *Just here* (indicates left shoulder).	Seeks specific location
And when red cardinal just here, what happens next? *I can stay where I am or maybe fly.*	Phase 4 time question for sequencing
And when you can stay where you are or maybe fly, what happens next? *I guess I have a choice.*	Sequencing question
And when red cardinal on your shoulder and you can stay where you are or maybe fly and you guess you have a choice, then what happens? *I can be myself freely.*	Sequencing question
And when you can be yourself freely, then what happens? *Oh, I fly.*	Sequencing question Signals potential for transformative change

In Part III, *Symptoms and Solutions*, we considered the propositions and basic practices of Clean Language. We deconstructed the three-part syntax and outlined a Four-Phase guide to Therapeutic Metaphor process utilizing twelve opening, describing, locating, and sequencing questions.

That may be all a client needs to reach a resolution or to experience an epiphany. But not all processes run as readily as Neil and the red cardinal, Vicky's vibrating peach, or Kay and the child within. Facilitators need to be light on their feet to follow the actual track a client takes. It means being open to any move and allowing for the introduction of more advanced strategies – and these are the subject of Part IV.

Notes to Chapter 15

1 Deliberate wording of the questions. Grove, his various collaborators, and the Clean Practise and Research Groups experimented over the years with variations. Few could be classed as 'clean'. See Appendix C for a current list.

2 Clients' first words. Tompkins and Lawley proposed a 'problem, remedy, outcome' model in 2006 in an article *Coaching for P.R.O.s* to help coaches and therapists facilitate clients in deciding what it is they really wanted and in orienting their attention to it.

3 Faster or slower perceptions of time: impulsive people are likely to perceive time as moving faster than more cautious types. Couples can have very different 'personal tempos'. Early in a romance, we may be attracted to our 'time opposite', but come to dislike it later: couples therapist Peter Fraenkel in *Sync Your Relationship*, 2011.

4 Strong stimulus and focused attention needed for unconscious processing to become conscious: Kate Douglas, *The Other You,* New Scientist 1 December 2007.

Part IV

COAXING INTO CONSCIOUSNESS
Adventures in Clean Language and Therapeutic Metaphor

The essence of knowledge is, having it, to apply it.
K'ung Fu Tzu

Introduction to Part IV

Unconsciously held knowledge has to be coaxed; it cannot be commanded. The Clean facilitator assists the client to unravel the relationships between their perceptions, to recognize the patterns across those relationships, and to decode the patterns in relation to their everyday life. In this forest of possibilities, a facilitator can lose track of where they are. Part IV looks at a number of strategies for keeping on course:

Chapter 16, *Rachel's Sadness*, deconstructs Grove's 'Four-Domain' Therapeutic Metaphor process.

Chapter 17, *Return of the Hamster*, compares six varied approaches to Clean questioning.

Chapter 18, *Sam's Freudian Blocks*, introduces twenty specialist Clean questions and various ways of seeking out redemptive resource.

Chapter 19, *The Special and the Unusual,* offers twenty tips for advanced facilitation.

Chapter 20, *When Change Happens*, considers three kinds of change experienced by clients and explains how Clean change is matured.

Appendix A outlines a Six-Step Exercise in Emotional Management utilizing client metaphor. *Appendix B* consists of three transcripts of Clean client sessions. *Appendix C* has a complete list of one hundred Clean Language questions covering Therapeutic Metaphor, Clean Space, and Emergent Knowledge.

Chapter 16
Rachel's Sadness

I will turn diseases to commodity.
Shakespeare, *Henry IV Part 2*

The Four-Domain Therapeutic Metaphor process: Narrative, Physiological, Spatial, Historical – Progressive resource, redemptive metaphor, intergenerational healing – Summary

Every problem we experience takes up a certain amount of space in our 'psychescape', a sizeable piece of metaphorical real estate divided by Grove into four distinct domains. He identified these by various labels, but typically 'here and now', 'biographical', 'spatial', and 'genealogical'.[1] My version opts for #1 Narrative, #2 Physiological, #3 Spatial, and #4 Historical.

Figure 10 Therapeutic Metaphor information quadrants
(an explanation of 'T – 1', 'T – 2' etc. appears later in the chapter)

The quadrants provide a structure for organizing disparate and often complex information related to the client's symptom or problem. They give the information a home. Grove pictured a gearstick at the center which he would use to shift the client's attention between domains. I imagined a crow's nest high above the center from which I could plot or pilot my client's progress. You might think that the idea of four quadrants is metaphor enough, however.

In this chapter, we accompany Rachel, a teacher in her thirties, from domain #1 through #2 and #3 to #4. The information she comes up with initially appears in the first, Narrative, domain; is developed and explored in the second and third, Physiological and Spatial, domains; and resolved in the fourth, Historical, domain. The unwanted symptom she identifies speaks for itself as she traces it back to its inception. Prior to the origin of the symptom, she identifies a powerful redemptive symbol and brings it forward through time to heal the complete etiology of the symptom: its cause or causes and the history and manner of its causation.

Rachel's progress #1 through #4 has a narrative logic, as you will see, but it is not the only plot she could have followed. A client's attention may shift, or be shifted by the facilitator's questioning, between any one domain and another. It is also possible for a symptom to appear, remain, and resolve in a single domain.

These are not so much problem or solution domains, then, as information domains. They can help a facilitator locate the source of a symptom; monitor symptom-related information held in different domains; and identify resources for healing at any point in the entire contributory history of the symptom.

1 The Narrative domain

Information held here tends to be cognitive in source and linguistic in nature. The client talks about themself in an attempt to make sense of their life. Questions and answers in the Narrative domain are linear and descriptive. Conventional counseling will generally remain in this quadrant, but Clean Language processes are unlikely to dally here long.

After the standard positioning and opening questions (*A Clean Start*, Chapter 12), Rachel's first words are:

I have a problem.

The full syntax of the standard response reflects and repeats the client's exact words:

> And you have a problem. And when you have a problem, what
> kind of problem could that problem be?

which is abbreviated here, as elsewhere, to:

> What kind of problem could that problem be?

For a reminder of the importance of the full syntax in practice, do
look again at Chapters 13 – 15.

> *I split up with my partner.*
> And is there anything else about that split up with your partner?

> *Yes, I feel an awful sadness.*

Rachel's eyes fill with tears. In domain #1, the head may
understand, but that will not heal the heart. The client's "awful
sadness" is a present feeling that could relate to any number of
things in the past. Rachel has given it a name. We can now ask for
an address.

> And where is awful sadness?
> *In my heart.*

2 The Physiological domain

Rachel's perceptions have shifted into domain #2. If she had
indicated that sadness was 'out there' somewhere, it might have
signaled a move into Spatial domain #3. Here in domain #2, we can
focus on the client's somatic experience. Our questions do not move
time along here. They go into a moment of bodily feeling, where a
tremendous amount of deep structural information resides.

If at this point we were to comfort the adult Rachel about what
are likely to be a six-year old or ten-year old's tears, we would be
removing the child from when and where she was originally sad.
"Clients experience a big difference between crying 'then' and
crying 'now'," Grove would say. "It's not enough to have the crying
now and assume that healing will follow." At best, the symptom will
not heal. At worst, the client's state will deteriorate.

In a domain that frequently holds inner child information, we
speak in a way the child understands. These are simple, direct
questions.

> And when awful sadness in your heart, whereabouts in
> your heart?
> *In the middle.*

And when awful sadness in the middle, does that sadness in the
middle have a size or shape?
It's huge.

And when huge sadness in the middle, that is huge sadness in
the middle like what?
Like a rock.

Had we asked Rachel, "Why do you feel sad?," we would have been
inviting the child in the adult to shift from direct feeling into
indirect thinking about her feeling in order to 'explain' herself. The
questions, *"Where* is sadness?" ("In my heart") and *"Whereabouts* in
your heart?" ("In the middle") help Rachel's inner child to access the
deep physiology of her sadness.

The *'size or shape?'* question does not ask for an adult's conceptual
explanation, but moves Rachel to a simple symbolic representation
("huge").

'Like what?' helps her identify an intuitive symbol ("rock") for her
huge sadness. In domain #2, Rachel can find out more about it.

And when like a rock, is there anything else about that rock?
It's hard and heavy.

We can speculate that tightly packed into Rachel's rock are her
sadness, the immediate cause of her sadness, and quite possibly the
entire history of her sadness. The rock is a foreign object and as
long as it remains in Rachel's heart, the cause of her sadness will
not be resolved.

And is there anything else about that hard and heavy rock?
It stops me breathing.

And when it stops you breathing, what would you like to
have happen?
To break the rock up and feel clean and clear again.

The rock, like all such symbols, is a 'container'. It holds critical
information. It has been doing an important historical job by
blocking or inhibiting a repeat of the original traumatic experience.
It will resist removal without some effort by Rachel and without
having something in place to compensate for its loss.
    If we take 'T' (for Trauma) to represent the worst moment of
Rachel's experience – the awful sadness that led to the formation of

the rock – then domain #2's 'T–1' (Trauma minus one) represents the unresourced spacetime *just before* the worst moment.

Figure 11 Rachel's present unresourced state in domain #2

The rock is Rachel's T–1. "It stops me breathing," she says. Here is confirmation that we are in physiological T–1 territory. The client identifies an ongoing activity that is keeping the problem in place.

Research by specialist trauma psychologist Anke Ehlers confirms Grove's thesis that intrusive trauma-associated memories commonly consist of stimuli that were present immediately before the traumatic event and shortly before the moment that had the largest emotional impact.[2] Grove suggested, and Ehlers' research concurs, that where there has been abuse or trauma, the child will pull back from the memory and dissociate from it in order to survive. In a desperate attempt to resolve irreconcilable conflict, the brain cuts off. Time stops at this dreadful moment of T–1, which will keep repeating in the adult in a noble, if desperate, effort (and it is an effort – it takes vital psychic energy) to prevent the original trauma from recurring.

> And when it stops you breathing, what would you like to
> have happen?
> *To break the rock up and feel clean and clear again.*

As long as Rachel continues in the rock-like state of T–1, it can seem as if the trauma T had never happened. Unfortunately, it will also mean that Rachel could go through the rest of her life manifesting the rock's obduracy, inflexibility, and capacity to block strong feelings whenever things became difficult or, conversely, whenever there is an opportunity for joy or emotional release.

T–1 will repeat until T is relieved by what Ehlers and her colleagues call "reprocessing" and we might call regenerative healing. The overall strategy of the Therapeutic Metaphor process is to facilitate the client to move to a new spacetime, 'T+1', where the trauma or problem has healed.

Meanwhile, whence comes this sadness in Rachel? What happened to her then that is taking up valuable space and energy now?

If we were to ask, "What happens next?" in T–1, we would be inviting things to go from bad to worse. What happens next in T–1, unfortunately, is T. We would be summoning the pain of then into the sensibility of now.

Rachel needs to find out how she came to form the rock before she can break it up and feel clean and clear again. It may have to be traced back in her biographical, genealogical, cultural, geographic, or cosmological memory.

3 The Spatial domain[3]

Spatial domain #3 can hold or yield information in three ways. It can act as a temporary transit camp in a move between Physiological domain #2 and Historical domain #4; it can give the client time and space to get information 'out there' physically in writing or drawing; and it is a place in which information can be mapped through movement. Each of these procedures allows information to be examined more readily than might be possible verbally or somatically. Chapters 18 and 19 have more on exploring written and drawn information (*Sam's blocks, Spaces between words, Metaphor landscapes*). Appendix C has more on movement and spatial sorting (*Clean Space*).

A client's symbolic shift into Spatial domain #3 signals a different kind of exploration from that in the Narrative and Physiological domains. Domain #3 has information about the places clients go before they speak (in #1) and before they acknowledge feeling (in #2). Eye movements, gestures, and "um" sounds can all be coded indicators of spatial storage.

Rachel is staring at the floor.

> And where are you going when you go there?
> *Down into where the rock came from.*

Working in the spatial domain allows the client to have more control than they are likely to experience in the narrative and physiological domains. Rachel's problem may still be scary, but is less likely to be overwhelming.

> And is there anything else about that down into where the rock came from?
> *It's dark and deep and cold.*

The client is locating and separating T–1 memories and perceptions relatively safely and naming them. The original trauma does not have to be re-experienced in order for its components to be identified and described.

In Therapeutic Metaphor process generally and in domain #3 in particular, clients often come across deeply buried fragments of themselves. As the ethno-archaeologists of their own lives, they can be invited to itemize and map these fragments. Space acts as their co-therapist. It helps organize the information, holds a record of what has been done, and will often give an indication of what needs to be done.

4 The Historical domain

Domain #4 contains biographical and genealogical information, and beyond genealogy to cultural, land of origin, and cosmological sources. Where and when is the genesis of Rachel's sadness? It could be in her lifetime or even in a spacetime beyond. The effects of a traumatic event that took place years before her conception could have passed through the generations like a virus.

How can the tears of 'then' be used to heal the pain of 'now'? Therapeutic Metaphor process works in such a way that clients can trace the history of their trauma (in Rachel's case, as we shall see, the history of the sadness and tears that predated her birth) back to a healing-related resource. Domain #4 is a holding place for both problem and solution-related information down the biographical, ancestral, geopolitical, and cosmological line. Both trauma and resource can have extensive roots.

In domain #4, we have the privilege of being able to 'look forward retrospectively' to the history of the symptom. It will be laid out before us in a series of steps or stages, which can be questioned separately to access the information they hold.

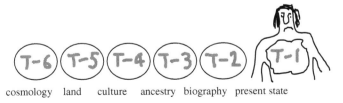

Figure 12 'Looking forward retrospectively' using domain #4 information sources

'T–2' (T minus 2) is the first source of information in domain #4 and typically holds biographical fragments related to childhood. 'T–3', ancestral information relating to parents, grandparents, and other ancestors. 'T–4', cultural and racial information. 'T–5' will take the client back to the land or to a place of origin. 'T–6' holds spiritual, cosmological, or nature of the universe information: possibilities beyond the usual boundaries.

Two basic sequencing questions pull Rachel back in time and space in domain #4:

And what happens just before it's dark and deep and cold?
It snows. (T–2 biographical)

And what happens just before it snows?
The storm clouds gather. (T–3 ancestral)

And where could those storm clouds come from?
From a terrible ideology. (T–4 cultural)

And where could that terrible ideology come from?
My homeland. (T–5 terrestrial)

Always available, meanwhile, are the default descriptive questions, "What kind of X?" and "Is there anything else about X?" which can help clients fill out some of the detail in their broader perceptions. Descriptive questions will normally be used sparingly here in order to maintain the historical flow.

And what kind of homeland could that homeland be?
A beautiful warm land. (T–5)

And where could that beautiful warm land come from?
From the sun and the rain and the stars. (T–6 cosmological)

In domain #4, we roll up our sleeves and pull the client back in time. This retrogression will often be at odds with most clients' sense of the 'forward' progression of events so, as we saw in Chapter 15, the pull back has to be evident in the facilitator's intonation and emphasis.

And what happens *just before*?
And where could that *come from*?

Physiological domain #2 might hold a single memory, but Historical domain #4 is likely to contain half a dozen or more contributory events. Rachel will need to identify and clean up the lot before she can heal.

She can do that in one of two ways: progressively, a step at a time, or, with a bit of luck, promptly, all at once. The step-by-step progressive approach prepares the ground for the client who may not be ready for the immediate redemptive journey.

Progressive resource, redemptive metaphor, intergenerational healing

As Rachel works back through Historical domain #4, she rediscovers qualities she is heir to – her mother's care, her grandfather's warmth, the survival instincts of ancestors, and the wealth of the earth they tilled and sowed. She takes these resources forward into the present through the upheavals and traumas of her generational timeline, and as she does so realizes that they have persisted in herself. She rediscovers the warmth of a once-imprisoned heart, the energy for caring that had been locked in self-absorption, and so on. The effect is cumulative. Successive additions of inherited resource build up the momentum for intergenerational healing and present redemption.

Prior to the history of the trauma and alongside the history of inherited resource, there will be a clean, original, unsullied time when the client and the world were one. This 'pristine' sense of self may take time to show itself, but when it does it can be tapped to generate a powerful healing symbol or redemptive metaphor.

The pristine suffused every cell of Rachel's bodymind when she was younger. In her case, it was present even before she was conceived.

> And what kind of homeland could that homeland be?
> *A beautiful warm land.* (T–5)

> And where could that beautiful warm land come from?
> *From the sun and the rain and the stars.* (T–6)

She has moved beyond genealogy, beyond culture, beyond land, to a further source.

> And is there anything else about that sun and that rain and
> those stars?
> *They make a ball of soft moist energy.*

A trauma originating in one spacetime may require a healing resource from beyond that spacetime. Grove drew an analogy with the familiar 'nine-dot problem', in which you are challenged to connect all nine dots with four straight lines without raising pen from paper.

To solve the problem, you need to go beyond its immediate boundaries.[4]

A facilitator should not stop too soon when pulling back time in search of a healing resource. Redemptive potential will only appear when the client has moved beyond the sources of trauma-related information in the historical line.

Once discovered, named, and known, a resource symbol can be invited to make contact with the symbol or metaphor that has been representing T–1; that is, to interact directly with the original symptom. If the system is ready, the symbol for the symptom, and as a consequence the symptom itself, will *transform*.

> And would that ball of soft moist energy [domain #4] be interested
> in going to rock in stomach [domain #2]?
> *I think so.*

> And can ball of soft moist energy go to rock in stomach?
> *Yes.*

> And as ball of soft moist energy goes to rock in stomach, then what
> happens?
> *It melts the rock and warms the cold.*

> And as it melts the rock and warms the cold, then what happens?
> *I'm on a beach in the Pacific.*

But what if potentially redemptive X has grave reservations about going to problematic Y, or if problematic Y is not yet ready to entertain otherwise willing X, and the momentum for change falters? Other things may have to be sorted out first.

In this example, the facilitator identifies a client's "greater love" as having transformative potential.

> And would 'greater love' be interested in going to a father who
> hit you?
> *Maybe. Not yet.*

> And when maybe, not yet, what needs to happen for greater love
> to go to a father who hit you?
> *It first has to forgive.*

And can it forgive?
(Hesitates) *I don't know. It's supposed to be bigger than petty human concerns.*

And when it's supposed to be bigger than petty human concerns, then what happens?
I think I have to make forgive bigger than it is.

A Clean facilitator will not attempt to superimpose a subjective sense of how the client should feel over how the client actually feels, or to replace an undesired state with a desired state by inference alone. The idea of introducing a potentially redemptive metaphor to an existing symptom is more like reminding a dormant seedling of the existence of the sun. If the ground has been well prepared and the season is favorable, the need of the seedling to grow will prevail. Rachel again:

And as you're on a beach in the Pacific, then what happens?
I'm not sad any more, I'm at peace.

Rachel is invited to develop the qualities of "peace" to give it more presence and power.

And what kind of peace could that peace be?
It's an active, not a passive peace.

And is there anything else about that active, not passive, peace?
It's compassionate and patient, it's a compassionate peace.

A resource has to be the best it can be to have the power to transform. Is "compassionate peace" strong enough to mitigate Rachel's original 'T-minus' sadness?

And would compassionate peace be interested in going to split up with your partner?
Yes, it would.

But is Rachel's construct of the original problem willing to interact?

And *can* compassionate peace go to split up with your partner?
Yes.

And as compassionate peace goes to split up with your partner, then what happens?
I'm no longer sad, he's reassured, we get on with our lives and remain friends.

An ending of a sort, if not the final act. Rachel's awful sadness was not only about the split with her partner, but also about a series of related, unconsciously coded events stretching into the past. The resource is taken back through every stage of Rachel's journey and invited to interact with each.

As "compassionate peace" meets with "huge rock in the middle of my heart," the space around the rock opens and the rock is transformed from a barrier into no more than an interesting feature of the landscape.

As "compassionate peace" meets with "dark cold night", the night evolves into a rosy dawn.

"Snow" settles quietly and insulates the ground.

"Storm clouds" dissipate.

"Terrible ideology" loses its power and is contained.

And in Rachel's "homeland", compassionate peace fills the gap left by the loss of awful sadness.

"I am made whole by my scars," wrote the poet Samuel Menashe. At the conclusion of a process that attends conscientiously to every contributor to the original trauma, Rachel no longer has cause for remaining in the frozen moment of T–1. She has moved into T+1. Her heart is her own again. Now tears of a different kind appear; cathartic tears from the relief she feels that something has healed.

Figure 13 The redemptive metaphor is taken forward to clean up the
upheavals and traumas of the client's generational and cultural timeline

Summary of the Therapeutic Metaphor process

Narrative domain #1, the client talks in everyday terms about the problem. As the client describes the symptom, Clean questioning moves in a typical, though by no means inevitable, sequence to:

Physiological domain #2, in which a metaphor for somatic, deeply held, inner child or preverbal information is elicited and developed. This may be followed by a move into:

Spatial domain #3, where the client is encouraged to develop information available in different locations. A key word, phrase, feeling, or gesture provides the cue for a move into:

Historical domain #4, in which the client is coaxed back in spacetime to discover component parts of the trauma, and further back yet to rediscover and develop a redemptive metaphor in pristine spacetime before the origin or onset of the trauma.

Rachel was invited to relocate the resource in herself and to clean up the chronology of the trauma at each stage of its appearance to heal its entire expression in history.

The Four-Domain Therapeutic Metaphor process is a general strategy. In the next chapter, we look at special tactics that can be employed as part of the process or as procedures on their own.

Notes to Chapter 16

1 For the background to this chapter I am indebted to U.S. therapist Rob McGavock's notes of a 1998 seminar with David Grove entitled *Problem Domains and Non-Traumatic Resolution Through Metaphor Therapy.*

2 Dissociating from the trauma in order to survive: Anke Ehlers et al, *The Nature of Intrusive Memories After Trauma: The Warning Signal Hypothesis*, Behaviour Research and Therapy 2002; Ann Hackman et al, *Characteristics and Content of Intrusive Memories in PTSD*, Journal of Traumatic Stress 17 (3) June 2004.

3 Grove went on to develop a complete methodology, 'Clean Space', from his work in spatial domain #4. Clean Space works on the proposition that when the client moves to a new space, they have access to new information. Appendix C, part 2, has a compendium of Clean Space questions incorporated into a model Clean Space process. Articles on the beginnings of Clean Space can be found at cleanlanguage.co.uk (James Lawley, *Clean Space: The First Workshop*, and Penny Tompkins & James Lawley, *Clean Space: Modeling Human Perception Through Emergence*). When the information from a network of six spaces iterates, new knowledge emerges that is greater than the sum of its parts. There is more on 'Emergent Knowledge' procedures in Appendix C, part 3, and at powersofsix.com.

4 The solution to the nine-dot problem entails going outside its immediate boundaries and beyond its apparent limits.

Chapter 17
Return of the Hamster

Each of us guards a gate of change that can only be opened from the inside.   Marilyn Ferguson

Six Clean procedures – The intervention question – Possibilities and pitfalls of intuition – Perceiver-Perceiving-Perceived: Ned's need to know, Janet feels worn out – Place-Object-Path: Clare's cage – The special case of transport symbols: Bridget and the chrysalis – Trust in the process: Simon and the raindrop

The genesis and evolution of Clean Language covers a period of twenty-five years or so.[1] In that time, a number of *modi operandi* have been created to help facilitators navigate their way through its processes theoretically and practically. Lawley and Tompkins produced several guides, including the 'Compass' and the 'Molecule', for their Symbolic Modeling trainings. Cei Davies Linn and Norman Vaughton made a specialty of 'epistemological metaphor' and 'wounded child within' procedures. In Chapter 15, we introduced a basic Four-Phase guide and in Chapter 16, Grove's Four-Domain Therapeutic Metaphor process. This chapter looks at six simpler approaches to tracking clients cleanly. They can be utilized on their own or in conjunction with the other procedures.

> The intervention question
> Intuition
> Perceiver-Perceiving-Perceived
> Place-Object-Path
> Transport symbols
> Trust in the process

The intervention question
The first of these is very simple indeed, but calls for a certain self-discipline to answer impartially. It is to ask oneself at intervals: are my interventions continuing to be Clean?

Inter-vene = come between

The intention of any intervention is to come between the client and their perceptions in some hopefully productive way. It is what every model of therapy and personal development aspires to. Even a Clean reflection or question can be said to come 'between' the normal relationship of the client and their problem – that is, the relationship that would exist if the facilitator were not present. At what point does an intervention interfere or become intrusive?

In-trude = encroach, usurp
Inter-fere = get in the way of, impede

The librettist W.S. Gilbert wrote, "It is rude, madam, to intrude, madam." To intrude is to butt in or trespass without permission. To interfere is to attempt to alter or interrupt a course of events without invitation or necessity.

> *I'm in despair.*
> I'm sorry to hear that. What do you need to feel good about yourself again?

This is a rude question. It intrudes. It also impedes. It has an inbuilt assumption that your despair is an undesirable state and that feeling good is better, which may be the case, but sidesteps the distinct possibility that there is valuable information in your despair that is indispensable to feeling good again. An intervention that skips directly from despair to the notion of feeling good again is an act of separation between the client and their perception.

Interceding, on the other hand, is an act of linkage. It is doing something on behalf of another.

Inter-cede = go between

A go-between brings together two parties – in this case, the client and their unconscious – who may desire to come together, but are under constraints of anxiety, timidity, or unfamiliarity.

> *I'm in despair.*
> And you're in despair. And when you're in despair, is there anything else about that despair?

The Clean question has implicit permission to intercede between the client and their unconscious on behalf of both. Those three honest brokers "And" (Chapter 13), "And when" (Chapter 14), and "that" (Chapter 19) are the tireless agents of intercession. Clean interceders get on familiar terms with them.

> *And* you're in despair. *And when* you're in despair, is there anything else about *that* despair?

Cleanish intervenors tend to acknowledge the first ("And"), while ignoring the second and third ("And when" and "that").

> **And* you're in despair. What kind of despair?

A nominally Clean intervenor will ignore all three:

> *What kind of despair?

A question that skims the surface of the client's perception and demonstrates little depth of concern.

Intruders are likely to be pursuing an agenda of their own. Intervenors like to move things along and make change happen. Interceders create and facilitate the conditions in which the most likely outcome is self-generated change that will last.

Most Clean facilitators work knowingly and some more intuitively.

Possibilities and pitfalls of intuition

It is possible as a facilitator to be so intent on staying out of the client's way that we become over-formulaic – word-perfect on the syntax and the format of the questions, but with a restricted view of the client's overall journey and limited sensitivity to their moment-to-moment little shifts, diversions, and changes of gear.

For the overall journey, we need a sense of the patterns the Clean formula is a part of, that is, to know what the formula is for. For the momentary shifts and diversions, we need acuity and flexibility, the ability to notice and respond to what is happening in the moment. This can get complicated. To do it consistently and coherently, we have to rely now and again on our intuition.

One way of thinking about intuition is as an involuntary impulse, an unmediated somatic response that can help manage our decisions – not necessarily well or badly, but with some justification. In the context of changework, it is not, or should not be, an instinctive emotional response derived from an attachment to the client, or to the client's desired solution, or to some unresolved personal issue. This is the kind of 'gut instinct' that is motivated by a need for personal gratification. I mean instead the kind of considered intuition that the bodymind is better at doing than many of us suppose.

For a few facilitators, the intuitive choice of what to ask clients comes naturally; for most, it comes from experience. Just as an athlete needs to balance concentration and relaxation to perform well, a Clean facilitator needs to combine intuition with deliberation, first impressions with second, and to do both pretty much at the same time. Clean processes are robust enough to accommodate both intuition and deliberation, and the occasional guess or assumption that turns out to be wrong.

There is a line or two to be drawn between 'admissible' and 'inadmissible' intuition.[2] In a Clean context, we can say it is *inadmissible* for a facilitator to formulate a question from their personal agenda rather than from the exact information the client presents. It is also *inadmissible* to trust entirely to intuition to the exclusion of other resources and to assume it to be incapable of making mistakes.

It may be *temporarily admissible* to come up with a question from our sense of the 'natural meaning' of the client's language. If the client identifies "water" in their metaphor landscape, it is not unreasonable to assume that it will have qualities of wetness, fluidity, and so on, though in the world of therapeutic metaphor conventional logic is often turned on its head, so every inference we draw from everyday meaning must be subject to constant review. (See *Provisional modeling*, Chapter 19.)

It may also be *temporarily admissible* to focus our questioning on a particular sub-set of the client's information that catches our attention – a repeated phrase, an unusual construction, a meta-comment like "There I go again" – though the same reservations about normal and metaphorical logic apply.

The only kind of intuition explicitly *admissible* in a Clean process is the hunch we may have about what the client means that we do not confuse with truth or reality, keep entirely to ourselves, and update at every opportunity. A gut feeling can help us decide on the next intercession without having to suppose some kind of empathic connection with the client, but only by keeping the intercession Clean can we be confident of not contaminating the client's response.

In preparing to intercede, we are witness to events on the frontiers of knowledge. Every step we take is on virgin territory. The client with the unique knowledge of a lifetime has new information. The facilitator with the meta-knowledge of watching a variety of client landscapes unfold has a particular experience; and together they form a unique system. When enough elements in the system have interacted, a pattern will emerge, and from there a direction in which to go next will follow. "A direction," as Lawley and Tompkins say in *Metaphors in Mind*, "that arises from the intelligence and wisdom of the whole system." At a certain stage of grace, the client's perception, the facilitator's intuition, and the intelligence in the system will be indivisible.

When that does not happen readily – and it is more likely to be the exception than the rule – there are two simple techniques for deconstructing client statements that will help serve the wisdom in the system. They are 'Perceiver-Perceiving-Perceived' (P.P.P) and 'Place-Object-Path' (P.O.P.).[3]

Perceiver-Perceiving-Perceived

In the nineteen-twenties, Korzybski declared that all we can know is the joint phenomenon of "the observer and the observed". The observed could only exist in a systemic relationship with the observer. In the nineties, Grove gave a name to the third element implied in such an equation. He called it, "The observer, the observed, and *the space in-between*," on the Korzybskian premise that to have an awareness of anything, we must be a part of a larger system. Grove's modelers, Tompkins and Lawley, preferred 'perceiver' to observer on the grounds that perceiving is an active, not a passive, role and the term supposes a more complete neurological process. To perceive is not merely to analyze the patterns of light entering the eye, but to engage one's experience and expectations of the world as affected by present needs and intentions and conditioned by psychopathology.

In terms of therapeutic process, the Perceiver is the client who presently wants or is aware of something, the Perceived is what they presently want or are aware of, and the Perceiving is the state in which the two are presently related. My client Ned's

I need to know the terrain ahead

deconstructs simply as:

Perceiver   *I*
Perceiving   *need to know*
Perceived   *the terrain ahead*

while Janet's

I feel worn out since my mother died, I have to clear up the house
and I don't want to die before my fiftieth birthday

is a little more complex. It breaks down into three perceivers, three
perceivings, and three perceiveds:

Perceivers   *I (who feels), I (who has to), I (who doesn't want)*
Perceivings   *feel worn out since, have to clear up, don't want*
        to die before
Perceiveds   *my mother died, the house, my fiftieth birthday*

Separating these out mentally or, with the client's active
involvement, graphically or spatially, will help client and facilitator
decide which to concentrate on first. Several simple pointers to
what to ask Janet have emerged from this deconstruction. Here are
two:

And when you [Perceiver] feel worn out since [Perceiving] your
mother died [Perceived], then what happens?

And when you [Perceiver] don't want to die before [Perceiving]
your fiftieth birthday [Perceived], what would you like to have
happen?

Drawing one part of a client's statement to their attention will
usually be more productive – it will certainly be more manageable –
than drawing their attention to the whole. Any number of "What
kind of?" and "Is there anything else about?" questions can be asked
of parts of these parts.

What kind of I is that I that feels worn out?
What kind of I is that I that has to clear up?
What kind of I is that I that doesn't want to die?
Is there anything else about that mother/house/fiftieth birthday?

In the simpler case of Ned's first words, the deconstruction itself
leads to an obvious question.

I need to know the terrain ahead.
And when you [Perceiver] need to know [Perceiving] the terrain
ahead [Perceived], where are you?

I'm stuck in the mud right here.

If the perceived ("the terrain") has a place in the metaphor
landscape ("ahead"), its perceiver ("I") must have a place too.

Clients are often able to locate themselves very precisely in relation to other elements of the landscape. From their perception of the nature of those relationships, new information will emerge.

'Perceiver-Perceiving-Perceived' offers a navigational route through the reefs, wrecks, and sunken treasure of the unconscious. It is a model of perception only. It is not an interpretive or explanatory model.

Place-Object-Path

P.O.P. is an explanatory model of the structure of the client's journey at a given point in time. 'Place' stands for either a point in spacetime or a context; 'Object' is a thing or a goal; and 'Path' signifies the relationship between them. P.O.P offers a metaphor map that will pinpoint the client's present position and make the topography more accessible.

Underlying the billions of bits of information that go into making up our experience of the world, all our literal and figurative constructions, all our verbal and nonverbal representations, are a mere handful of concepts related to where things are, what they are, and how we get to them or find a way round them. Evolutionary biologist Richard Dawkins suggests how this came about:

> Each of us builds, inside our head, a model of the world in which we find ourselves. The minimal model of the world is the model our ancestors needed in order to survive in it [...] the world familiar to our ancestors on the African savannah: a three-dimensional world of medium-sized natural objects, moving at medium speeds relative to one another.[4]

Our brains have evolved beyond what Dawkins calls "the mediocre utilitarian one" our ancestors made use of in order to survive on the savannah, but we continue to view the world in terms of its evident dimensions of space and time and our familiar experience of matter. They are at the heart of the fundamental 'African savannah' metaphor of places, objects, and paths. Whether we are building a model of the universe, working out where we are in our immediate environment, or developing an imaginative landscape of the mind, the basic structure is the same. And just as we have invented special technology (telescopes, microscopes, particle accelerators) to obtain information about extremely large cosmic events or extremely small sub-atomic events outside the limited mid-range of our sensory abilities, we have special psychological tools to access mental events beyond the restricted mid-range of our intellectual capacities. Clean Language is just such a tool. It encourages our symbolizing minds to divulge and decode the information they hold.

P.P.P. and P.O.P can be employed separately or complementarily. The use of one may suggest a use for the other.

I'm stuck in the mud right here

says Ned in a Perceiver-Perceiving-Perceived view of his present situation. Switching to a Place-Object-Path analysis of how he is *constructing* it, we find that his 'Place' ("right here") and 'Path' ("stuck in the mud") evidently lack an 'Object' or goal. We can then enquire:

And when stuck in the mud right here, what would you like to have happen?
I need to step out on to dry land.

At which point, an 'Object', "dry land", and a new 'Path', "step out", appear, with all the advantages for movement and direction they imply. A signpost has appeared in the African savannah.

Clare's cage
Clare (Chapter 9) is the young graduate who suffered from claustrophobia while driving.

I'm like a hamster in a cage on a wheel going nowhere.

A client's first words are not always models of simplicity and clarity. They may be as full of misleading clues as the opening pages of an Agatha Christie novel. The exercise of deconstructing the protagonist's language into a universal metaphor of places, objects, and paths can help a facilitator decide how to proceed.

I'm like ... [metaphor of]
a hamster [Object]
in a cage [Place]
on a wheel going nowhere [Path].

Traditional linear, analytical, or cognitive approaches to change have difficulty finding their way round these three- and four-dimensional landscapes. Clean algorithms are perfectly at home here.

And what kind of hamster [Object] could that be?
And is there anything else about that cage [Place]?
And when on wheel going nowhere [Path], then what happens?

Clean Language is the optimal traveler's aid. It enables clients to create a model of what they have encountered to date, the better to know what is needed to reach their desired destination.

And when on wheel going nowhere, then what happens?
I realize I have to get off the wheel or get out of the cage.

It is temporarily admissible, as we have seen, for a facilitator to suppose a certain similarity between the way things happen in a metaphor landscape and the way they happen in reality. For the moment, we can assume that the wheel in the hamster's cage is fixed (though it may not be) and that the door to the cage is closed (though it may be open or ajar). And there are differences too. Symbolic events are not in thrall to the laws of reality physics. In the metaphorical world, a small rodent may fashion a key to unlock its own cage, just as it might fire a bullet that leaves a large hole through a pursuing cat without affecting the cat physically in any way. I have witnessed a client convey himself deep into the earth's core to see what his problem looked like from below and another who was able to squeeze a symbolic pebble with her bare hands to produce a soothing balm. Whatever happens in the metaphorical world, 'real' or not, has meaning.

The compound metaphors of 'Perceiver-Perceiving-Perceived' and 'Place-Object-Path' can yield a certain kind of perception that points the way to another strategy for questioning.

The special case of transport symbols
Dorothy is swept up by a tornado and transported from a mundane existence on the farm to the magical world of Oz. A cloud brings soft rain on the west wind to comfort an anxious client. The pattern in a curtain carries the pristine spirit of a child from the reality of abuse into a realm of escape and survival.

'Transport' symbols come in many forms – streams, vehicles, arrows, patterns in the carpet, and so on. They can signal benefice, resource, release, or transit to a new land. Their merits and potential are not always obvious when they first appear.

Bridget and the chrysalis

At the age of seven, Bridget constructed a metaphorical shell to protect herself from violence in the family. In adolescence, the shell became a prison that isolated her from others and prevented her from expressing herself satisfactorily. In her late twenties, she became depressed and in her thirties, suicidal. At thirty-eight, she made the decision to come into therapy.

After several sessions, Bridget feels safe enough to honor the protective intention of the shell she had fashioned those many years past. Some sessions later, in a moment of creative insight, she converts the carapace into a chrysalis. And after a few weeks more, she finds herself emerging from a transitional state of quiescence into a transformed state of being. From a 'T–1' problem state, she has transported herself to a 'T+1' solution. The fluttering of Bridget's butterfly wings is one of those tiny, unexceptional events with unanticipated and far-reaching consequences.

Trust in the process

Whatever tactic or strategy facilitators follow, in the final analysis the client can simply be trusted to self-model. It is no part of a Clean facilitator's job description to make change happen. Change is often a spontaneous by-product of client self-modeling.

Simon is a 50-year old television producer beset with regrets about the past and confusion about the immediate future. He is gazing outside. I follow his line of sight:

> And where are you going when you go there?
> *To the tree ... a leaf ... to a raindrop on the leaf ...*
>
> And when that raindrop on leaf, where are you?
> *I am the raindrop.*

I now have a strategic choice to make. If I want a clear direction for my questioning, I can privately deconstruct Simon's, 'I am the raindrop on the leaf' into 'Place-Object-Path'. If "the leaf" is a place, "the raindrop" an object, where is the path? I am aware of the symbolic function of a path for the client's journey, but my question may not impose any idea of a direction or impetus for Simon-as-raindrop.

> *And when you are that raindrop, what happens next?
> *I trickle down the leaf ...*

A path has appeared. Alternatively, I could map Simon's "I am the raindrop" onto 'Perceiver-Perceiving-Perceived'. If "I" is his perceiver and "the raindrop" what he perceives, there may be information for him in their 'in-between' perceiving, which in this case is likely to be their spatial relationship. I can ask:

*And when you are that raindrop, where is leaf?

I am not obliged to have a clear direction for my questioning or to be following a predetermined strategy, however. Simon is already self-modeling. If his raindrop is a potential transport symbol, I can simply facilitate him to find out more about where it is taking him. And this is what happens:

And when you are that raindrop on that leaf, what happens next?
I trickle down the leaf ... perch for a moment on the edge ...

And then what happens?
I fall ...

And then what happens?
I continue falling ...

I am concerned about where Simon's path is taking him, but I keep going and trust in the process.

And then what happens?
I hit the ground.

And then what happens?
I smash into a thousand pieces.

Simon has passed what is almost certainly a point of no return. It feels like – it is – a kind of death.

And when you smash into a thousand pieces, then what happens?
The droplets soak into the earth.

And then what happens?
They feed into the roots of the tree.

And as the seasons change and warmth comes to the earth, new growth appears. Simon models a transformation that came about from following the natural logic of his perceptions and allowing the story to unfold as it would.

The underlying principles of Clean facilitation are as always reducible to two rules:

- operate from a state of not knowing
- ask questions that have no imputation of meaning
  beyond the questions themselves

The protocol is the same even when the basic questions and methods we have employed so far are going nowhere and we want to go further.

Notes to Chapter 17

1 For more on the historical development of Clean, see *Clean Language Revisited: The Evolution of a Model*, and *Symbolic Modelling, an Overview*, at cleanlanguage.co.uk

2 Admissible and inadmissible intuition: acknowledgments to Caitlin Walker's 'Levels of Inference', a model for training police officers to interview vulnerable witnesses using Clean Language.

3 'Perceiver-Perceiving-Perceived' (P.P.P.): Tompkins and Lawley currently prefer 'relating' to 'perceiving' and separate out a fourth element, 'context' (thus P.P.R.C). Maurice Brasher points out that in quantum terms, the 'perceived' is just as active as the perceiver, emitting signals that Arny Mindell, the American psychologist known for his integration of psychology with physics, calls "quantum flirts".
   'Place-Object-Path' (P.O.P.) is adapted from a 1998 model by Lawley and Tompkins after Lakoff and Johnson. Lawley and Tompkins now use 'relationship' rather than 'path' (thus 'Place-Relationship-Object' or P.R.O.) on the grounds that it is less metaphorical and more inclusive. I prefer 'path' because of its intimations of the client's pursuit of their mission or desire as an archetypal journey.

4 Model building on the African savannah: Richard Dawkins, *The God Delusion*, 2006.

Chapter 18
Sam's Freudian Blocks

It's a very good question, very direct, and I'm not going to answer it.   George W. Bush

Specialist questioning – Graphic information: Sam's blocks – Re-entry questions: Anthony goes blank – Specialist describing, locating, sequencing, relating questions: Gordon's brilliant dawn, Vicky's star – Maturing questions – Use of 'as' and 'when' – Seeking resource: Sylvia connected, Ted and the apple, Janet's happy feet

This chapter looks at more specialist material: graphic information; thirty specialist questions; and a detailed guide to seeking resources. The information here will generally be more relevant once the procedures in Chapters 15, 16, and 17 have done their work and something more may be indicated.

Graphic information
'Graphic' means both visual and overt. Writing and drawing are not only visible means of expression, but also explicit and undeniable. They are at least as informative as speech in conveying the life of the mind. As entry points into client process, they are as useful as doors are to houses.

I shall concentrate here on the written version of graphic information and in the next chapter, under *Metaphor landscapes*, on the drawn version.

Sam is an Orthodox rabbi in his late thirties. His first words to me are:

> *I want to get rid of the blocks to my creativity.*

I could question this statement as a whole, or break it down into its constituent parts, or use it as the starting point for a process of spatial sorting. Instead, I invite Sam to represent what he has said on the flipchart. He takes a thick felt nib pen and scrawls:

I Want to Get Rid of the Bolocks to my Creativity

Invited to *re*process a problem, remedy, or statement of need – in this case, by writing it up – a client will often develop it further. Sam has made several interesting choices.

Grove called our analysis of written statements an examination of

| The | Architecture | of | the | Text |

Since the emergence of glyphs and pictographs for keeping accounts thousands of years ago, writing has always had more significance than as the graphic equivalent of speech. Not only is every word a symbol having cultural and personal significance, every letter is too. And there is meaning in the way we assemble our statements: their placing and spacing, the gaps left, the shapes made, the appearance of 'mistakes'. The way Sam has configured his statement is likely to be one of those ambiguous tricks of the mind that points the way to more information.[1]

Mistakes in spelling can be the result of dyslexia or unfamiliarity with the language, but more often than not reveal unconscious determinacy. Freud called these determinants *Fehleistungen*, or faulty performances, and we know them as Freudian 'slips' – the thoughts that slip silently past the guardians of decency and end up making a scene of themselves in public places.

Sam notices his mistake and laughs. He tells me that for years he has been keeping his generative instinct in check while he devoted his energies to religious teaching, a profession he suspects may no longer express his true vocation. What he really wants to be, he assures me, is a body therapist.

A mistake like Sam's can free up something. It can even lead to the discovery of a latent resource, particularly when humor is involved. Sam self-mockingly celebrates the appearance of the truth by returning to the flipchart and correcting his statement. He meant "blocks", he says. The correction he makes on the flipchart, however, is:

I Want to Get ^Back *Rid of the Bolocks to my Creativity*

He has retained the original conflation of 'blocks' and 'bollocks', and has given it a new twist. He now wants to "Get Back" his creativity rather than "Get Rid" of it.

Sam goes on for half a dozen sessions and discovers a great deal more about himself. He struggles with what he sees as a choice between an obligation to himself and a commitment to family and community. For a while, he considers resigning his rabbinical post in order to take up Feldenkrais training, but finally decides that, for the time being at least, it is enough to be a happier rabbi.

We can reasonably assume (with the usual mental reservations) that a client's use of Capitals, as in "I Want to Get Back ...," is an Indicator of Importance, a means of wittingly or unwittingly drawing attention to or favoring the words they initiate. Capitals have been making distinctions in written and printed English for over five hundred years and have an undeniable influence on the conscious and unconscious choices we make. Every letter of the alphabet is a signpost to our literal and figurative literary inheritance.

> "Of course you know your ABC?" said the Red Queen.
> "To be sure I do," said Alice.
> "So do I," the White Queen whispered. "And I'll tell you
> a secret – I can read words of one letter!"[2]

Language-based therapeutic modalities have traditionally revolved around words rather than letters, the walls of the building rather than the bricks, in the way that 19th century chemists based their work on the existence of molecules while remaining highly skeptical of the reality of atoms. In fact, the alphabet is an inexhaustible resource for the symbolic modeler.

A A a A A A A A

Every letter holds idiosyncratic information about the writer. Every element of the client's depiction or scripting of their present state is a potential source of information and can be interrogated (not interpreted, we are not graphologists) as such.

Here are thirty more questions for this and every other purpose. They cover the four categories of process in the Four-Phase guide in Chapter 15 – opening, describing, locating, and sequencing – and three further categories: relating, maturing change, and seeking resource.

Specialist opening / re-entry

> How do you know? [of a feeling or belief]
> What are you drawn to? [of a symbolic landscape]
> What is happening now? [of silent processing]
> Where are you going when you go there? [of a line of sight]

How do you know?
can help a client shift from narrative mode in domain #1 into the discovery and developmental potential of physiological domain #2.

> [Everyday narrative] *I'm very depressed
> And how do you know you're very depressed?
>
> [Crosses threshold] A feeling of heaviness.
> And where is that feeling of heaviness?
>
> [Arrives domain #2] Here (hand to stomach).

"How do you know?" can also take a client into spatial domain #3 or historical domain #4.

> *And how do you know you're very depressed?
> I see a dark cloud above me [spatial domain].
> I hear the voice of my grandmother [historical domain].

"How do you know?" is a useful question for clients who are more familiar with their cognitive than with their sensory or somatic experience. It can encourage them to acknowledge an emotion ("How do I know? Because I feel sad/angry/unhappy"), which is generally a more accessible entry point to what is going on for them than a conceptual statement such as "I'm thinking of leaving him" or "I need to stop drinking."

If the question, "How do you know X?" prompts an "I don't know" response, a facilitator might choose to go for one of the somatic signals that frequently accompanies words like these: a sigh, a gesture, a shift of position, a pursing of the lips: all alternative ways into the cryptic world of the unconscious.

> *And what does that [reflect sigh, gesture, shift, purse] know?

And what would that [reflect sigh, gesture, shift, purse] like to have happen?

Beware that "How do you know?" also has the power to provoke.

Anthony goes blank
Anthony is a highly conceptual client who takes all references to 'knowing' as a challenge. I ask him:

And what would you like to have happen?
I don't know.

And how do you know you don't know?
If I knew that, I would know.

It would be facile to dismiss a response like this as 'resistance'. Systems analyst Peter Senge suggests that resistance is merely a response by the system trying to maintain an implicit system goal and that until that goal is recognized, any attempt to change or redirect the person will be doomed to failure.[3]

What is Anthony's implicit system goal that he is so adept at maintaining? It isn't at all obvious. His response to my next question ("And is there anything else about that 'If I knew that, I would know'?") is:

I don't know what you mean.
And how do you know you don't know what I mean?

I don't know.

I acknowledge this and gently persist:

And you don't know. And when you don't know, what kind of don't know could that don't know be?

Something happens. Anthony glimpses a door he has left an inch ajar. He peers through the gap:

I see a room that's kind of blank inside.

'Blankness', 'emptiness', and even 'I-don't-know-ness' invariably have active lives of their own.

And what kind of kind of blank inside?
I don't know – fuzzy and thick and grey.

And where could that fuzzy and thick and grey come from?
Way back.

And where way back?
Father.

Does Anthony mean "father" or "farther"? His English accent does not distinguish between them. It makes no difference to the form of my next question, but the way I ask it hints at the ambiguity:

And what kind of father could that way back farther be?
A father who a long time ago told me I was stupid when I couldn't answer questions like, 'Is this the best you can do?'

Anthony's original "I don't know" turns out to have the implicit system goal of surviving the countless shocks of rejection he endured as a child who found himself unable to answer an abnormally critical father's questions correctly. He is reliving a reminder of that now, but rather than risking a 'wrong' answer, he is closing down – the familiar frozen moment of 'T minus 1' we met in Chapter 16 – to save himself from reverting all the way into trauma.

The question "How do you know?" can also invite clients to examine their evidence for a dogmatic statement of belief.

And how do you know you are certain / giving up / responsible?

The response may well contain feeling-related information – "My heart tells me so," "I'm churned up inside," "It's like my head is in a vice": metaphors that can be questioned more readily.

What are you drawn to?
In a later session, Anthony comes up with another metaphor for his blankness.

It's like I'm driving along a long road with no trees or buildings in sight.

I invite him to map this out on the flipchart. After only a moment, he stops. He studies his minimalist depiction of two straight lines going off into the distance. I wait a while, then ask:

And what are you drawn to?

A 're-entry' question that can be asked after a hiatus. Normally it invites the client to make a selection from a number of elements they have mapped out in a metaphor landscape, but it can work equally well when there is almost nothing to go on. Anthony responds:

I want to find out why I am so hard on myself.

A response with three perceivers: an "I" that wants to find out, an "I" that is hard, and a "myself" that is probably feeling hard done by. I ask him to decide for himself which (or what else) we should attend to:

And when 'I' wants to find out why 'I' am so hard on 'myself', what are you drawn to?

The three perceivers might benefit from an opportunity to express themselves separately. It is at least possible that one of them will have something interesting to say about the others.

"What are you drawn to?" originated in the need to invite clients to consider whether any part of the metaphor landscape had an indefinable quality that took their special attention. A Clean coach I know has qualms about the question. She thinks of it as metaphorical in a way that other Clean questions are not. In fact, the construction 'drawn *to*' has a long and respectable history. It derives from the Old English *dragan* ('being drawn or pulled towards') and not from the much later meaning of 'draw' as in 'drawing a line'.[4]

What is happening now?
is another re-entry question. I asked it of Lorraine in Chapter 12 after she had been quiet for a few moments.

And what is happening now?
I'm focusing on my goals.

The question has to be finely timed and spoken gently. It should neither interrupt the client's processing nor be delayed until they they have altogether stopped processing. The right moment, improbably, is *just before* their attention begins to shift away from themself. There is no protocol for calculating such a moment! It is matter of intuition. There could be as little as half a second in which to make a decision and intercede.

Where are you going when you go there?
may be asked of a line of sight that the client is taking, often
unconsciously. We first encountered the question in Chapter 13
when Rachel was staring at the floor.

> And where are you going when you go there?
> *Down into where the rock came from.*

There could be information *at any point* along a line of attention.
This could be a spot on the carpet or an imaginary space beyond
physical reality. It might represent a mental space to which the
client escaped during past abuse or trauma, so the question should
be followed up with care.

Specialist describing

> The same or different?'
> How many?'
> How old? / What age?
> What could X be wearing?'

The same or different?
It is easy to assume that a new client perception with the same
name as an earlier one will be the same perception, when it will
always be least a little, and at most a great deal, different. The
question can help the client relate or differentiate the two things.

> *And is that bird in the bush [new symbol or perception] the same
> or different to that bird in hand [earlier symbol or perception]?

It can also help authenticate or differentiate a homophone without
having to spell it out. We might have asked Richard the Third

> *And is that son of York the same or different to that sun of York?

How many?
can be asked when the client has unequivocally identified the
existence of more than one thing. There should be clear evidence.

> *It's a habit that has to coaxed down the stairs a step at a time.*
> And how many stairs could those stairs be?

> And when a step at a time, how many steps?'

Answers to "How many?" can be surprisingly precise.[5] The number
identified by the client may itself be a significant source of information.

So many steps, I've no idea.
How many steps?

Three. No, four.
And what could the first step be?

There is a more subtle role for number. When I asked Anthony, "Where could fuzzy and thick and grey come from?" he answered "Way back", which led him to uncover a single generational influence in a "way back father". Another client who answered a similar question with an intuitive, "Oh, way way way back," went on to identify the origin of the problem as three generations back.

The number of times a word is repeated is rarely arbitrary. The number may have echoed throughout the client's life. It may relate to the way they retrieve certain kinds of information. Not infrequently, it turns out to be the number of stages the client's unconscious has calculated as necessary to arrive at the solution to a problem.

How old? / What age?
can be asked when the client has moved from third- to first-person narrative with the appearance of a personal pronoun.

I froze. / My heart stopped.
How old could you / that I / that heart be? /

or

What age could you / that I / that heart be?
I'm five or six.

The client may be reverting to a time before trauma, or more likely – if this is early in the process and relates to a painful or disagreeable memory – associating into a 'child within', a spacetime linked to early trauma that impacts still on their present state.

What could X be wearing?
is a useful follow-up to 'How old?' It encourages the client to build up the characteristics of the memory or the image representing who they were at the time in question.

And what could five or six be wearing?

The party dress or the pattern on the T-shirt may trigger more information. The facilitator has no need to be sure whether the client's memory of how old they were or what they were wearing is real or imagined, intact or incomplete. Some memories are verifiable by other means, but most are not. Clean Language and Therapeutic Metaphor processes are not so concerned with the 'false memory syndrome' that exercises some therapists.[6] All memories, associations, fantasies, figments, impressions, and recollections can be treated as *symbolic* – constructed in, or reconstructed by, the unconscious for reasons relevant to the client's present need or intention.

Specialist locating

Inside / on the surface / outside?
Above / over / on / under / below?
Left or right? / Front or back?
In which direction? / How far?
What is beyond?

Once the general location of a symbol has been established (via "Where?" and "Whereabouts?"), these specialist vector-related questions invite the client to pinpoint its exact location or direction, or its position in relation to other symbols.

The more precisely a symbol is located, the more likely it is to be trusted by the client; the more trusted, the more engaged the client will be; the more engaged, the more likely the symbol will be to reveal the information it holds.

Inside or outside?

Round and hard like a tight fist (gestures to stomach).
And is tight fist inside or outside?

I feel a kind of constriction (touches chest).
And is constriction inside, on the surface, or outside?

The 'inside/outside' question can be asked of any container that appears or is indicated in a client's metaphor landscape – box, body, consulting room, solar system – or of any virtual 'boundary' that separates one zone of information from another. It is a simple either/or question, so we need to be alert to the possibility that the symbol in question could be straddling the boundary or be half-in, half-out of the container.

The implied restriction of an either/or question can be neutralized by adding an unstressed open conjunction:

Over or under X or ...?
Left of X or right of X or ...?
Front or back of X or ...?

In which direction? / How far?

In which direction is that mountain?
Over there.

The client glances and gestures towards the location of the mountain in space, but its exact location is unclear.

And how far over there?

The nearness or farness of an item can have relevance in terms of its likely influence, but symbols located a few feet or many miles away may share the same line of sight. Having assumed this client's mountain to be on a distant horizon, I was surprised to find that he was already climbing the foothills and seeking a route that would take him to the top. The converse has also happened. A client identified a father figure who seemed to be standing nearby, but she had actually placed him on the dark side of the moon. A careful study of eye focusing patterns can help locate the items on a client's line of sight, but is likely to yield little more than the difference between 'near' and 'far'.

Once we know the precise location of a symbol, we are better able to 'place' our questions in the space it occupies, which helps considerably in maintaining the client in process. There is more on *Placing the questions* in Chapter 19.

What is beyond?

A question offering possibility without limit. My colleague Clive Bach brought it to the Clean Practise Group some years ago when we were renting a room in a Marylebone convent. It was no surprise when it took one volunteer client to a metaphysical place. "What is beyond X?" works on a similar basis to 'Is there anything else about X?' Just as there is always something that can be added to what has already been said, it is reasonable to suppose that, given the microscopically small corner of the universe we inhabit, there will always be something beyond the limits of our present perceptions.

And when you are in that vale of despond, what is beyond?
A range of possibilities.

And when that vale of despond and that range of possibilities,
what is beyond?
A happier land.

And when that vale of despond and that range of possibilities
and that happier land, what is beyond?
Mother earth. The solar system. The Milky Way.

'What is beyond?' led this client to a powerful resource in a distant
galaxy. The question has implications not only for searching beyond
apparent physical limits, but also for seeking information beyond
the boundaries of conventional thought.

Having named, described, and located their perceptions, clients
normally find it helpful to become familiar with the order in which
things happen.

Specialist sequencing

In addition to the standard time-related questions, "What happens
just before?" "What happens next?" and "Then what happens?"[7] we
can call upon four specialist time-related questions:

Where could X come from?
What happens after X?
How long? [duration]
What time? [time implied and implied by time]

Where could X come from?
is likely to take a client into historical domain #4 without further
ado. It is a powerful question and calls for some sensitivity from the
facilitator when responding to the answers. It may be taking the
client to a time and place that they have been avoiding or denying
for years.
   Time is, of course, as measurable dimensionally as form and space
in the metaphor landscape. The basic "What happens just before?"
and "Then what happens?" questions help slow or stretch the time
that a momentary sequence of events takes. "Where could X come
from?" pulls back time, space, or matter to an historically earlier
perception. It has a built-in hint that the place or event in question
– where or what X came from – had a contributory influence on X,
that the influence had an agency that predated it, and this in turn
an earlier contributor, and so on.

Sylvia is a male to female transsexual whose fear of parental and
peer rejection has led her to a disturbing place:

I'm having to deal with a lot of things that are troubling me.
And where could that troubling you come from?

From a fear of not having the answers.
And where could that fear of not having the answers come from?

From a stepmother who hit me for not understanding her.
And where could that stepmother who hit you for not
understanding her come from?

*From her father who chased her upstairs with an axe and buried it
into the banister just missing her fingers.*
And where [etc.] ...?

A client may need to experience a thorough process of inter-generational healing to deal with the information that comes up in historical domain #4, so it is not a trip to be undertaken lightly. The 'come from?' question pulls perceptions back to memories of places, people, and events that played a part in the current problem, and often back to perceived antecedent cause.

When we look at the night sky, we see into the past. We see the moon is as it was a second ago, the galaxy Andromeda as it was two and a half million years ago. Spectacular images of distant reaches of the universe taken by powerful telescopes and orbiting instruments mean that we are becoming increasingly familiar with the fact that the past exists in the present, a reality with enormous significance for therapy and personal development. However distant, tainted, or distorted an image or a memory might be in our minds, it is a present phenomenon. It means that troublesome events formerly thought of as rooted forever in the past can be changed or transformed as much as everyday problems. They respond, as do the moon and the stars, to our active attention.

What happens after X?
is a part-time question compared to the regular employment prospects of "What happens next?" and "Then what happens?" It offers clients an opportunity to evolve time beyond their immediate concerns; to move on from event-in-time X to new event-in-time Y. The question can be asked when the client has given an indication of an ending of some kind.

*And when you have reached the top of the crest, what happens
after you have reached the top?
I stop and rest.*
And what happens after you stop and rest?

I move on to the next.

Clients are able to work with many more concepts of time than the simple 'before and after' order in which things usually happen. A resting event, no less than a climbing or reaching the top event, may also respond to questioning that relates to 'duration time' or 'actual time'. These specialist questions help clients expand their knowledge of regions of the landscape that they may have neglected or ignored, or which are simply *terra incognita*.

How long?
questions the duration of an event. It presupposes that the client has already indicated that its duration has some significance.

> *It may take time.*
> And how long could that time take?

> *It happened very quickly.*
> And how long could that very quickly be?

> *And then there's peace.*

The natural logic of this client's "then" supposes a 'before' before it.

> And when then there's peace, how long before that peace?

What time? (time implied)
The time of day, night, or year in a metaphor landscape can have a significance that has barely been hinted at. The existence of shadows implies the presence of the sun or a source of light. The length of the shadows suggests the time of day or the height of the light source. The strength of the shadows or the intensity of the light has implications for the time of day, or year, or the presence of something obscuring the light. A tree in the metaphor landscape may have leaves, buds, blossom, or bare branches that signal the season. And so on. All time implied references can be questioned according to the inference they make in the mind of the listener.

> *And what time could that moonlight be?
> It's the middle of the night and I'm scared.*

> *And what time of year could that frost be?
> My birthday.*

A client traverses a metaphorical ocean enveloped in perpetual fog.

He realizes that the noonday sun is present, unseen above the fog. As he focuses his attention on the sun, it disperses the fog, brings color to the sea, and lightens his journey.

What time? (implied by time)
A client whose depression tends to deepen towards the afternoon makes use of 'implied by time' questioning to recall a difficult childhood in Singapore.

> And what time of afternoon could that afternoon be?
> *About four o'clock when it always seemed to rain.*

> And is there anything else about that always when it always seemed to rain?
> *Every day I had to leave school and go home to my stepmother.*

Another client is stalked by a long shadow, which follows him constantly.

> And when long shadow, which follows you constantly, what time could that long shadow be?
> *It's seven or eight in the morning.*

> And is there anything else about that seven or eight in the morning?
> *When it's midday, the shadows will be shorter.*

The client finds himself able to move time forward there and then until a higher sun and shorter shadow trouble him less. In the universe of the mind, the laws of physics are at the client's disposal.

One person's internal representations of time, just as of form, can be very different from another's. Some clients gesture ahead when referring to the future. Some point to the side or behind them. Some signal a straight line as a measure of events over time; others a wavy line or a zigzag. Facilitators should be aware of their own eye, head, or hand movements when asking time-related questions. They could be indicating a direction for the future or the past that is at odds with the client's. Time, we may remind ourselves, is always relative to the perceiver.

Specialist relating

> Is there a relationship between Y and X?
> What does Y know about X?
> When Y, what happens to X?

> Would Y be interested in going to X?
> Can Y go to X?
> When/as Y goes to X, then what happens?

These questions explore the relationships between symbols, where Y is a newly developed solution-related symbol and X the original problem-related symbol.

As the client discovers more about the form, location, and sequencing of their perceptions, information accumulates. More of the landscape comes into awareness and coded messages from the unconscious begin to decode of their own volition. Already the client may be getting a sense of how their symbols interact and relate.

Is there a relationship between Y and X?
Every symbol in the landscape will have some kind of systemic relationship – direct and dynamic or distant and quiescent – to every other symbol. The relationship will not always be apparent. Even when apparent, it will not always be immediately relevant. Asking, "What is the relationship between Y and X?" would suppose that a relevant relationship existed already, which may not be the case.

It may be reasonable to suppose an existing relationship of some kind between, say, "head" and "tail" or "sunlight" and "moonlight", in which case "What is the relationship?" is a reasonable question, but in most cases the construction "Is there a relationship?" will be cleaner, just as "Is there anything else?" is cleaner than "What else is there?"

Gordon's brilliant dawn
Gordon is addicted to alcohol, but is having some success in tracing the roots of his dependency. I ask him:

> And is there a relationship between brilliant dawn ...

– a newly developed symbol [Y] that has appeared in his landscape –

> ... and great wave of blackness?

– an earlier metaphor [X] for the onset of the depression that led to his drinking. It is possible that the juxtaposition of brilliant dawn and great wave of blackness has the potential for benefit.

> *Yes, they kind of need each other.*

Whereas

> *And is there a relationship between brilliant dawn and [e.g.]
> screwdriver?

would be a less likely juxtaposition in terms of its natural logic
unless the client had already intimated a connection.
   Alternatively, I can ask Gordon:

What does Y know about X?

> *And what does brilliant dawn [Y] know about great wave of
> blackness [X]?
> *Brilliant dawn knows it has the power to lighten it.*

Or a simple but exceptional specialist question that can help
consolidate a new learning:[8]

When Y, what happens to X?

> *And when brilliant dawn [Y], what happens to great wave of
> blackness [X]?
> *It has lifted and dissipated.*

In fact, I take Gordon through a sequence of three key questions
that bring his symbols together, probably for the first time.

Would Y be interested in going to X? / Can Y go to X? / When Y goes
to X, then what happens?

> And would brilliant dawn [Y] be interested in going to great wave of
> blackness [X]?
> *Yes.*

> And can brilliant dawn go to great wave of blackness?
> *Yes.*

> And when brilliant dawn goes to great wave of blackness, then
> what happens?
> *I am lighter, everything is lighter.*

The repetition built into the sequence energizes the transformation
and confirms its effect.

Metaphor is the first language of resource, a carrier of multiple
messages from deep levels of wisdom. A resource may derive from a
variety of sources: personal qualities, genealogy, forces of nature,

symbolic objects, the reaches of space, or a further dimension. There was an example of the discovery and utilization of a redemptive resource in Chapter 16, when Rachel's "ball of soft moist energy" was invited to go to the "rock" in her stomach and the rock melted.

> And when the rock melts, then what happens?
> *I'm not sad any more, I'm at peace.*

Here is an example from a client who first appeared in Chapter 5.

Vicky's star
Vicky is working with the "over-excited nut" and "cold angry peach" symbols she developed for her alternating bouts of elation and depression. When Vicky first brought nut and peach together, they formed a "vibrating peach", a resource with a useful transitional role, but which turned out not to be strong or persuasive enough to meet the deeper need her symptoms were signaling. A couple of sessions later, Vicky is journeying back in inter-generational time in historical domain #4.

> And where could that father working the farm come from?
> *From his father before him and from the earth they worked.*

> And where could that earth they worked come from?
> *From a distant star.*

> And is there anything else about that distant star?
> *It's radiant, powerful.*

I invite Vicky to bring the new resource into contiguity (near-proximity or actual contact) with the original symbol for her depressive state:

> And would radiant powerful star be interested in going to cold angry peach?
> *Yes, it would.*

> And as radiant powerful star goes to cold angry peach, then what happens?
> *It warms the peach.*

> And as radiant powerful star warms cold angry peach, then what happens?
> *The peach reassures the nut.*

A nut 'going haywire' was Vicky's original representation of her manic state.

> And as peach reassures nut, then what happens?
> *I don't feel crazy, I feel warm and energized and okay.*

Vicky has transformed the metaphorical outcome of the encounter ("star warms peach ... peach reassures nut") into a reality solution ("I feel warm and energized and okay"). Putting resources to work in this way is like inviting rain to go to the parched earth: if the conditions are conducive, new growth will appear.

Encounters between symbols can have less obvious promise. A client's "Siamese cat" agrees to go to a "tangled knot of fear," whereupon the knot is gently unraveled. Not all encounters between symbols observe the normal laws of physics or biology: a client's "apple blossom" rises to reattach itself to the branch from which it fell. Not all encounters fulfill their potential: a client answers "No" to "Would kindness be interested in going to hurt?" She is signaling that hurt is not yet reconcilable or that kindness is insufficiently powerful. The ground has not been fully prepared and the system is not yet ready for change.

A facilitator can lose rapport in a second if the "Would Y be interested in going to X?" question is poorly timed. The client could perceive Y as a violator of process rather than as a potential collaborator. Y and X may need more time to establish trust.

Introductions between symbols are more likely to succeed when the elements concerned are well formed in themselves, when the context is amenable, when the timing is propitious. The aim of the Clean facilitator, like that of the good midwife, is to be sensitive to every condition that will encourage the client's self-system to persevere in its own being and give birth to itself.

Maturing questions

> What needs to happen for X?
> What is the first thing?
> What would X like to do next?

What needs to happen for X?
predicates the existence of a desire in the client that something has to happen in order for progress to be made.

Raj is a law student preparing for his final exams. He identifies a potential remedy:

Somehow I have to look after uncertainty.
And what needs to happen to look after that uncertainty?

Faith needs to ally itself to belief.
And what needs to happen for that faith to ally itself to that belief?

Faith has to relax.
And what needs to happen for that faith to relax?

Faith has to go back to square one.

What is the first thing?
can be asked when the context indicates that a process has to be initiated. Raj finds himself needing "to go back to square one" in order to achieve a particular end. A series of steps may be called for.

And when faith has to go back to square one, what is the first
thing that faith needs to do?
To take an overview.

What would X like to do next?
might be appropriate when a particular symbol or perception has already embarked on a process.

And as faith takes an overview, what would that faith like to do
next?
To sit the exam.

And as faith sits the exam, what would that faith like to do next?
To make all the right connections.

Use of 'as' and 'when'
You will have noticed the word "as" appearing in recent exchanges.

And as faith takes an overview ...
And as faith sits the exam ...

It also appeared in Vicky's process.

And as peach reassures nut, then what happens?
I don't feel crazy ...

"And as ..." and "And when ..." are alternative ways of bringing a client's attention to the functioning of a new resource.

And when you feel warm and energized and okay ...

"And when ..." can sound a mite uncertain. It could be interpreted by Vicky as meaning 'if' or 'whenever' she feels warm. This is more likely to be the case at the start off her process, when she would still be familiarizing herself with what was going on:

> *And can nut and peach come together?
> *Erm ...*
>
> And when nut and peach come together ...
> *I'm not sure they can just yet.*

"And as ..." assumes greater confidence and affirms Vicky's experience of having the feelings now.

> And as you feel warm and energized and okay ...

The ongoing event is followed by an invitation to notice what is likely to be its maturing effect on the system as a whole:

> ... then what happens?

Seeking resource

> Where could X [problem-related perception] come from?
> What kind of [noun] was that [noun] before it was [negative qualifier]?

The word 'source' comes from Old French *sourse,* 'risen', so it is no surprise to find that springs or fountainheads are often identified by clients as reserves to be drawn on for assistance or healing. A 're-source' is simply a 'risen again', a quality the client possesses that they can be facilitated to rediscover.

Resource symbols often appear spontaneously in the metaphor landscape. They also appear as a result of conscientiously tracking information back in historical spacetime to 'source'.

Where could X come from?

Sylvia is the transexual patient who lost what she calls her "sense of connection" to her children, her former wife, and her purpose in life. She is puzzled and angry. Notice below how the information in her responses gradually loses its power to disturb and becomes more comforting. A trauma that originates in one cosmology may be first eased, then resolved, by contact with a healing resource from another.

As usual in these transcripts, the first and second parts of the syntax are omitted for easier reading.

And where could that fear of not having the answers come from?
From a stepmother who hit me for not understanding her.

And where could that stepmother who hit you for not understanding her come from?
From her father who chased her upstairs with an axe and buried it into the banister just missing her fingers.

And where could that father who chased her upstairs with an axe come from?
(Pause) *The war. The blitz.*

And where could that blitz come from?
War. Explosions.

And where could those explosions come from?
(Pause) *From a release of brilliant energy.*

And where could that release of brilliant energy come from?
(Long pause) *A greater source.*

And what kind of greater source could that greater source be?
(Longer pause) *Connection. Feeling held. Not needing to know the answers.*

Sylvia connected
Every level of Sylvia's perceptions includes and transcends the earlier levels. Her original presentation of the problem, "I'm having to deal with a lot of things that are troubling me," can now be seen to have contained a hint of its solution, identified here by the client as "connection". Not only has Sylvia been able to trace a chain of *sources* – an abusive stepmother, an unstable grandfather, and so on – for her troubled feelings, she has also been able to rediscover a chain of *re-sources* ("brilliant energy, "greater source," "connection"), which help her re-connect to an earlier pristine sense of herself "feeling held", at a time – as a baby, presumably – when there was no fear of "needing to know the answers."

And when connection, feeling held, not needing to know the answers, the greater source, and brilliant energy ... all that is like what?
(Long pause) *Joy.*

After a couple of developing questions, "joy" evolves into "sublime joy". Is it ready to go to work?

> And would sublime joy be interested in going to explosions?
> *Maybe. Yes, why not?.*

> And as sublime joy goes to explosions then what happens?
> *There's a kind of sudden increase in goodwill.*

> And would sublime joy be interested in going to blitz?
> *Yes. There was a lot of support among people of goodwill at that time.*

Now "sublime joy" goes to "war" and a truce is declared. It goes on to distract the madman with the axe and to find common cause with the abusive stepmother.

There is sometimes a case for inviting a potentially redemptive resource like "sublime joy" to take a single leap through the ether to confront the original problem directly, but in most cases the longer route that takes in every stop along the way will be more rewarding. Repetition gives the process rigor and persistence, dependable strengths in these subtle and sensitive negotiations of the mind. The new network of neurons established in the first encounter will be reinforced and enhanced with each iteration.

> And would sublime joy be interested in going to stepmother who
> hit you?
> (Hesitates) *Yes.*

> And as sublime joy goes to stepmother who hit you, then what
> happens?
> *She cries. She holds me. She knew no better. There's nothing to say.*
> (Sylvia weeps)

The question "Then what happens?" gives no hint and makes no assumption about the nature of the interaction. Sylvia must make what she will of the opportunity the question affords. Note too that the process I invite Sylvia to consider is not in the past or the conditional tense ('What happened when ...?' or 'What might happen if ...?'), but in the present, when sublime joy "*goes to*", and the question is "what *happens*"? The encounters take place, as always, in the here and now (the only time, etc.).

Even with extensive preparatory work, the search for a resource powerful enough to neutralize or transform a persistent problem can take time. Like every voyage of discovery, it can expect to run into fickle winds and unpredictable storms. Here is a particularly powerful aid to navigation.

What kind of [noun] was that before it was [adjective]?
This is not a question to be asked glibly, but in the context of a diligent process it can help the client clean up a state of mind that has been around for so long that it feels inescapable. Take the client who repeatedly identifies a "cruel father" or a "broken heart" as their nemesis. The disparaging adjective is consistently found to be corrupting what would otherwise be an innocent noun. Yet questioning "cruel" or "broken" would only tend to get more of the same; what Grove called "the blood and guts of the story."

Ted and the apple
My client Ted grew up with a very poor opinion of himself.

> *I was called a rotten apple.*

If I were to ask Ted:

> * What kind of rotten?
> *Oh, you know, unpleasant, aggressive, badly behaved ....*

I would only be inviting him to confirm what he has always felt. If instead I ask a question about the apple that separates it from the rotten and pulls it back in time, what does that look like and then what happens?

> And what kind of apple was that apple *before* it was rotten?
> *Bright, green, firm, and whole.*

There is precision and grace in both the intention and effect of this simple exchange. Ted has a glimpse of himself at his best, perhaps even in a pristine state. The question acknowledges the historical affinity of adjective and noun by appearing to be in the past tense, but actually invites the client to seek new information from a present perspective. The new information is then acknowledged, reinforced, and developed.

> And bright, green, firm, and whole. And when bright, green, firm, and whole, is there anything else about that bright, green, firm, and whole?
> *Yes, it's more me.*

Ted identifies the qualities of the apple as resources in himself.

Janet's happy feet
You will remember Janet from Chapter 17:

> *I feel worn out since my mother died, I have to clear up the house
> and I don't want to die before my fiftieth birthday.*

Janet had been rejected for long-term counseling at the mental
health charity where I was working at the time. A
psychodynamically trained assessor had deemed her to be
"cognitively unsophisticated" and "incapable of benefiting". Janet
found her way into short-term counseling instead and responded to
Clean Language questioning without hesitation.

> And when you don't want to die before your fiftieth birthday,
> what would you like to have happen?
> *I'd like to dance again. I used to dance a lot but my feet are
> worried.*

> And what kind of feet were those feet before they were worried?

I invite Janet to attend to the nature of the innocuous noun before
it became saddled with its noxious qualifier. Janet's poor feet were
not ever thus. And lo, "worried feet" are reborn as

> *Happy feet.*

A metaphor that Janet quickly decodes as relating to her truer
nature. I offer happy feet an exceptional opportunity:

> And would those happy feet be interested in going to worried feet?
> *Oh yes!*

> And as happy feet go to worried feet, then what happens?
> *They're not worried, they're happy!*

Janet recalls carefree times when she and her mother went dancing
together. The rediscovered resource is invited to keep dancing:

> And would those happy feet be interested in going to 'clean up
> the house' / 'feel worn out' / 'don't want to die' (etc.)?

What happens next is not a wholesale transformation, but a series
of smaller transitional changes. Janet's bouts of anxiety and
confusion continue, but with more self-awareness and greater
control. And after a few sessions, she is ready to benefit from more
sophisticated work, cognitively and otherwise.

Notes to Chapter 18

1 Another example of information arising in the spaces between words comes from an early research workshop with Grove when a colleague was asked to say whatever was on her mind. "Things are coming together," she said confidently. Grove invited her to write this out on the flipchart. When she had finished, it looked more like, "Things are coming to get her," which had an altogether different meaning.

2 "Of course you know your ABC?" Lewis Carroll, *Through the Looking Glass and What Alice Found There,* 1871. More about the symbolism of letters in Richard A. Firmage (note that 'A'), *The Alphabet Abecedarium,* 2000.

3 'Resistance' as maintaining an implicit system goal: scientist-philosopher Peter M. Senge in *The Fifth Discipline: the Art and Practice of the Learning Organization,* 1990, 2006.

4 "What are you drawn to?" 'Drawn' derives from Old English *dragan*, 'to pull towards', and not from the much later meaning of draw, 'to delineate'. It can't be denied, however, that the construction of the question engaged Grove's sense of poetic mischief, combining as it does two ideas – attraction and depiction – in one. When asked of a metaphor map, the allusion to drawing makes the question too artful for some, but in the absence of better alternatives, the wording has stuck. 'What do you notice?' is too broad. 'What attracts you?' is too strong and has other connotations. 'What pulls you towards it?' and 'What invites your attention?' are clumsy and don't quite have the meaning desired.

5 Unconscious significance of number: more in *The Power of Six: A Six Part Guide to Self Knowledge,* op. cit.

6 'False memory syndrome' is *not* an official mental health diagnosis. We all have inaccurate memories recovered by unreliable means which label them genuine. A false memory can only be harmful when it is so deeply ingrained that the person resists evidence that challenges it. Clean Language and Therapeutic Metaphor process do not challenge memories or beliefs, but can question them in such a way that the client discovers their true relevance, source, and underlying purpose: 'Where could that [memory/belief] come from?' etc.

7 'Then what happens?' is also a specialist maturing question. See the end of 'Maturing questions' on page 232.

8 The astute relating question, "When Y [new resource state], what happens to X [old problem]?" is a maturing question too. It was devised some years ago by psychotherapist Teresa Sherlock while facilitating me in a research session.

Chapter 19
The Special and The Unusual
Advanced Clean Language

Ah, it's a lovely thing to know a thing or two.
Molière

Symbols in limbo – Words to listen out for – Prepositions – Words with momentum – Spaces between words – What is present – What may be missing – Dreamscapes – Props and costume – Vocal qualities – Timing – Placing the questions – Use of 'the' and 'that' – Gathering and tracking information – Metaphor landscapes – Provisional modeling – No such thing as 'resistance' – Client outcomes – Unconscious thinking – Tips from trainees

Here are twenty suggestions for taking facilitator competence to another level.

1 Never leave a symbol in limbo
Once a symbol has been raised into consciousness, it should not be left in a void or in a state of neglect. It will have a location in the client's perceptual space. Where is that? It will have characteristics that distinguish it from other symbols. What are they? It will have a purpose in being there. What might that be?

'Never leave a symbol in limbo' is a rule with one obvious exception. If a large number of similar symbols appear at the same time, the client can be asked to decide for themselves which, if any, to select for their attention. We might ask:

> And when a myriad stars / a profusion of signs / a hundred and one Dalmatians, what are you drawn to?

2 Words to listen out for

- Words that pop up out of nowhere. They come from somewhere.

- Words with ambiguity or multiple meaning. Date, dawn, deal, dear, defect, etc. Open the dictionary anywhere. Which meaning holds the relevant information? It could be more than one of them.

- Unusual or obscure words or constructions. They could point the way to information that a more conventional line of enquiry would miss. How did they get there and what might they be saying?

- Non-sequiturs. Something that does not follow logically from what came before. A sports commentator said of the Arsenal defender, Thomas Vermaelan: "He's done well. Apart from his goal, he's made no outstanding errors." What is the nature of the illogic? Does it indicate a conflict of some kind (the commentator may have been a Spurs supporter) or something unresolved?

- Puns and wordplay. "When I married I got a new name and a dress." The punning may be conscious or not. It may be obscuring the truth or acknowledging it.

- Repeated words. One mention is interesting and may be noted; two mentions are intriguing and should be questioned; three mentions and there is really no choice, the word is demanding attention.

- 'Knowing' words. The client is reflecting in some way on the contents of their own mind. What kind of knowing is it – appreciation, awareness, consciousness, perception, realization, recognition, seeing, sensing, understanding? Where does the knowing come from? What happens as a result?

- Indicators of limitation, neglect, or unresolved need: 'can't', 'won't', 'need', 'never had', etc. Counter-examples will also be present: occasions when the client 'can', 'will', 'has', etc.

- Shoulds: "I should do this. I shouldn't do that." Shoulds usually hold a message from the past. "Where could that 'should' come from?"

3 Prepositions

A preposition normally precedes a noun or pronoun and expresses a *relationship* such as position or direction between the noun or pronoun and another word in the statement. "Between" and "in" are the modest shapers of relationship in that sentence. Prepositions do their work quietly and have a significance that is often neglected.

Ellen is the executive in Chapter 9 who wished to act "with more abandon". I could have asked her about that "with", a demure little helper that lends itself to a number of tasks around the house – accompanying, employing, possessing, supporting, joining, and so on – but I overlooked it at the time. I asked Ellen the more obvious question:

> What kind of abandon could that abandon be?
> *Oh, like blossom in spring.*

I picked up on this one instead.

> And what kind of 'in' could that 'in' spring be?
> *Well, when blossom is in spring it can spring anywhere.*

"In" is one of the most remarkable of the 130-odd prepositions in the English language and deserves a chapter to itself. It actually has one in Seth Lindstromberg's *English Prepositions Explained* (1997). Suffice to remind ourselves here that by 'in' a client might mean 'within', 'inside', 'in the centre of,' 'in the substance of,' 'during the act of,' 'in the space of,' 'in the state of,' 'after the style of,' 'by means of,' 'with reference to,' and many, many other expressions of relationship. 'In' can be hired as a preposition ('in reach'), an adjective ('in joke'), an adverb ('come in'), and a prefix ('in-ability'). It can signal activity, location, circumstance, relevance, movement, ratio, or time. "In" is a very smart word and should not be taken for granted.

Ellen, you may remember, was left behind by her mother when her parents divorced.

> And when blossom in spring can spring anywhere, can it spring to a mother who left you behind?
> *Yes!*
>
> And then what happens?
> *She says sorry and puts it in her hair and takes hold of my hand.*

It is all too easy to make up the meaning of a preposition, or to make assumptions about its function, or to walk by without a second glance. Six words of prepositional significance ("to", "up", "of", "about", "by", and "without") appear in that one sentence alone. Like the relationship of higher civil servants to government ministers, they hover in the shadow of more conspicuous words, yet have a compelling effect on their masters.

4 Words with momentum

Language is imbued with 'movement' words, words that hold 'energy', provide 'impetus', supply 'driving force', or offer 'transport' of some kind. Most of the time, again, we are hardly aware of them.

> *My depression is lifting.*
> *I'm drawn towards the light.*
> *It's like being pulled in all directions at once.*
> *Things are spiraling out of control.*
> *I'm going round in circles.*

What happens if we draw the client's attention to the movement?

> And when depression is lifting, is there anything else about that lifting?
> And when you are drawn towards the light, what kind of drawn towards could that drawn towards be?

A client, Andy, finds himself in a state of mild trance as he likens his mental state to

> *A dark cloud drifting in from the west ...*

Here is a transport symbol ("cloud") with ready, if uncertain, momentum ("drifting"). Andy has already expressed a desire for change, but that doesn't mean the impetus for change is present or inevitable. How should I facilitate his metaphor cleanly? In the first part of the syntax, I can only confirm what Andy has said:

> And dark cloud drifting in from the west ...

In the second part, I have a decision to make. After "And when ..." I can simply repeat his words evenly or I can make a selective emphasis. In this case, I underline the potential for movement in the metaphor:

> And when that dark cloud *drifting in, then* what happens?

What happens next is entirely up to Andy. The cloud may stop, continue, build, accelerate, or dissipate. If Andy still has the motivation to change, the momentum for change is likely to follow, but it will not always follow as a matter of course. There may be a vulnerable, relatively slow-growth phase at the start as the client's information base expands and impetus builds.

What happens if we extend the idea of selective emphasis? Another client:

> *I'm going round in circles.*
> And you're *going round in circles.* And as you're *going round in circles* and *going round in circles ...*

The further repetition intensifies the energy and momentum that are already present. Instead of offering the client a way of slowing, stopping, or stretching time in order to consider a rapid sequence of events in more detail, we are in effect speeding up time by projecting the absence of change into the future.

Alternatively, what happens if we amplify the apparent *lack* of momentum in words with latent energy?

> *I'm holding on to my principles.*
> And you're *holding on,* and *holding on,* and when you're *holding on ...*

The client might simply be confirmed in the endless loop in which they are caught – useful information in itself, in that going round a few more times may give them a better sense of how they have constructed the loop and what may be required to change it – or the system might nudge itself into breaking out of the loop.

A Clean purist might cavil at extending emphasis in this way, on the grounds that it does not reflect *exactly* what the client has said. It could also be argued that it does reflect it exactly, but twice or more over, and is an elegant way of drawing the client's attention to a repeating pattern. This is endlessly debatable and one shouldn't get too precious about it. I have used the technique on a few occasions when the client was on a perpetual roundabout and had already expressed a desire to get off. I have no clear evidence as to its efficacy.

5 Spaces between words

Terry gets severely depressed at times. He has difficulty holding down a job and sustaining a relationship. "I fall into a pit of despair" is the way he puts it. Rather than responding with an instant question, I help Terry deconstruct the architecture of the text using 'Perceiver-Perceiving-Perceived' (Chapter 17). And what he gets is a statement with three parts and two spaces in-between.

I		fall into		a pit of despair
perceiver		*perceiving*		*perceived*

Deconstruct it further and we can see that it has in fact upwards of eleven parts, including six spaces before, after, and between the words.

| |I| |fall| |into| |a pit| |of despair| |

What lies between the lines? Spaces may contain as much information as words and can be questioned as readily.

> And what happens just before fall?
> *I'm playing happily.*

A breathing space appears in which Terry may be able to redefine the nature of the problem. There is also potential resource in his "playing" that might be traced back, developed, and brought forward again to clear up the present "pit of despair".

> And what happens between 'fall' and 'into'?
> *A moment of realization – here I go again.*

"Realization" is a 'knowing' word. There might be a resource in the moment of realization that could be developed to cushion Terry's fall or to discourage it from repeating.

What else do we notice? That "despair" does not have to be attached forever to "pit". In Terry's original statement, they were strongly conjoined. Simple surgery will show them to be separable.

> And what kind of pit was that pit before it was a pit of despair?
> *Just a hole in the ground.*

Pulling a dominant qualifier off a submissive noun demonstrates that their embrace does not have to be forever. Terry now has an opportunity to re-source the pit. He might wish to transform it into a playpit or an orchestra pit. He might be moved to fill it, bridge it, or dig deeper and mine it for reserves.

6 What is present
What else can a facilitator keep an eye out for? Is there information in the client's rate of breathing or blinking, or changes in skin tone? An increase or decrease in these vital physiological signs could be an indicator of a rise or fall in the emotional temperature.

7 What may be missing
Is there some discrepancy in the client's story or metaphor? Is there a 'child' in the landscape who has not been identified? Is the client fluent in one time-frame (past, present, or future), but hesitant in another? Given the natural or inherent logic of what is there, what may be missing?

8 Dreamscapes

Freud and Jung interpreted their patients' dreams according to their theories, but that need not deter us from questioning them cleanly. A dream is as much a source of coded information for the dreamer as their waking imagery or any other manifestation of their inner life.

Cleanly facilitated, the decoding of dreamful information is a matter for clients themselves. Whether a dream relates to wish fulfillment (Freud), universal symbolism (Jung), emotional processing (present day analysts), or is a by-product of routine repairs and maintenance (more recent theory), by the time it appears in the consulting room it is a subjectively sourced memory as valid as any other.

Dreams can be explored as ready-prepared metaphor landscapes. In the way that they bring together apparently unrelated ideas, they can be a rich source of creativity for problem solving. They can be useful convincers for clients who are doubtful or dismissive of their waking metaphors. In the metaphor landscape, as in the dreamscape, waking reality suppositions do not apply.

9 Props and costume

A client having difficulty articulating what they want to talk about can be invited to select an object or a prop to talk about instead. They can be asked to bring a symbolic object of their own with which they have an existing relationship: a souvenir, a brooch, a photograph. In the case of inner child work, a particular toy can trigger memories and associations.

Clients can be offered a large mirror and asked what they know when they look at themselves (see the Emergent Knowledge questions in Appendix C). They can be invited to choose an item of costume and dress up. Hats and masks are good for getting things going. Everything has the potential for facilitating a client's entry into the sacred halls of their psychoactivity.[1]

10 Vocal qualities

As the questions and syntax become second nature, facilitators can concern themselves less with what clients say and more on how they say it. Information that has never before seen the light of day or has been incarcerated for years may not appear at all unless the conditions set by the facilitator are favorable. Here we consider in particular the roles of

       pacing the syntax
       emphasis
       tonality
       vocal matching
       rhythm and integral markers

in optimizing the difference between everyday language as a communication tool and Clean Language as a healing art.

Pacing the syntax
A normal turn and turn about conversational style is inadequate for the delivery of Clean Language as a healing art. Subtle variations of pace are called for.

      Client *I'm determined to get it right.*

In the first, reflective, stage of the facilitator's response, rapport is established by repeating the client's words at the same pace as that which the client themself has used:

      Facilitator And you're determined to get it right.

In the second, selective, stage, the pace slows a little to help focus the client's attention on what they have said. At the same time, emphasis is placed on both the "when" of the question and the key word or phrase selected (in this case "determined"):

      A n d when y o u ' r e determined to g e t i t r i g h t ...

In framing the question in the third stage, the slower tempo is maintained, the voice takes on a quality of curiosity, and a slight emphasis is placed on "that":

      I s t h e r e a n y t h i n g e l s e a b o u t that d e t e r m i n e d?

The syntax should be delivered with a certain *élan*: confidence, artistry, and mindfulness combined. The variations of pace help focus the client's attention on what is being said, create a forward momentum for the question, and encourage a self-induced state of receptivity to the authentic voice of the unconscious. The whole has a mild trance effect not dissimilar to that created in the early stages of hypnotic induction.

Emphasis
There are choices, inevitably. Try saying the following out loud:

Is there anything else about that need to change your life?

Say it again with stress on the word "need". Again, emphasizing "change". And again, highlighting "life". Let the questions sink in. Notice your internal response. It will be different each time. I have heard it argued that a no-emphasis choice is 'cleaner' in that it encourages the client themself to select where to place their attention. But when every one of a client's words is a part-pattern that relates to the whole, and when coping with the whole is what most clients find confusing, selection by the facilitator can be very helpful indeed. It is an invitation to the client to engage in a powerful simplicity. Attention is most effective when it is undivided. The bigger picture will build, if it will, a little at a time.

Tonality
In the first two stages of the syntax, the tone or pitch of the facilitator's reflection and selection should convey that what the client has said is clearly of interest and value. In the third stage, the tone of the question should convey curiosity and care. The more a facilitator communicates their genuine interest, respect, curiosity, and care, the more seriously the client will take themself.[2]

Vocal matching
Vocal matching is not mimicking. The human voice is an exquisite barometer, sensitive to tiny shifts in emotional pressure. The modulations that convey the client's individual cadences of anxiety, affection, grief, and joy should be hinted at by the facilitator rather than imitated. Subtle physical mirroring that reflects the client's general body orientation is an aid to vocal matching. Mirroring the movement and positioning of facial muscles and lips can also help.

Rhythm and integral markers
In transcribing my exchanges with clients in this book, I have made little attempt to reproduce their patterns of tempo and flow or the presence of 'integral markers', those little pauses and hesitations that have a major effect on how we say what we say. I have snipped out most of the dithers, hums, stumbles, and stammers because in general they distracted from the point I was making. Here they are the point. In Chapter 10, I reported Colin's desired solution as:

To come out of the dark corner of my life into open sunshine and see the road ahead as sunny and bright.

Something was lost in the transcription. It could have been presented more on the lines of:

> (Pauses, makes as if to speak, pauses again) *Well, to come out of the dark corner ... er, the dark corner of my life ... into open sunshine ...* (pauses, purses lips) *... and see the road ahead as, um, sunny and bright.*

Reprising the client's repetitions and hesitations in a live session calls for some delicacy. In Colin's case, I have only to hint at his ums and ahs for him to launch into a defense of his need to be accurate. Later he acknowledges that what goes on for him in the consulting room mirrors what goes on for him outside: a continuous, at times overwhelming, barrage of internal self-correction that inhibits his spontaneity, obscures his best sense of himself, and keeps friends, colleagues, and possibly small furry animals at bay. Colin discovers the positive intention of this compulsive behavior. It saves him from the certainty that his spontaneous responses will be disparaged and rejected, which was his traumatic experience as a child who was never quite good enough for a critical father. Colin's integral markers are intensely psychoactive.

11 Timing

"Pauses are tremendous servants," said Grove. "They are response-inviting gaps in which psychoactivity takes place." Sometimes it will not even be necessary to get to the question.

> **I'm drinking because the wife left me.*
> And you're drinking because the wife left you ... (deliberate pause)
>
> *Well no, I'm drinking because I lost my job.*
> And you're drinking because ...
>
> *Okay. I know. It must be me.*
> And ...
>
> *You're saying I'm the only one who can do something about it.*

Like any performer, a facilitator needs an intuitive sense of timing to know how long to allow for the audience to respond; to determine whether a silence is psychoactive or not; and to judge the right moment to come in with the next line. Over-zealous questioning can nip psychoactivity in the bud. Equally, an overlong delay in responding can dissipate the client's attention and leave them wondering whether they left the gas on at home.

12 Placing the questions

You will know it when you feel it. There is no doubt that of the subtler skills associated with Clean Language, the precise placement of the question within the client's psychoactive space is one that challenges practitioners the most.

The aim of accurate placing is to optimize psychoactivity and the best indicator of success is that at the end of a session the client will have been so immersed in their own process that they will have little or no memory of the questions they were asked.

Questions about the client's perceptions should not go directly to the client, but *to the location of the perception to which they are addressed*. If I ask:

> *And whereabouts in your stomach could that knot be?

while looking you in the eye or gazing into space, the less embodied and relevant your response will be. Your attention is likely to be more on me than on your symptom. If instead I direct my question to your midriff, your attention will be more on the whereabouts and characteristics of the knot that has taken up residence there.

I train my attention on the spot on which I want the client to train *their* attention.

A good place to practise combining delivery and placement skills is the timespace question, "Where could X come from?" Coaxing a client into shifting their attention to the past in order to bring it into present awareness requires a tone of voice that delivers genuine curiosity with a generous helping of resolve. The client will be more inclined to make a move back in time if they believe the facilitator to be already there. Whatever metaphor you employ for the process (Grove used "pulling back" or "hauling back"; some facilitators prefer "guiding" or "coaxing"), the deed is done by conviction and tonality alone.

> And when knot in stomach, where could that knot ... [slow down, half-speed, emphasis, conviction] ... *come from?*

If the client has mapped out a metaphor landscape, we may be tempted to direct our questions to the map rather than off-map to its location in space.

There are two scenarios here: one when a symbol to which the client refers is already on the map; the other when the client comes up with a new symbol that is not on the map.

Symbol on map
The client, having first developed the symbol in imaginary space, refers to its location on the map and says something like:

I need to come down from that hilltop.

In the first phase of the syntax, we look at the hilltop on the map:

And you need to come down from that hilltop ...

Now we shift our gaze *to the location of the hilltop in the client's perceptual* space and 'place' the question there.

And when you need to come down from that hilltop, what needs to happen to come down? / What is the first step you could take? / Is there anything else about that hilltop?

Symbol not on map
While considering the map, the client comes up with a new symbol.

I need to find a good path.
And you need to find a good path ...

As before, we look first at the relevant place on the map to which the client has referred. Now the choreography changes. Having no idea where the path might be, we look *into general perceptual space.*

And when you need to find a good path, where could that good path be? / In which direction is that good path?

The question is placed off-map, but the look is not aimed in any particular direction and does not settle on any particular spot. We are inviting the client to precisely locate the symbol for themself.

13 Use of the and that

These pivotal determiners first appeared in Chapters 13 to 15. Here is a little more about them. A facilitator's first reflection will be exactly that: it will mirror what the client has said, including the definite or indefinite article ("the" or "a") if it was present.

| *It went to the heart.* | *An uneasy feeling.* |
| 1 And it went to the heart ... | 1 And an uneasy feeling ... |

The second, selective, reflection may omit the article if grammatical sense allows.

* *It went to the heart.*	**An uneasy feeling.*
1 And it went to the heart.	1 And an uneasy feeling.
2 And when it went to heart ...	2 And when uneasy feeling ...

The second part directs the client's attention unequivocally to the heart or feeling that they have just identified and not to any other heart or feeling, including any the facilitator may have imagined. The difference is small but significant. The construction "And when it went to the heart ..." would be a hint that the facilitator knew the heart too, which would not only be untrue, but could imply shared responsibility for both the metaphor and the outcome. Whereas the construction:

And when it went to *heart* ...

is directly concerned with the specificity and subjectivity of the symbol or symptom. This is personal. The client can be certain that the reference is to no other heart than theirs.

The third part of the syntax, the question, makes considered use of the demonstrative pronoun "that".

3 Is there anything else about that heart?
It's an anxious heart.

Compare two ways we can follow up on this.

* And when an anxious heart, what kind of anxious?
Oh, you know, worry, nerves, not relaxed, etc.

The generality of the question is likely to evoke a non-specific response. Whereas the subtle but unambiguous formality of

And it's an anxious heart. And when anxious heart, what kind of anxious could *that* anxious be?

respectfully invites client-specific information to appear.

After the bombings, I'm scared to go to work.

The facilitator's percipient placing of "that" invites the client to identify what distinguishes this particular instance of anxiety from any other anxiety they may have felt and from their experience of anxiety in general.

14 Gathering and tracking information

Images, sounds, and feelings hold different kinds of information and need different storage systems. How should one go about recording and retrieving live client sessions which almost always make demands on all three? The best way, I suggest, is to get clients to do it themselves (see *Metaphor landscapes* below). Some trainees take verbatim notes (think of all the nonverbal cues you may be missing). Others record sessions (tedious to transcribe), or use mind mapping (don't get carried away), or draw little diagrams of key symbols and symptoms (okay if you can decode them reliably later). Some depend on memory alone (dodgy, but you can at least give the client your total attention). I use a kind of visual-kinesthetic memory to watch the landscape unfold, but I make a point of writing down, or getting the client to write down, the exact wording of key statements, metaphors, unusual constructions, and so on. One client used to take copies of my notes away with him for homework. Not recommended for everyone, but it cleaned up my questioning and note taking no end.

Sometimes the obscure becomes dazzlingly obvious when we look back at it later. Backtracking with the aid of a verbatim record can bring to light patterns that went unnoticed at the time. It was easier to appreciate my client P's progression from perceived problem ("Too much pressure," session #1) to possible remedy ("To be less anxious," session #5) to a desired solution ("To have a strategy for dealing with my discomfort," session #9) when I was able to match the words he used to the actual sessions in which they appeared; but that was more for my education than his.

There are other uses for backtracking as a training aid: checking for common patterns across different metaphors; feeding back exactly what clients have said rather than what they think they said; reviewing a case where momentum has faltered; keeping continuity with clients who return months or years later; and, last but not least, reviewing one's own patterns of questioning: am I concentrating on one or two things to the exclusion of others?

15 Metaphor landscapes

The information that accumulates during an extended process more often than not needs a place where it can be consolidated, stored, and retrieved for review. To that end, clients can be invited to gather their ancestral, biographical, cultural, cosmological, emotional, fanciful, physiological, spatial, and temporal perceptions into a single 'self-information model', 'map', or 'metaphor landscape' as an *aide-memoire* to further work.

Andrea begins her first session with the statement

> *I feel there's a record of rejection playing in my head over and over and over.*

After an hour or so of questioning, I invite her to draw a picture incorporating the various elements that have emerged during the session:

- difficulties with her parents and brothers [narrative/biographical]
- history of gastrointestinal and menstrual problems [physiological]
- sinking feeling having three interconnected places: throat, stomach, and gut [physiological/spatial]
- second generation Greek immigrants [historical]
- belief in reincarnation [spiritual/cosmological]

If words are the poor servants of consciousness, images are the elected representatives of the unconscious. What Andrea actually draws is an outline of herself with a blob in the area of her throat and a thick line down to her stomach, where it is attached to a big weight below which is an old anchor.

Figure 14   Andrea's metaphor map

This is the view from a world beyond words. A metaphor landscape is a personalized virtual reality comparable to any physical environment; a psychoactive space in and around the client in which information resides and is represented in kind. Andrea's drawing offers her two kinds of perspective: a view of the relative shapes, sizes, and dispositions of the symbols in her landscape; and a guide to the weight and significance of the feelings and problems represented there.

Metaphor landscapes may be in any medium: a collage, a mime, a poem, a flow chart, a set of sticky notes, a tableau of cushions. They are limited only by the inclination and imagination of the client and the materials to hand.

There is nothing illusory about the mental images from which metaphor landscapes are composed, by the way. The images are as real as any other internal sensation. The notion of a personal metaphor landscape as a kind of projection theatre for the unconscious is closely allied to Kant's basic model of the mind as an active originator of experience rather than its passive recipient. For visually related information to exist at all, our minds have to actively produce and perceive it. We do in a real sense create and construct what we see.[3]

Psychiatrist Gerald Epstein, founder of the American Institute of Mental Imagery, calls image:

> the natural and true language of the inside life; a silent language communication from invisible reality and visible reality.

There is a long history of therapists working with their clients' mental imagery, from Jung's 'guided imagery' to Desoille's 'rêve evéillé' or 'waking dream', Shorr's 'psycho-imagination therapy', and Frederking's 'deep relaxation symbolism'. Each of these practitioners acknowledged the autonomy of their clients' imagery and the value to clients of exploring their inner worlds in their own way, but in practice all intervened and interpreted the imagery in varying degrees. "Some set the initial metaphor," notes creativity researcher John Martin; "some offered interpretations to the client; some formed their own interpretations – possibly based on their prior theories about the nature of therapy – and then used these to direct the action."[4]

In contrast, Clean Language process dispenses with direction and avoids therapist interpretation altogether.

Metaphor mapping can be done relatively quickly. It allows complexity to be parked; it provides a resting place for what may be a fast-moving dynamic process; and it allows the client time to assimilate information: to notice it, process it, and find new connections. A map makes the implicit relationships between features in the mental landscape explicit. The act of plotting and portraying information invariably prompts more information to appear. It is a live, not an archival, act.

16 Provisional modeling

"Doubt is not a pleasant condition," wrote Voltaire, "but certainty is absurd."[5] Working assumptions have always formed the basis of our exploration of the unknown. If I go in this direction, I might find food. If I don't find it, I can take another direction.

Any assumptions I make about Andrea's "I feel there's a record of rejection playing in my head over and over and over" will be beset by reasonable doubt. I will assign every one of my assumptions, beliefs, and their attendant uncertainties to a 'provisional model'. After all, my sense of what Andrea means by what she says is based on my internal representation of my perception of my experience of her description of her internal representation of her perception of her experience! The original feelings that resulted in "a record of rejection" playing in her head "over and over and over" have been obscured under multiple layers of mental processing. I shall get nowhere near them using conventional tools. Any particles I detect will only be the tiniest trace of her experience. Any suggestions I offer on the basis of that faint echo can only distract or confuse her.

Like most difficulties in life, in relationship, and understanding, they will spring from what systems researcher Maurice Brasher describes as:

> our failure to understand that every individual is operating out of *their own individual epistemology* [his italics]. This explains why people's systems are so resistant to conventional intervention, held together as they are in a structure composed of experience and perceptions glued together by beliefs and values.[6]

If instead I question Andrea's "record of rejection" cleanly, she will update my provisional model of her model with every response. Even if one of my questions is prompted by a supposition that turns out to be false, the question itself will make no reference to the supposition. Given the strict protocol of the syntax, my question can only refer to what Andrea herself has said. I will abandon any interim theory that I may have concocted the second it is corrected and incorporate any part of it the moment it is confirmed. I am like a child building a tower with toy bricks. Any brick I place wrongly will topple off. The tower will only grow with the bricks that fit.

When Colin first expressed his desire to "move out of the dark corner" of his life, I privately supposed that the "dark" of his corner represented something unpleasant or sinister. The question I asked, however, was:

And when dark corner, what kind of dark could the dark of
that dark corner be?

which allows for my suspicion, but contains no hint of it. The
strength of the art and science of Clean Language lies in its ability
to work with every scintilla of uncertainty in the gap between client
reality and facilitator fantasy.

17 No such thing as 'resistance'

One way of maintaining an open attitude towards provisional
modeling is to acknowledge that there is no such thing as a
'difficult' or 'resistant' client, only "the client's way of training the
facilitator to ask a better question," as Grove described it.
'Resistance' is in any case a therapist-generated metaphor. It is also
a nominalization, a noun formed from a perceived action (resisting)
or the perceived nature of that which is resisting (resistant).
Therapists who encounter resistance could do worse than ask
themselves what it is they are resisting or where they feel resistant.
If we consider the carefully arranged zones of authority in some
consulting rooms, the definition of 'resistance' as an underground
movement engaged in secret operations against an occupying force
might reasonably describe a patient's natural reaction to a certain
kind of therapist – not so much resistant or hostile as heroically
resilient in the face of persistent emotional encroachment.

A Clean Language client might respond with reluctance or
equivocation to a poorly timed intervention, or might ask for a
question to be repeated. It can happen if the client is still
processing their response to the previous question or, having
considered the question in one way, is responding to it in another.
Psychoactivity takes place in the moment and if a facilitator is
insensitive to the moment, a Clean question might well be, at that
moment, the 'wrong' question. Client responses such as "I don't
understand the question" are a sure way of reminding the
facilitator to update their provisional model. The ground on which
change happens is always shifting, and always helpfully.

18 Client outcomes

Every seeker after change boards an open-top bus with an
uncertain destination. As psychoanalyst Darian Leader puts it:

> most therapies offer precisely what can't be predetermined. You
> can never know what you're going to get, and that's why it's an

inherently risky process. Indeed, therapy often fosters a recognition that life isn't predictable, neat or safe.[7]

Getting something one wants invariably means giving up on something else. It can be difficult to predict what that will be, because every developmental process is unique and neither client nor facilitator can have any certainty about the precise outcome. This is why attempts to restrict psychotherapy to an externally regulated system that permits customers to sue the service provider if they don't deliver the goods must fail, because it is in the nature of self-derived change to evolve, and to continue to do so long after the original work has concluded.

Critics of Clean Language's all-inclusive approach to client outcomes question whether a facilitator should ever work with a client outcome that is at odds with their values. What if a client desires something the facilitator believes to be pernicious or dubious?

I start from an acknowledgment, shared by most of the facilitators I know, that every preference, need, or desire is formed from within a client's existing limitations. The work clients undertake is aimed at surmounting those limitations. That said, I have yet to come across a client with an outcome such as "I want to be really nasty to everyone." If I did, I might ask:

*And where could that want to be really nasty come from?

A question that would probably lead to a hidden vulnerability or to a feeling of shame or guilt that the client-victim would rather not possess. One of my client M's early offerings was

I'd like to land one on my dad that he'd never forget.

It had me thinking twice about how to respond. In fact, the Clean syntax permits me to acknowledge – even honor – a statement like this as present and provisional, without the least need to approve or disapprove, confront or appease, interpret or even believe it.

And how do you know you'd like to land one on your dad that he'd never forget?
How do I know? Cos I get this really sick feeling here.

The rest of the session is spent discovering more about M's really sick feeling. And at the start of the next session, he says:

I feel better for getting things off my chest, I've given it a lot of

thought, I want to learn how to control my temper, and to lose the
nausea it causes me, and gain confidence.

Not unusually, the client has moved on. Values that might be
dormant or half-formed at the start of a process tend to mature and
become more explicit as the client's knowledge of themself develops
and their requirements of others change. M went on to work at
separating the aim of his vexatious behavior – to deflect the critical
expectations of others – from the means he had been using to
achieve it – belligerence and abuse. As Edward de Bono once said,
"Sometimes you have to journey south for a while in order to
journey north."

19 Unconscious thinking

'Unconscious thinking' is not a contradiction in terms. To think is to
direct one's mind to something, and that can be done consciously or
unconsciously. There has been a great deal of research to show that
people who rely overmuch on the linear process of conscious
reasoning tend not to make the best choices. A study by Dutch
psychologist Ap Dijksterhuis found that conscious thinkers and
reasoners can only focus on a few things at a time.

> Although consciousness can be said to be 'smart' and rational, it is
> also of very limited capacity. This means that when making
> decisions about rather complex, multifaceted issues, conscious
> thought can be maladaptive and lead to poor decisions.[8]

A predominantly cerebral facilitator faced with emotional
complexity in a client is likely to give some factors undue
importance at the expense of others. Unconscious thinkers do not
suffer from this capacity limit. Large amounts of information can be
integrated and evaluated without reference to conscious reflection.
It is true that a question arising from an immediate response to
what the client has said will have been heavily influenced by a
disorderly mix of the facilitator' own associations, needs, and beliefs
– a mishmash that cannot always be trusted to come up with the
best question. But if the question is Clean, it can never be entirely
wrong. Members of our Research Group tried hard on occasion to
ask the 'wrong' Clean question of each other and failed. In the
examples below, the questions were the least likely the facilitators
could think of in response to what their clients had said.

I've always had a fear of flying.
And when 'a' fear, what kind of 'a' could that 'a' be?

Actually it's several fears rolled into one.
(Client goes on to explain.)

I'm having some problems with anger.
And is there anything else about that 'with'?
I guess the feeling is with *me, not against me. It's doing something for me.* (Goes on to discover what.)

It's like I'm watching my life instead of getting on with it.
And does that 'watching' have a size or a shape?
Yes, the shape of a fob-watch in a waistcoat pocket, I can choose to leave it there or take it out. (Proceeds to work on choices.)

The information that came up for these volunteer clients turned out to be no less relevant than information that came up from more 'sensible' questioning. One learning for our researchers was not to concern themselves overmuch with being 'right'. Another was to continue gathering experience in the knowledge that intuition feeds best off the accumulation of reserves.

20 Tips from trainees
A general practitioner halfway through Clean Language training said this:

> I'm glad to be reminded that the facilitator's primary purpose is to get the client to model symbolically, not to change or to challenge their model. Coming from a medical model where the practitioner is supposed to have a body of knowledge that is imposed on the patient, this has been the most difficult aspect for me to change. I'm having a crash course in boundaries.

The comments below come from by a life coach, a therapist, and a teacher.

> The format supports me in not contaminating client process with my own assumptions about the client. This is going to help me in meeting the needs of others.

> When I'm in counseling mode and working intuitively and empathically, I tend to be 'ahead' of the client and readily interrupt them. The difference with Clean Language and Metaphor is that I'm staying with the client and not moving ahead of them. I'm a part of them rather than separate from.

> I appreciate the simplicity of the questions and what they can evoke. It's a process in which those questioned process themselves. They themselves know where they need to go.

And these words of advice to their peers come from other trainees:

> Trust the process.
> Don't worry if nothing seems to happen.
> Keep it simple.
> Be one hundred per cent present.
> No matter how much theory and experience you have,
> remember you know nothing.
> The client does not have to change.

The client will often change anyway. And then what happens?

Notes to Chapter 19

1 Use of props, costume, and mirrors in therapy. See the *Reflections* exercise in Chapter 5, Part Six of *The Power of Six*, op. cit. In France, Silvie de Clerck and Jennifer de Gandt have created a set of 'Clean Cards Nature' with images that invite the client to take a walk through their inner landscape and a set of 'Clean Cards Passages', which can be used in a game about change. Visit metaphores.eu. A set of 'Clean Change Cards' and 'Metaphor Cards' with tips for facilitating group and individual work can be found at cleanchange.co.uk.

2 Delivery of the Clean Language syntax: the video *A Strange and Strong Sensation* (cleanlanguage.co.uk) features a client session facilitated by Penny Tompkins and James Lawley working in tandem. Every practitioner has their own way of asking the questions, but Tompkins and Lawley offer two excellent models.

3 The mind as active originator rather than passive recipient of experience: Immanuel Kant, *Critique of Pure Reason* ('Kritik der reinen Vernunft'), 1781.

4 History of guided imagery and differences to Grovian metaphor: researcher John Martin in his *Review of 'Metaphors in Mind'* by Lawley and Tompkins, in *Metaphor and Symbol* 22 (2) 2007.

5 "Doubt is not a pleasant condition, but certainty is absurd." From one of Voltaire's many letters to Frederik II of Prussia, 1767 ('La doute n'est pas une condition agréable, mais la certitude est absurde').

6 Why people's systems are resistant to conventional intervention: Maurice Brasher, personal communication.

7 A political dimension to client outcomes: psychoanalyst Darian Leader in an article in *The Guardian*, 10 December 2010: *Therapy shows us life is not neat or safe. So why judge it by those criteria?* More on therapist regulation at psyreg.co.uk

8 "Unconscious thinkers" make the best choices: social psychologist Ap Dijksterhuis, *When Not To Think: The Role of Conscious and Unconscious Processes in Decision Making*, University of Amsterdam 2003.

Chapter 20
When Change Happens

Of suffering comes ease.   Shakespeare, *Henry IV Part 2*

Three kinds of change: rearrangement, translation, transformation – Andy's path to the sea – Maturing the change – Roz's resilience and grace – Limits which have no limit

As clients learn to discern and decode the patterns in their drawn, spatial, or imagined metaphor landscapes, the information held there is released and one of three things will happen.

> 1   Change of a kind. Symbols will *rearrange* or be *reassigned.* There will be some learning by the client, but no fundamental change in the pattern.

When ice melts a little and re-freezes, some internal crystals and air bubbles change size and shape, but the overall structure stays the same. The client will know a little more about themself, but life goes on much the same. The system remains in self-preservation mode. It may even shift its organization sideways so as not to change. The facilitator's job is to continue drawing the client's attention to any part of the landscape with the potential for change (which may be any part), or inviting the client to move one element forward in time to see how it evolves. Any one such move could be the first of a series of incremental steps to change.

Alternatively or subsequently, there will be:

> 2   Some change. Symbols *translate* in their relationship to one another. Patterns repeat, but in a different guise, resulting in new but not necessarily wholly different modes of behavior, feeling, or belief.

Ice melts to form water. There is some fluidity and movement, but water can only take the shape and gradient of whatever contains it. The client's perceptions will modify to a certain extent, but problem patterns will repeat, albeit in a different form.

There is nothing inherently bad in translation. Time spent re-experiencing the pattern in other ways can have considerable value. Clients can use it to test and confirm a pattern; or to recognize when they are and when they are not in the pattern; or to explore what have hitherto been unacknowledged patterns with new insight. Holistic philosopher Ken Wilber maintains that translation is a necessary and important function for the greater part of our lives; those who cannot translate adequately, he suggests, fall into severe neurosis or psychosis.

At some point, repeatedly doing the same old thing and just getting by will cease to console. To maintain health or sanity, the nature of the related feeling, thinking, or behavior has to change fundamentally. It may require only one of the elements that make up its circularity to change. One question can make all the difference, just as a single instruction can dramatically change a computer program's behavior. And what happens next is:

3 Radical change. Symbols and their relationships *transform*.
New patterns of being, thinking, or feeling emerge.

As water heats, its molecules move more freely and eventually metamorphose into steam, which can travel in any direction. Rather than merely translating as a result of self-modeling, a client's patterns change fundamentally. And what results is a qualitatively new pattern of organization. Transformation may occur suddenly and spontaneously or gradually and cumulatively.

As I was looking for examples to illustrate these three phases of change, I realized that my journalist client Andy (Chapter 19), had been through all three in quick succession.

Andy's path to the sea

At the age of nineteen, Andy made a difficult decision to leave his home in the western isles and travel to London. Twenty years later, he came into therapy. And after several sessions during which the theme of water in all its forms has been a constant companion, a source of both misery and consolation, he summarizes what he calls his "impending depression" in a metaphor of

A dark cloud coming up on me ...

An image he relates to the fear and shame that shadowed his days as a child and the self-doubts that follow him now. He continues:

> *... a dark cloud drifting in from the west.*
> And when dark cloud drifting in from the west, then what happens?
>
> *The cloud is blown to the mountains.*

A symbolic *rearrangement* or *reassignment*. The form of the symbol has not changed, but Andy has shifted its location, upped the ante ("drifting" has evolved into "blown"), and a new symbol ("mountains") has emerged. Mountains are attended by both promise and peril. If they represent the guardians of change, they have the power to both assist and obstruct Andy's progress. Either way, they are not going to make his progress inevitable.

> And when that cloud is blown to mountains, then what happens?
> *There's heavy rain.*

A significant *translation* of form. The challenge of the mountains has compelled Andy to make another adjustment. Although the form of the new symbol ("rain") has characteristics in common with the old symbol ("cloud"), it represents movement of a different kind. If dark cloud cannot get past mountains, perhaps heavy rain can.

> And when that heavy rain, then what happens?
> *The rain becomes a stream.*

A further *translation* of form. A new pattern emerges. Stream may have more transport potential than cloud and conceivably greater potential for progress than rain.

> And what kind of stream could that stream be?
> *The stream becomes a river.*

Another *translation*. The momentum for change seems to be growing. (My private and provisional hypothesis about what is happening. It does not necessarily reflect the client's experience or intention; nor does it affect my next question.)

> And when stream becomes river, then what happens?
> *The river meets the sea.*

> And what kind of meets could that meets be?
> *Joining, connecting, becoming part of the bigger whole.*

A *transformation*. A series of translations have resulted in a qualitative change. Andy's patterns around water – cloud, rain, stream, river, sea – have shifted onto a higher level of organization. Now he is "joining, connecting, becoming". A series of thresholds have been crossed and a new way of being has emerged.

Andy goes on to relate the idea of connecting and becoming part of a bigger whole to his home life, work, and relationships.

Rearrangement, translation, and transformation are not in the habit of eliding one into the other as readily as this. Clients normally have to spend time in one phase of change before being ready for the next. Thresholds to change are personal and relative. They can appear in the metaphor landscape in the form of natural barriers like mountain ranges and rivers, crossing points like doors and bridges, or social constructs like rituals and ceremonies.

Facilitators can draw the client's attention to unrealized or unrecognized thresholds to change and assist in developing their potential.

Maturing the change

Transformation is not the end of the process, but it is likely to be the beginning of the end. The client has journeyed to a new place and needs time and space to acclimatize. Andy is invited to become more familiar with his "joining, connecting, becoming" and then to develop them into a single, potentially more powerful symbol.

> And when joining, connecting, becoming part of the bigger whole,
> all that is like what?
> *A channel of light.*

> And what kind of light could the light of that channel be?
> *A soothing light.*

> And would that channel of soothing light be interested in going to
> dark cloud drifting in from the west?
> *Oh yes, I think so.*

> And as channel of soothing light goes to dark cloud drifting in from
> the west, then what happens?
> *The cloud fades and disappears.*

And as cloud fades and disappears, then what happens?
I am in the light.

And as you are in the light, is there anything else about that
light?
It gradually brightens.

And as it gradually brightens, then what happens?
I absorb its rays.

And as you absorb its rays, then what happens?
I feel myself again.

And as you feel yourself again, then what happens?
No doubts. No fears.

Roz's resilience and grace

Roz is a hospital administrator who lost her sight through retinal
cancer at the age of six. As a child, she had the idea that growing
up meant suppressing all feeling. Being able to hold back on
expressing fear or joy was closely aligned in her mind with the idea
of restraining uncontrolled cancerous growth.

> *As if I were afraid that letting myself out would result in unleashed
> destruction and death.*

Over the course of her therapy, Roz develops an imaginative
landscape featuring gardens, woods, and a freshwater spring. She
explores these resources, develops their relationship with each
other, then packs them into a portmanteau resource she calls
"maple tree". As maple tree takes root, Roz readily identifies with
its redemptive potential: its beauty, growth, fullness, and bounty.
But as the natural logic of the metaphor takes her through summer
and fall to the chill of winter, she becomes concerned about the real-
life implications of a time of no-growth and death. She persists,
however, and learns to accept the winter branches of maple tree as
an essential part of her identity. And after a few more sessions, she
reaches a point where she feels able to mature the transformative
process on her own.

In an email several months later, she describes how she decoded
her symbolic perceptions and applied what she learned to her life.
There may be lessons here about challenges we all have to face.

> *I saw that my winter branches were made up in part with healthy
> muscles, their shape and movement showing flex and strength. And*

I noticed that having accepted winter into my formation, I could take another step in my understanding. Suddenly I came to see that my failures – losses, breakages, weaknesses, particularly the public ones – were actually a kind of ministry.

She explains her 'ministry' in terms of both healing and teaching.

Before I realized the wholeness, comprehensiveness, inner and native balance of my tree, I feared failure in the view of others. Now it seems to me that when my experiences of vulnerability happen, they are occasions for modeling survival – potentially a great benefit to others suffering from fear of public humiliation or loss.

Since childhood, I always had the gift of survival. The difference now is that I embrace it. I feel the artful beauty that comes from a tree: scarred, broken, windswept, under, then over-nourished, too close and then too far from shelter; growing strong with resilience and grace.

I am reminded to cherish the capacity for healing and teaching in every one of us and to note, again, that the work does not end when the facilitator is no longer present.

Limits which have no limit

Clean Language is a simple, resilient technology for self-realization and change. Anyone can pick up the basics in a day or two and learn to do no harm with the questions. At a deeper level, it is an exceptionally responsive model of psychotherapy, counseling, and coaching; a synthesis of principle and procedure in which the facilitator must continually be asking themself, "At this precise moment, what is the question my client's system requires?" It is the client, after all, who determines the significance of their perceptions. And as the system learns about its own organization, it is the client who determines what needs to happen for that to adapt, translate, or transform.

A thousand years from now, when mental well being is deemed as universal a human right as the right to life, when cognitive-enhancing drugs and microchip implants are as common as aspirin, when, who knows, we might even be on the verge of eliminating poverty, injustice, oppression, and corruption, we will still want to feel better about ourselves and to help others feel better in turn. The least we can do then, having long since embraced the self-psychology of change and the role of symbol and metaphor in subjective experience, is to stick to the disciplines of accurate reflection, selective attention, and non-assumptive questioning – *and to trust in the process.*

"I rarely end up where I was intending to go," wrote science fiction author Douglas Adams, "but often I end up somewhere that I needed to be." He gave this line to holistic detective Dirk Gently in *The Long Dark Tea-Time of the Soul.* Detective Gently may not have realized it at the time, but he was describing the transformational journey.

Journey's end may appear as gradually as the dawn or it can pop up out of nowhere. My client Tim reported just such a moment as he stepped out of the shower one morning. After fourteen years of depression and paranoia and eight weeks of Clean changework, he suddenly heard a voice saying:

You are a worthwhile person.

It was followed immediately by another saying:

I am a worthwhile person.

He recognized the voice as his own. Tim was nourishing his original breath. No journey of the mind is impossible, he knew at that moment; it is only a matter of navigation.

References and Further Reading

Steve Ayan, *Psychotherapy on Trial*, Scientific American April/May 2006

Judy Barber, *Good Question! The Art of Asking Questions to Bring About Positive Change*, Bookshaker 2005

Max Born, *Symbol and Reality*, in *Physics in My Generation*, Springer 1969

Fritjof Capra, *The Web of Life: A New Synthesis of Mind and Matter*, HarperCollins 1997

Francis Charet, *Spiritualism and the Foundations of Jung's Psychology*, New York 1993

Daniel C. Dennett, *Freedom Evolves*, Viking Penguin 2003

Antonio Domasio, Looking for Spinoza: Joy, Sorrow, and The Feeling Brain, Heinemann 2003

Angela Dunbar, *Essential Life Coaching Skills*, Routledge 2009

Moshe Feldenkrais, *Body and Mature Behavior: A Study of Anxiety, Sex, Gravitation, and Learning*, Frog Books 1949

Jerome A. Feldman, *From Molecule to Metaphor, A Neural Theory of Language*, MIT 2006

Richard A. Firmage, *The Alphabet Abecedarium*, Bloomsbury 2000

Sigmund Freud, *The Interpretation of Dreams*, 1900, translated by A. A. Brill 1913

Eugene Gendlin, *Focusing*, Everest House 1978, Bantam 1981

Malcolm Gladwell, *Blink: The Power of Thinking without Thinking*, Allen Lane 2005

David Grove and Basil Panzer: *Resolving Traumatic Memories: Metaphors and Symbols in Psychotherapy*, Irvington 1989

Philip Harland, *The Power of Six: A Six Part Guide to Self Knowledge*, Wayfinder 2009

Aldous Huxley, *The Doors of Perception*, Chatto & Windus 1954, Vintage 2004

C.G. Jung, *Synchronicity, An Acausal Connecting Principle*, 1952, translator R.F.C. Hull, Routledge & Kegan Paul 1972; *Man and his Symbols*, Aldus 1964

Arthur Koestler, *The Act of Creation*, Barnes & Noble 1976, Penguin 1990

Alfred Korzybski, *Science and Sanity: An Introduction to Non-Aristotelian Systems and General Semantics*, Institute of General Semantics, 5th edition 1993

James Lawley and Penny Tompkins, *Metaphors in Mind: Transformation through Symbolic Modelling*, Developing Company 2000

Joseph LeDoux, *The Emotional Brain*, Weidenfeld & Nicolson 1998

Seth Lindstromberg, *English Prepositions Explained*, John Benjamins 1997

John Martin and Caitlin Walker, *Practical Thinking*, UK Open University course 2004

Jeffrey Masson, *Against Therapy*, HarperCollins 1989

George Orwell, *Politics and the English Language* (1946), in *Why I Write*, Penguin 2004

Steven Pinker, *How The Mind Works*, Penguin 1999

Barry Posner and James Kouzes, *The Leadership Challenge*, Jossey-Bass 1987, 2003

Martin Rees, *Will the Human Race Survive the Twentyfirst Century?* Heinemann 2003

Carl R. Rogers, *On Becoming a Person*, Houghton Mifflin 1961

Jacqueline Rose, *Psychoanalysis and the Modern World*, Chatto & Windus 2003

Anne Wilson Schaef, *Beyond Therapy, Beyond Science*, Harper 1992

John R. Searle, *Mind, Language, and Society*, Weidenfeld & Nicolson 1999; *Mind*, Oxford 2004

Wendy Sullivan and Judy Rees, *Clean Language, Revealing Metaphors and Opening Minds*, Crown House 2008

Kathryn L. Taylor, *The Inner Child Workbook*, Tarcher 1991

Francisco Varela, *Neurophenomenology*, Journal of Consciousness Studies June 1996

Caitlin Walker, *Clean Language and Systemic Modelling*, Training Attention DVD 2007

Carol Wilson, *Best Practice in Performance Coaching*, Kogan-Page 2007

Ken Wilber, *The Collected Works*, Shambhala 1994-2008

Stephen Wolfram, *A New Kind of Science*, Wolfram Media 2002

Irvin Yalom, *The Gift of Therapy*, Perennial 2002

Appendix A
Metaphor in Emotional Management

You are not thinking, you are merely being logical.
Neils Bohr to Albert Einstein

An exercise that adapts to almost any developmental or therapeutic need.

1 ELICIT 'HOW IT IS NOW' (METAPHOR #1)
Invite client to generate a metaphor for a feeling (anger, frustration, sadness, etc.) that they would rather not have, or for when they act inappropriately as a result of the feeling: *That is like what?*
Ask basic Clean questions of the metaphor or its constituent symbols to clarify: *What kind of X could that X be? Is there anything else about that X?*
The intention is not to seek change or to develop the metaphor, but for the client to get more information about it as it is.
Invite client to map/draw Metaphor #1 and place it where it needs to be.

2 ELICIT 'HOW YOU WOULD LIKE IT TO BE' (METAPHOR #2)
Invite client to generate a metaphor for how they would prefer to feel or respond: *That is like what?*
Ask basic Clean questions of the metaphor (as step #1).
Invite client to map/draw Metaphor #2 and place it where it needs to be.

3 COMPARE
Invite client to find a space that knows about both #1 and #2. Ask: *Within the context of the metaphor, how can [Metaphor #1] become [Metaphor #2]?*.

4 APPRAISE
What is the first thing that needs to happen for [#1] to become [#2]?
If indicated: *What is the next thing? And the next?* Invite client to map/draw any intermediate stages.
Finally: *What is the last thing that needs to happen?*
Invite client to generate and draw a new metaphor that represents the whole process of #1 becoming #2.

5 FUTURE PACE
How will the information in the metaphor guide you in the future?
Invite the client to start getting used to being/feeling/acting like #2 by embodying its qualities: *What is your posture? What do you feel? Where is your attention? What do you say and how?*

6 ACTION PLAN
What will you do? When? etc., as end of Emergent Knowledge, Appendix C.

After an original exercise by Penny Tompkins and James Lawley

Appendix B
Clean Case Histories

"I want everyone to love me" – "Can stop me feeling sad?" – "Did you know that people on average eat eight spiders in a lifetime?"

These cases select themselves for a number of reasons, not least the existence of verbatim transcripts and the fact that the work lasted a matter of weeks rather than months, so that you can see a beginning, a middle, and an end to the client's process fairly succinctly. The only elements I have altered are any that might have identified clients, but I have not done this to a pattern, so no key exists that would unlock the lot. Here and there, I have summarized chunks of what took place in a single sentence and omitted sidetracks that might have diverted the reader from the client's main path. As elsewhere in the book, I have omitted the repetitive elements of the full syntax, though if you are not already familiar with these, I urge you to remind yourself of their importance in practice by revisiting Chapters 13, 14, and 15.

The effect of the editing decisions I have taken might give the impression that clients for Clean Language and Therapeutic Metaphor get what they want in an efficient and orderly way. This is not always the case! For reasons of space, I have selected cases where the clients were more self-aware than average and got where they wanted to be relatively quickly. You can imagine for yourself those who needed more time.

The success attached to the stories here is not mine, but that of the methodology – drawing attention to exactly what the client has said or expressed and asking Clean questions of it. The cases celebrate the ability most people have in the right circumstances to focus their attention and to tap into their resources in the most remarkable way.

It so happens that each of these examples is a love story. The client sets off in pursuit of a certain kind of love and ends up finding love of another kind.

♥

"I want everyone to love me"

The phone rings.

> Hello. I'm Chris, I've been recommended to you by J. She told me you wouldn't be bamboozled by my language.

Chris goes on to talk about himself at length. He is a history lecturer in his early thirties, confused about the discrepancies he perceives between his attitudes to work and to his private life. Eventually I get to ask him:

> And with all that what would you like to have happen?

Chris is thrown for a moment, then answers carefully and precisely.

I want everyone to love me and to be something special. (Pauses) *And I want to be honest, but I don't want to hurt people.*

He launches off again, talking at length about what he calls his "high sex drive," which gets him into trouble on a Tuesday night after playing rugby and going drinking. He makes an appointment for 9 a.m. on a Wednesday a couple of weeks ahead. At 8.30 a.m. on the day, he phones to apologize. He spent the night at the pub, he says, got into "a bit of a thing with someone," slept through two alarms, and is going to be late. When he arrives, I ask him what he would like to have happen in the time remaining. He thinks for a moment, then states:

I want to be able to make the decision to behave in an ethical way.

I invite him to write this up on the flipchart. Unusually, he uses three colors and divides his outcome neatly into three parts.

I want to be able [in grey]
to make the decision [in red]
to behave in an ethical way [in blue].

He explains the significance of the colors: grey because he presumes he is able to do this; red for importance – this is what he needs to work on; and blue is "me when my head and heart are together." I ask him:

Is there anything else about that want to be able to make the decision to behave in an ethical way?

Under the words, Chris draws three little figures. The figure on the left is "a thoughtful Chris behind a big clear window." The figure on the right is "a passionate Chris on the edge of the chair ready for action." And the figure between them is "a balanced Chris assessing the situation."

And when a thoughtful Chris, a passionate Chris, and a balanced Chris, now what would you like to have happen?

He looks at the drawing for a moment.

I'd like the thoughtful Chris to walk out of his house that protects him and travel some way with the passionate Chris in the balanced Chris that they both are ... so that I can stop and look at things.

It is the end of a short session. A week later, he tells me:

I've been trying to be honest with people. There's no point in being loved if it's not for what you are.

And he asks:

Do you think people change just by thinking about themselves and talking?

He goes on:

I am changing. I am being more honest.

He develops a metaphor landscape of his ideal, ethical self at home in what he identifies as "a Tudor tithe barn". It is very open and light, with a fireplace, sofas, and a gallery. I pick up on the unusual words he has used.

And is there anything else about that Tudor tithe barn?
Well, a tithe barn was used to hold produce given as a local tax, usually to support the parish church.

And when you are at home in Tudor tithe barn [etc], what happens next?

Chris finds himself in the 16th century, representing the village laborers in a dispute with the local landowner. In a light trance state, he likens the role to mediating between the two conflicting parts of himself: the remote academic and the promiscuous drinker. He is beginning to decode his metaphor. After a while considering the mediating role, he realizes:

It is possible to be lonely and gregarious. I don't have to be one or the other. I am the teacher in the middle, trying to improve communication between both sides.

After another three sessions of intense work, he is able to say:

I'm more settled. More sure of my place, and my importance or my lack of importance. I'm less arrogant. More open to hearing other people. I can stand back a bit.
And when you can stand back a bit, then what happens?

I can sit on the shore and watch the tide and watch the world go by.

His metaphor landscape has transformed. I invite him to map out the differences. He studies his new drawing. I ask:

And when you can sit on the shore [etc], what happens to 'I want everyone to love me' and 'I want to be honest and not hurt people'?
It's easier to be able to make decisions.

And when it's easier to be able to make decisions, then what happens?
I'm much stronger.

And as you're much stronger then what happens?
Thoughtful Chris and passionate Chris are more of an entity.

And what would thoughtful Chris and passionate Chris like to do?

He looks at his drawing.

To go for a walk or swim to somewhere I don't know and taste the pure air.

And a few sessions later:

Probably 80% of the time now I'm just whoever I am. I can be thoughtful with my rugby friends and playful with my history lot.
And when [I repeat this back to him], then what happens?

He refers to his picture of the figure on the beach.

I'm walking now. I'm not afraid of meeting people along the way and interacting properly. I don't have such a high self-image to project. I've worked out how to be happy on my own. I can be who I prefer to be.

♥

"Can you stop me feeling sad?"

Gina is a personal assistant in her late twenties who laughs and cries readily. She has just left her boyfriend and is fearful of ending up as depressed as her mother had been after leaving Gina's father when Gina was sixteen. Gina's first words are:

Can you stop me feeling sad?

She dissolves into tears and takes a tissue. I ask her:

What would you like to have happen?
I want to feel I'm on the road to recovery.

And when you want to feel you're on the road to recovery, what kind of road could that road be?

She laughs. I invite her to map out her road.

It looks like an angry road, but it's not meant to be angry.
And is there anything else about that road that looks like an angry road, but is not meant to be angry?

It's an internal road that leads to and from anger.
And where is that anger?

She puts a hand to her chest.

I want to have left him not having so much regret. I want to stop torturing myself with the past and what might have happened. I want forgiveness for myself for leaving him and being angry. I want freedom from the past. I want to feel loved.

Gina seems to have constructed an equivalence between leaving her boyfriend and freeing herself from her mother's depression, but in doing so, she is finding herself in what must feel like an impossible bind. In leaving her boyfriend she feels depressed, and in feeling depressed she cannot escape from her mother. I invite her to write her last words, "I want to feel loved," on the flipchart. She hesitates, then writes slowly and in a childish hand. I ask her what happened for her while she was doing this.

I felt very young.
And where is that very young?

Somewhere here. (She puts a hand to her middle)
And whereabouts here?

Just above my tummy button.
And whereabouts just above your tummy button?

About an inch, half an inch.
And how far in is that very young, or is it on the surface?

It's just inside.
And is there anything else about that very young just above your tummy button and just inside?

She opens her mouth. She looks sad.

It's like an open mouth.
And is there anything else about that open mouth?

It's going ... (she mouths 'waaah') ...
And where could that (I mouth 'waaah') come from?

She starts to cry and takes another tissue.

A seven or eight year-old tomboy.
And where could that seven or eight year-old tomboy come from?

A five year-old girl.
And what could that five year-old girl be wearing?

She brightens again.

A bright yellow dress.

It is near the end of the session. Gina's homework is to map out the seven or eight year-old tomboy and the five year-old girl in the bright yellow dress. The following week, she says:

I was breaking down in tears last week. But now I feel stronger, because I'm concentrating on me. I don't feel guilty about burdening you, because I'm paying you. I feel regret for giving up my boyfriend who loved me.

She looks at her drawings.

I'm just going round in circles. That's my life. Too much is going on.

She maps this out. In the center of a body outline she draws a large pink oval and inside this, a small black circle surrounded by five yellow circles.

Figure 15 Gina "just going round in circles"

She points to the black circle at the center.

It's a black evil knot in the middle. It's depression. (She laughs) *I suppose it's healthy to be able to see yourself 'doing depression'!*
And what would you like to have happen now?

To feel more positive and not to feel so lonely. To acknowledge it's okay to feel lonely sometimes. It's wanting to make everything right.

She refers back to her original 'road to and from anger'.

I'm always looking back to it, and then to the circles.

She decides to redraw the circles.

Figure 16 Gina transforms her circles into petals

The five yellow circles now touch the black circle, so that they look like petals round the heart of a flower. Gina suddenly sees the resemblance.

Oh! It's like a flower. Like a gerbera. It's got good things in it as well as bad. Excitement and hope coming from depression.

She captions her drawing, "A flower of excitement and hope."

And what does that flower of excitement and hope want?
Rain – my rain. Care.

Gina's unconscious has come up with three potentially redemptive symbols – "road that leads to and from anger," "flower of excitement and hope," and "my rain, care". I remind her of her original outcome ("I want to feel I'm on the road to recovery") and ask:

And is there a relationship between flower of excitement and hope and road to recovery and your rain – care'?
(She laughs) *The road is the flower, of course!*

This is one of the ways change may happen: in the moment and out of nowhere.

And when the road is the flower, what happens to 'I want to feel I'm on the road to recovery'?
I am!

And what happens to 'feeling sad'?
It goes!

And what happens to 'torturing myself with the past?'
I see it for what it is.

And what happens to 'forgiveness for myself?'
That's okay, there's no need.

And what happens to 'want to feel loved?'
I acknowledge I do feel loved.

She starts to weep again, but these are cathartic tears. The feeling of "loved" is developed with a succession of "And then what happens?" questions. Finally, Gina takes another tissue from the box, which I notice is covered in yellow chrysanthemums. This time she smiles through the tears.

♥

"Did you know that people on average eat eight spiders in a lifetime?"

Alan is the sports psychologist we met in Chapter 9 as *puer in silva*, 'the boy in the woods'. Here is his full process. He starts by telling me he has what he describes as "an overwhelming phobia about spiders."

Did you know that people on average eat eight spiders in a lifetime? Apparently, wherever you are you're never more than three feet away from one? If I see one in the house, I'm terrified. (His eyes widen) *It's so overwhelming. I can't be alone in the house with one.*
And with all that, what would you like to have happen?

To be able to relax.

I take a speculative short cut:

And when you *are* able to relax, then what happens?
(His shoulders drop slightly) *A sense of peace and balance.*

And when a sense of peace and balance, then what happens?
(He pauses) *Feeling honored and cared for.*

What kind of honored and cared for?

The question prompts something from the past. We work on it. Alan is beginning to decode his phobic construct. At the next session, he brings a representation of some part of it in the form of a dream.

> *It was about a window covered in webs, and I was really small compared to the window.*
> And how old could that 'I' be who was really small compared to that window?

> (A younger voice tone) *Six or seven. The webs were very dirty.*
> What kind of dirty?

> *Layers. Years of webs. But there was no over-riding panic when the Hoover didn't suck them up.* (Pause) *I could be quite fond of spiders. An odd thing, that. It would be nice not having to kill them. But if I see one at home ...*
> And what happens just before you see one at home?

> *I'm feeling jumpy, scared.*
> And that's jumpy, scared like what?

> *Like being lost in the forest. A big old dark forest. Like Hansel and Gretel left by their parents, who were upright moral citizens.*
> And what happens just before upright moral citizen parents left Hansel and Gretel?

> *They lost all their money, they couldn't afford their children, but Hansel and Gretel kept finding their way back again.*

The analogy with the fairy story takes him back to traumatic events in his childhood. He recalls:

> *Our house being possessed, moving into a caravan, being sent to boarding school paid for by an aunt. My mother tells me that me and my sister changed at that time. I had bad school reports, they were waved in my face. I was no good at exams. I only remember one thing from my Latin: 'puer in silva', boy in the woods.*

The relationship between metaphor and reality is captured by Alan in this ambiguous phrase from Latin class. It describes what he still feels himself to be – the boy in the woods who was poor in silver. He maps out a thick green forest, with a cozy-looking house glimpsed through the trees in the distance. He studies the picture. I ask him:

> And where is your attention now?
> *The house. It's light, warm, everyone is there, it's a party.* (He frowns) *I'm not wanted. I'm scared and lonely.* (He moves his body slightly back) *I keep my distance, like a lone wolf.*

Is there anything else about that lone wolf?
It's the sort who goes off for a long time and comes back. (Long pause, then)
I took the boy's hand, and smiled, and reassured him.

Alan seems to have assigned a compassionate adult in himself to take care of the traumatized child. In his next session, there is another surprise.

I kind of thought this week that I don't really have a problem with spiders and I don't know what the fuss was about. I've been thinking about whether the fear allows me to feel vulnerable and let other people sort out them out. Home should be a place of happiness and sociability, but my home wasn't. It was there I was fearful of spiders.

The decoding of the phobia seems to be complete and the next stage, change of some sort, is under way.

And what would you like to have happen now?
To go into the garden and get a spider and bring it into the house.

We go into the garden. It is a time of year when there are a lot of spiders about. He allows one to run over his hand. His eyes open wide and he laughs.

I have never ever done that before.

In his understated way, Alan has achieved a major transformation. He begins the business of maturing the change by coaxing the spider into a jar and taking it back to the consulting room. He keeps jar and spider close for the remainder of the session. Two weeks later, in what turns out to be his final session:

I've thought a lot about the phobia being some sort of displacement for needing other people. I depended on my parents and I lost that when I was sent to boarding school. Now I'm linking spiders to a need in me to be less alone, less alien. I acknowledge spiders rather than avoid them. I'm getting to know them more. I've stopped thinking of spiders as alien.

Two years after this work, he reports:

I've been in contact with many small spiders in the last two years and I'm little bothered by them. Instead of killing them or having someone dispose of them, I generally leave them alone. A couple of times I've needed to pick up a big house spider in a glass and put it outside. Not a pleasant task, but possible. I speak to them sometimes. I apologize. Actually, I quite like them.

Without a single suggestion from the therapist, Alan has transformed "an overwhelming phobia about spiders" into "I quite like them" and in doing so has generated a range of behavioral and emotional choices for himself.

♥

Appendix C
The Complete Clean Questions

40 Clean Language and Therapeutic Metaphor questions – 30 Clean Space questions
– 30 Emergent Knowledge/Power of Six questions

Clean Language and Therapeutic Metaphor

POSITIONING
Where in the space would you like to be?
Where would you like me to be?

OPENING / RE-ENTRY
What would you like to have happen?
What would you like to have happen now?
When all that, what would you like to have happen?
When [identify change], what would you like to have happen?
How do you know X?
What is happening now?
What are you drawn to?

THE SYNTAX   1 And X ...   2 And when X ...   3 Question about X

DESCRIBING
What kind of X could that X be?
Is there anything else about that X?
Does that X have a size or a shape?
That is an X like what?
Are X and Y the same or different?
How many?
How old? / What age?
What could [age] be wearing?

LOCATING
Where is X?
Whereabouts is X?
Inside or outside? / Above or below? / Over, on, or under?
How far? / In which direction?
Left or right? / Front or back?
What is beyond X?

SEQUENCING
What happens just before X?
What happens next?
Then what happens?
Where could X come from?
What happens after X?
Between / How long? / What time?

RELATING
What does X know about Y?
Is there a relationship between X and Y?
Where is X in relation to Y?
When X, what happens to Y?
Would X be interested in going to Y?
When X goes to Y, then what happens?

SEEKING RESOURCE
Where could X come from?
What kind of [noun] was that [noun] before it was [negative adjective]?

CHANGING AND MATURING
What needs to happen for X?
What is the first thing?
Is that a left or a right-footed step?
What would X like to do next?
When [identify change] then what happens?

Clean Space

Of all the things that are, the greatest is Space, for it holds all things.
                                                    Thales of Miletus
Space is not just my co-therapist, but a greater participant. David Grove

Our inability to answer a question may simply be a function of where we are. When we move to a new space, something different happens. "Why is a grown man crying just because he took a step forward?" one of my clients asked himself. He was viewing events from a different place and information that made a radical difference to his sense of himself had appeared. It may be difficult on occasion for a client to move emotionally, but moving to another space can achieve the same objective quickly and easily.

This 10-step exercise in Clean Space (with an optional 5-step extension) is one of several similar processes utilizing the principles of Intergenerational and Prior Cosmology Healing. The client's responses may be clarified at each stage with a standard Clean question of two, but no one stage should be developed in detail or delayed. The intention is to maintain a flow so that the information in each space networks together and iterates, in the expectation that new information and healing that is more than the sum of its parts will emerge. The exercise prefigures the full Emergent Knowledge and 'Power of Six' methodologies that follow it.

1 CLEAN START
Write or draw what you want to work on.
Place [statement or drawing] where it needs to be and place yourself where you need to be in relation to it. [Space #1]

2 HERE AND NOW SPACE #1
What do you know about that [the statement] from there?
What is between you and [the statement]?
What does [client's description of what is between] know?
Is there anything else you know from there?
Give this space a name [X].
Find a space that knows about X. [Space #2]

3 INTERMEDIATE SPACE #2
What do you know about X from there?
Is there anything else you know?
Give this space a name [Y].
Find a space that knows about Y. [Space #3]

4 FURTHER SPACE #3
What do you know about Y from there?
Is there anything else you know?
Give this space a name.
Go back to [Space #1].

5 SPACE #1 REVISITED
What do you know about that [the original statement] now?
Is there anything else you know?
How might you change that [statement] or does it stay the same?

6 ITERATION
*Whatever the response to step 5, invite client to iterate between spaces #1,
#2, and #3, using the names the client has given them. Then:*
What do you know now about [statement, or X, or Y]? *Then:*
Find the place where you were born. [Space #4]

7 BIRTH SPACE #4
What do you know from there?
Is there anything else you know?
Give this space a name.

Map out your life from [Space #4] to [Space #1] in a number of life events –
ages, stages, places, or changes. [Spaces #5+++]
Give each space a name.
Step into [Birth Space #4].
What is your mission or purpose at this time?
Step into [Space #5].

8 SPACES #5+++
In each life event space:
What is your mission or purpose at this time? *Then:*
Consider the shape or pattern your life events make.

9 THE SHAPE OF YOUR LIFE
What do you know about that?
Is there anything else you know?
Return to [Space #1].

10 SPACE #1 REVISITED
What do you know about that [the original statement] now?
Is there anything else you know?
Does it stay the same or is there anything you would like to change?

Five more steps are possible where a more thorough process is indicated.

11 GENEALOGY SPACES
Invite client to map out where they came from before they were born with a succession of 'Where could you come from before [Birth Space #4]?' *questions. One or two clarifying questions can be asked at each stage of the mother's lifeline, the father's lifeline, and maternal and paternal parents' lifelines. Then:*
Is there a space that knows how far back you can go? [Prior Spacetime]

12 PRIOR SPACETIME
What do you know from there?
Give this space a name.
Find a space where you belong. [Alternative Spacetime]

13 ALTERNATIVE SPACETIME
What do you know from there?

NB: there may be new physics here. Alternative universes are unlikely to have the same rules as this one.

Give this space a name.
Return to [a previous space].

14 ITERATION BETWEEN SPACES
In each: And now what do you know?
Finally:
Return to [Space #1].

15 SPACE #1 REVISITED
What do you know from there now?
Do you want to change your original statement or does it stay the same?

Emergent Knowledge and The Power of Six

The swarm knows more than the sum of what every bee knows. Kevin Passino

For a full explanation of the principles of Emergent Knowledge, the methodology of The Power of Six, and a full range of exercises utilizing the questions, see powersofsix.com and the book *The Power of Six: A Six Part Guide to Self Knowledge.*

BASIC
What do you know here and now?
And what else do you know? [Repeat 5 more times]
And now what do you know? [or] And what do you know now?

OF VERBAL STATEMENT
What do you know about [that]?
And what else do you know about [that]? [x 5]
And now what do you know?

OF WRITTEN OR DRAWN STATEMENT
What else could go on there?
And what else could go on there? [x 5]
And now what do you know?

UTILIZING 'CLIENT SPACE A'
Find a space [A]. What do you know from there?
Find a space that knows about that [x 5].
What do you know from there? [x 5]
And now what do you know?

UTILIZING 'PROBLEM SPACE B'
And what does that know?
And what else does that know? [x 5]
And now what does that know? / And now what do you know?
And what does that know about you?
And what else does that know about you? [x 5]
And now what does that know about you? / And now what do you know?

CLEAN START IN RELATION TO WRITTEN OR DRAWN STATEMENT
Choose the size of paper you would like to work on.
Write or draw or find a way to represent what you want to work on.
Place that [the statement or drawing] where it needs to be.
Are you in the right place? / Is that in the right place?
Are you facing the right direction? / Is that facing the right direction?
Are you at the right angle? / Is that at the right angle?
Are you at the right distance? / Is that at the right distance?
Are you at the right height? / Is that at the right height?
Are you in the right position or posture? / Is that in the right position?

UTILIZING 'SPACE BETWEEN C'
And what does the space between know?
And what else does the space between know? [x 5]
And now what does the space between know?
And now what do you know?
And what does the space between know about you?
And what else does the space between know about you? [x 5]
And now what does the space between know about you?
And now what do you know?

MOVING FOR A CLEAN START
Find a space. *[Ask Clean Start questions]* 'Are you in the right place?'
'Are you facing the right direction?' [etc.]
What do you know from there?
Is there another space you could go to / that would like you to go to it?
Are you in the right space/place? [etc., ask as for Clean Start]
And what do you know from there?
Repeat these questions four more times for four more spaces, then:
And now what do you know?

CLIENT TURNING
Turn slowly in either direction until you know something else.
And what do you know there?
Keep turning until you know something else.
And what do you know there?
Repeat invitation and question four more times, then:
And now what do you know?

WORKING WITH CLIENT SYSTEM
Having worked with client space A, problem space B, and space between C.
Find a space that knows about all that [A B C].
And what does it/all that know?
And what else does it/all that know?
Repeat question four more times.
And now what does it/all that know? / And now what do you know?

AFTER A WHILE
(Applies to all Emergent Knowledge exercises)
And what is the difference between what you knew at the start and what
you know now?

And finally
ACTION PLAN
List six specific behavioral things you are going to do to follow up what you
have learned. For each action, ask yourself:
What exactly am I going to do?
When will I do it? / Where?
By myself or with whom?

Index

Printed in Great Britain
by Amazon.co.uk, Ltd.,
Marston Gate.